D0272846

PREP SCHOOL CHILDREN

Continuum UK, The Tower Building, 11 York Road, London SE1 7NX
Continuum US, 80 Maiden Lane, Suite 704, New York, NY 10038

www.continuumbooks.com

First published 2009

British Library Cataloguing-in-Publication Data
A catalogue record for this book is available from the British Library.

ISBN 978 1 84706 287 1

Typeset by Pindar NZ, Auckland, New Zealand
Printed and bound by MPG Books Ltd, Cornwall, Great Britain

Prep School Children
A Class Apart Over Two Centuries

Vyvyen Brendon

continuum

For my sons, George and Oliver,
and my grandsons, Beau, Sonny and Lucas.

Contents

Illustrations

Acknowledgements

I owe a great deal to the many people who have helped me with the research for this book. My greatest debt is to the sixty men, women, boys and girls who have given up their time and expended emotional energy by talking to me about their prep school experiences. They are listed in the bibliography at the end of the book.

The staff of the libraries and archive collections I have worked in have provided expert and patient assistance at all times. I am especially grateful to those who pointed me in the direction of valuable material: Nicholas Aldridge of the Summer Fields Archive; Sophie Bridges, Allen Packwood, Andrew Riley and Katharine Thompson of the Churchill Archives Centre; Roderick Suddaby of the Imperial War Museum; Patricia McGuire of King's College, Cambridge; and Clare Fleck of Knebworth House Archive who also identified and scanned illustrations from Knebworth family letters.

I am also grateful to those who have been so generous with their help in other ways, particularly by suggesting useful sources, books or interviewees: Julia Boyd, Marion Dixon, Jane Ellwood, Alan Findlay, Judith Findlay, William Greenwell, Maureen Gruffydd Jones, Alex Hamilton, Richard Ingrams, Tim Jeal, Jeremy Lewis, Andrew Lycett, Christine Outhwaite, Neil Smith, Ann Thwaite, Henrietta Twycross-Martin, Fiona Unwin and Rosemary Wood. Others have kindly entrusted me with letters, theses, memoirs and old school magazines: Richard Aldwinckle, Johnny Bell, Gillian Bickford-Smith, Martin Bluhm, Douglas Hurd, Rupert Morris, Tony Orchard and Philip Steadman. Still others have given me the benefit of their own knowledge and expertise: Nicky Blandford, Pam Gatrell, Tim Heald, Teresa Outhwaite, Rosalind Rayfield, Gordon Robinson and Gillian Sutherland. Simon Hitchings of St Aubyns and Robin Badham-Thornhill of Summer Fields welcomed me into their schools and put me in touch with charming pupils who showed me round and answered questions. Tom Sharpe and John Burningham have generously allowed me to use their graphic representations of prep school life.

My special thanks are due to my agent, Laura Morris, who has worked hard on my behalf and given me much encouragement; to my publisher, Robin Baird-Smith, who had faith in the project, as well as to my production editor, Alice Eddowes, project manager, Kim Pillay and cover designer, Nick Evans; to my friend, Anthony Heath, whose enthusiasm and knowledge of the prep school world have been of inestimable value; and to my husband, Piers, whose support has been unfailing.

Introduction: 'How Would You Know?'

Fiction and fact tell the same tale. Tom Brown, a proud nine-year-old setting off from home in the 1820s, supposed that all English boys were sent away to school.[1] At the age of seven, Winston Churchill felt 'perfectly helpless' in the face of the 'irresistible tides' which propelled him towards the prep school his parents had selected for him in 1880.[2] Half a century later, Diana Athill lamented her eight-year-old brother's dispatch to prep school from their upper-middle-class Norfolk home: 'Boys had to go to boarding-schools, it was what always happened to them, poor things, and there was nothing anyone could do about it.'[3] Seven-year-old Stephen Fry accepted the same fate in the 1960s, because 'all the friends I had in the world went away to boarding school'.[4] And Harry Potter's name was put down at birth for Hogwarts School for Witchcraft and Wizardry.

Just as Harry is removed from non-magic folk (or Muggles) because he is a wizard, children from the upper and middle classes have habitually been detached from their lower-class contemporaries at a tender age. This book is about that separate system of education which, until recent years, nearly always took place in secluded boarding schools. Its focus is the preparatory school, with its aim of grooming boys aged between seven and thirteen for public school. But it also contains some references to boarders of that age group in other schools: early nineteenth-century public schools which accepted boys as young as eight; girls' boarding schools with a starting age of eleven; and other weird (or wizard) educational establishments.

Sending young children away to school is a peculiarly English phenomenon. In *The Victorians*, A. N. Wilson expressed surprise that 'otherwise kind parents were prepared to entrust much-loved children to the rigours of boarding-school', and he regards the practice as 'one of the mysteries of English life from the 1820s to the present day'.[5] Some historians account for the custom as a means of perpetuating the class system. Others explain that Britain's empire demanded both nurseries for the children of distant parents and training grounds for its hardy leaders. It is not so much my purpose to debate these matters as to shed light on the experience of separated children, most of whom did not question why they had been sent away. If they did, they often assumed that their parents simply did not want them at home.

The timescale of the book is the same as that mentioned by A. N. Wilson. It begins in the early nineteenth century, because by that time there were many small private boarding academies which prepared boys for 'great schools' such as Eton, Harrow, Winchester and Rugby. During Queen Victoria's reign, as public schools standardized their age of entry at thirteen and became choosier about the background and calibre of their entrants, specialized preparatory schools developed apace. The Industrial Revolution increased the number of prosperous families able to afford them. By late Victorian and Edwardian times, prep schools were well established and they had also evolved their characteristic manly and Christian ethos.

In the twentieth century, they survived two world wars, the Depression, several Labour governments, Dr Spock and the Swinging Sixties, by which time they were educating one in twenty ten-year-olds.[6] Generation after generation of parents assured their offspring that these schools were less harsh than they had been in their day; but it is only in the last thirty years or so that this claim has had any real foundation. In the new millennium, prep schools have become stronger than ever, but they have had to adapt to modern requirements. Teachers cannot use corporal punishment, parents like to see more of their offspring, boys often sit in classes alongside girls and, I am assured, pupils are less likely to be bullied than in former years. The evidence for these developments and their impact upon the growing child is as interesting as it is various.

Children's fiction of these two centuries often conjures up the world of boarding school. There is plenty to choose from, for J. K. Rowling and others have found an ideal background for adventure in this setting, free of intrusive parents and complete with its own codes of behaviour. Moreover, novelists usually draw on real life. Thomas Hughes based Tom Brown's friend, George Arthur, on Arthur Penrhyn Stanley, later Dean of Westminster; as a delicate and devout young boy Stanley went to Rugby, where he was immediately nicknamed Nancy and needed the protection of a more robust character.[7] The schoolboy hero of radio plays broadcast on post-war *Children's Hour*, Jennings (known always by his surname in true prep school fashion), had his origin in Anthony Buckeridge's old schoolfellow, Diarmid Jennings. Another fictional schoolboy (who has delighted adults as well as children) is nigel molesworth, conjured up from the teaching experiences of his creator, Geoffrey Willans, at a school bearing some resemblance to st custard's. And Groosham Grange, a wizards' school which predates Hogwarts, might never have been created had Anthony Horowitz not been sent to a boarding school he compares to the grisly horror plays of the Grand Guignol.[8] It could also work the other way round. Ten-year-old Arthur Quiller-Couch was so excited by tales of derring-do in *Tom Wildrake's Schooldays* that he begged to be sent away to school.[9]

Real schools and teachers have also prompted adult fiction. In the preface of *Nicholas Nickleby*, Charles Dickens explained that Dotheboys Hall was inspired by his own research in Yorkshire, where several schoolmasters would proudly lay claim to being the original Wackford Squeers. Evelyn Waugh's Llanabba Castle, portrayed in *Decline and Fall*, emerged from the author's teaching experiences in prep schools. P. G. Wodehouse came as close as he ever did to autobiography in depicting Bertie Wooster's feelings about his former headmaster, the Rev Aubrey Upjohn of Malvern House. This 'prince of stinkers' is not just a comic character. The name of Upjohn's school is the same as that of Wodehouse's own naval prep school, 'a very bad choice', says his biographer, 'for a dreamy impractical boy who loved reading'.[10] There is uncharacteristic venom in Bertie's description of Malvern House as a chain gang and a horror from outer space. No wonder he is appalled to find that Upjohn, an unwelcome guest at Aunt Dahlia's house party, has published a book describing the formative years at a preparatory school as the happiest of a boy's life. Luckily, Bertie's old school chum, 'Kipper' Herring, manages to set the record straight in the *Thursday Review*: 'Aubrey Upjohn might have taken a different view of preparatory schools if he had done a stretch at the Dotheboys Hall conducted by him at Malvern House, Bramley-on-Sea, as we had the misfortune to do.'[11] Other writers, such as C. Day Lewis, Pamela Hansford Johnson and John le Carré, have used the prep school rather as Agatha Christie did the country house, its self-contained environment forming the ideal background for misdeeds and mysteries.

Fictional schools crop up in many published and unpublished memoirs – the prime source for this book. Some writers recall how they were misled by preconceptions gained from schoolboy tales such as *Tom Brown's Schooldays* and *Eric or Little by Little*.[12] Alistair Horne uses two analogies with fiction to convey the horrors of Ludgrove in the 1930s. He regrets that there was no Tom Brown to speak up for him when he was singled out for bullying and he reckons that the school 'made Dotheboys Hall seem like the Club Med'.[13] More cheerful alumni sometimes liken their scrapes and larks to those of Jennings and Darbishire, while others identify more with nigel molesworth, the curse of st custard's. Fraser Harrison recalls that he and his fellow pupils at a Welsh prep school found the molesworth series 'the funniest our literature could possibly afford'.[14]

Again and again, the British memoir paints a vivid picture of schooldays. Spent as they often were so far from domestic affections and comforts, they permeate the collective consciousness of the race. Some critics assert that early memories cannot be authentic, arguing that they are unreliable and often vary from one member of a group to another. I have found authentication, however, in the wealth of corroborating detail both about the schools themselves and about reactions to them. Of course, careful judgements have to be made, since memory plays all sorts of tricks. As sometimes appears in my book, two pupils from the same school (like siblings from the same family) may have very different remembrances of things past. But, as Hilary Mantel argues in defending her own childhood record, *Giving Up the Ghost*, 'it doesn't mean that either of you is wrong'. She makes a convincing case for 'the power and persistence of memory', for our ability to capture the moment when 'the adult slips away and the child appears, wide-eyed and gleeful, reporting back to you with sensual precision.'[15]

That moment is frequently associated with food. Leonard Woolf conjures up not only the 'dense boredom' he experienced in classrooms at Arlington House 'smelling of ink and boys', but also 'the deliciousness of a large, hot Cowley bath bun which we were allowed to buy after bathing in Brill's Baths'.[16] Less happily, General Sir Ian Hamilton conveys the shame he felt as a ten-year-old new boy at Cheam School, when he was ridiculed by the headmaster after asking for some more butter at breakfast: 'the troubles of Oliver Twist were cheap stuff compared to mine'.[17] And Stephen Fry can never forget his 'lips-parted, heart-pounding, face-flushed state' when he broke into the headmaster's study at Stouts Hill, opened the desk and found bags and bags of confiscated sweets: 'Foam shrimps, fruit salads, blackjacks, flying-saucers, red-liquorice bootlaces, every desirable item of Uley village bounty that could be imagined.'[18] This book is packed with such tasty morsels, the fruit of autobiographies that together make such a crucial contribution to history.

Surprisingly often, writers have used poetry to convey their feelings about the rather prosaic world of school. A few lines can capture a key episode in a child's life. Samuel Taylor Coleridge is lulled to sleep by visions of his far-off rural birth-place. Henry Newbolt's Victorian schoolboy goes in as the last batsman with 'an hour to play' and ten runs needed for victory. A precocious Wystan (W. H.) Auden rags 'elderly grey' stand-in teachers during the First World War, while a fearful John Betjeman gets out of a fight with the Dragon's school hero by inventing 'rotten news from home'. In more recent times, Edward Lucie-Smith evokes a boy's realization that the genuine news of his father's death, baldly conveyed by a bald headmaster, 'Could bind the bully's fist a week or two'. (In 1942 six-year-old John Ellwood had the same experience; he was informed of his father's death by the headmaster at Beachborough and promptly sent back into class with the blunt instruction that he must be brave.)[19] Hugo Williams remembers his first day at Lockers Park:

> I was eight when I set out into the world
> Wearing a grey flannel suit.
> I had my own suitcase.
> I thought it was going to be fun.

But it is not long before the little boy starts to dream of 'leaving school' with that same suitcase.

One of Hugo Williams's collections is entitled *Writing Home*, which is the subject of several of the poems and points to another major source of evidence. 'A Letter to My Parents' consists of thirty-five lines which sound as though they come from one of the letters he wrote as a schoolboy. They recount a hit in the face, an accident to a dog, the position of his bed in the dormitory, plans for a new gang, some forthcoming sunray treatment, a lecture on the Headhunters of Borneo and a complicated game of charades, before giving his parents information on 'going out days'. The child ventures to say that the sunray treatment 'seems a complete waste of time', which suggests that the letter is not going to be as closely inspected as they often were.[20] This scrutiny varied from one school (or one master) to another, but letter-writing sessions were usually conducted under supervision. Even if there was no actual censorship, the lack of privacy could be inhibiting. Morgan (later known as E. M.) Forster complained in a letter to his mother that there were boys looking over his shoulder as he wrote. Nevertheless, some school letters are remarkably revealing and most give clues about their writers' state of mind. Whether they were frank or formal, messy or neat, they were frequently preserved, surviving to this day either in books or (more often) in archive collections and private houses. With their shaky grammar and erratic spelling (which are retained in quotations in this book), these missives bring to life their inky-fingered authors as they struggle to convey their everyday lives and suppressed emotions to distant parents.

For more recent experiences of prep schools there is an additional source – personal interviews. I have quizzed about sixty people from different walks of life and aged between ten and ninety, usually face-to-face but by telephone or email where this was not possible. I was surprised, as I was when doing research for my previous book, *Children of the Raj*, by how willing people were to talk about their childhood. Often my studiously neutral questions stirred memories of forgotten incidents or released long-buried feelings. Many found that they enjoyed the experience but in a few cases it acted, in the words of one man, as 'the final sting in the long tail' of prep school. For some, who were wary of living parents or teachers or for other reasons preferred to be anonymous, I have used pseudonyms which are indicated by an asterisk when the name is first used. All interviewees have seen the material I have quoted and given permission for it to be used.

Many contemporary pupils (especially in boarding schools) are questioned regularly by Ofsted inspectors, anxious to ensure that recent reforms have been implemented. The resulting reports form another valuable source of evidence, as can visits to schools' Open Days and anniversary celebrations or to the archive collections which some schools are accumulating. Prominent in these repositories are sets of old school magazines which some former pupils have also preserved. While these rarely contain any contributions from boys, they afford interesting contrasts between past and present. The histories and websites of schools, whether defunct or surviving, sometimes use such documentary material as well as the recollections of their more loyal old boys.

I have drawn on this varied and abundant evidence to look at prep schools through the eyes of children in a way which has not been attempted before. This is not a painstaking institutional history such as that written by Donald Leinster-Mackay, with its wealth of important detail. Nor is it simply a 'delightful collection of prep school reminiscences', like those composed by Arthur Marshall and Michael Gilbert.[21] It illuminates an area of childhood hardly mentioned in recent histories, such as Hugh Cunningham's *The Invention of Childhood* or Harry Hendrick's *Children, Childhood and English Society*, both of which try to encompass the 'whispers and muted articulations' of children themselves. Anthony Fletcher's *Growing Up in England* does touch on 'boys' experience of being at school' up to 1914, but he judges that this is 'hardly susceptible to analytical treatment on the basis of authentic source material'. It is true that the childhood diaries which Fletcher values most highly are rare. But he underrates the material which can be gleaned from letters and memoirs and he was not, of course, in a position to talk to past pupils.[22] A comprehensive blend of sources enables us to hear the shared laughter and the private sobs, the recited lessons and the playground cries of prep school pupils down the years.

It was not my aim to produce an affectionate apologia for the preparatory school of the type written by the fictitious Aubrey Upjohn in 1960 or by the real-life headmaster, Philip Masters, in 1966. Nor do I presuppose with Nick Duffell that former boarding school pupils are all victims.[23] Instead, I have followed the evidence where it leads. These pages encompass a fascinating and sometimes bewildering spectrum of views on the prep school experience, ranging from 'a pleasant sunlit state' through 'a rite of passage' to 'a fascist state'.[24] Such opinions were rarely sought or expressed by pupils at the time, for ironically these privileged children did not attract investigations such as the Victorian inquiries conducted by Lord Shaftesbury and Henry Mayhew into the circumstances and thoughts of young factory workers and street-traders. Many of those deprived youngsters longed for an education; one orphan flower girl told Mayhew how proud she was of having put her younger brother through Ragged School so that he could read and write – 'and I pray to God that he'll do well with it'.[25] These waifs would have been astonished to learn that Shaftesbury always 'shuddered at the thought' of the 'filth, bullying, neglect and harsh treatment' he had endured at his prep school, or that Mayhew had been so bored with 'the dead tongues' he was taught at Westminster School from the age of nine that he ran away to sea.[26] Any complaints Shaftesbury or Mayhew might have uttered at the time would have gone unheeded. And in the twentieth century, too, it remained 'a fact of life that adults never believed thirteen-year-olds'.[27] One man I interviewed told me that when his mother referred to his time at prep school as the 'happiest days of your life', his unspoken reply was 'How would you know?' This book strives to give a voice to prep school children, a class apart over two centuries.

1

'A Little Roughing It'
Georgian Boys' Schools

Pick from the shelf a memoir or biography of an eminent Victorian man and the chances are that its early pages will reveal him as a small boy making the journey by stagecoach to a distant boarding school in the early nineteenth century. The fictional departure of nine-year-old Tom Brown from his quiet old-fashioned country village in White Horse Vale conveys Thomas Hughes's somewhat idealized vision of this English custom. Tom goes off in the coach (accompanied by Squire Brown) with 'his small private box full of peg-tops, white marbles, screws, birds' eggs, whip-cord, jews'-harps, and other miscellaneous boys' wealth' donated by the heartbroken village companions he is leaving behind. The stalwart young hero is sad to be losing his childhood playmates, but he also feels 'the pride and excitement of making a new step in life'. This emotion carries him through the parting with 'dear Mamma' – though he becomes dreadfully unhappy in the first week when the school housekeeper fails to seal and post his first letter to her.[1] A contrasting account comes from the pen of William Makepeace Thackeray, who never forgot the day in 1811 when, at the age of six, he departed for school alone in a 'Defiance' stage coach:

> Twang goes the horn: up goes the trunk; down come the steps. Bah! I see the autumn evening: I hear the wheels now: I smart the cruel smart again; and, boy or man, have never been able to bear the sight of people parting from their children.[2]

It was a lament that would echo down the ages.

Both Tom Brown and Thackeray were heading for one of the many private academies which proliferated in late Georgian times. Typically these were in the charge of clergymen, aided by sundry family members, but some of the larger, more expensive private establishments, such as Twyford (the model for Tom Brown's first school), Temple Grove or the Rev George Nicholas's academy at Ealing, were run 'on the Eton lines'.[3] All these forerunners of the later preparatory schools aimed to impart enough of the Latin and Greek required for entrance to the great public schools of England, such as Eton, Winchester, Harrow, Rugby, Shrewsbury, Westminster and Charterhouse. These ancient foundations had originally been endowed for needy local boys but, by the late eighteenth century, they had become elite schools patronized largely by fee-paying pupils who lived in boarding houses. With their exclusively classical curriculum, the 'vocationally useless' learning that was 'the symbol of the gentleman's education', they were the means by which suitable boys would enter the universities of Oxford and Cambridge.[4]

Some of the private schools, run by particularly learned clergymen, also prepared boys for university. Devout parents like the Wilberforces preferred this homely form of education to the 'hard world atmosphere' of the public schools, 'capital training for the world', no doubt, but less beneficial to a child's 'eternal state'.[5] Other parents, like Squire Brown, were so confident of the great schools' ability to produce 'good English boys' that they curtailed their sons' days at the private academy and moved them on when they were as young as nine. One way or another, as a German mother observed of the English upper and middle classes:

> Hardly anyone brings up his children at home, where they would cause too much noise and commotion. As soon as boys and girls emerge from the nursery they are packed off to these establishments, and only return to their parental homes when their education is complete and they themselves nearly grown up.

Actually, daughters were often educated at home. But they could be sent to polite institutions, where they were prepared for marriage by learning 'a little of everything' and a lot of graceful accomplishments.[6]

The choice of a school for sons was a thorny matter. At this time of sharp religious controversy, parents might select a schoolmaster of their own Evangelical or High Church leanings. More often the determining factor was simply financial. In Dickens's novel *Dombey and Son*, the prosperous Mr Dombey sees the high cost of Doctor Blimber's academy in Brighton as 'one of its leading merits', since he wants an establishment from which his little son can rise to his proper eminence.[7] But down-at-heel parents of 'gentle standing', such as those of Anthony Trollope, were glad to accept the 'almost gratuitous' places that some endowed schools like Harrow still offered to a few local youngsters, even if this meant their being subjected to ignominy when they got there.[8] For boys who could sing like angels a choir school was a possibility; but parents had to be careful, since many of these medieval foundations no longer prepared choristers to go on to further schooling once their voices had broken. King's College, Cambridge, linked by its royal charter to Eton, now offered only the most elementary curriculum to its choirboys. And at Wells Cathedral, idle choristers were in the habit of kicking balls and throwing stones in the nave, leaving as their legacy a hole in the stained glass where St Andrew's nose should have been.[9] Such lax discipline would not do for lads who were bent on a career in Britain's omnipotent navy. They had to be toughened up, like the 'King's Boys' at Christ's Hospital, 'for the rough element which they were destined to encounter'. As Admiral Sir Robert Barlow observed before sending his nephew to the Naval Academy at Gosport, 'nursing is not a good initiation to a life of enterprise and hard work'.[10] This criterion was applied not only to future naval cadets. Many parents of this era shared the second Marquess of Salisbury's idea 'that the more boys roughed it in every way, the stronger and better they grew up'.[11]

How well did schools meet the varied expectations of parents? If it was difficult for them to make well-founded judgements, how much harder it is for historians to find out about conditions in schools, many of which have long since disappeared. Only the children really knew. From their dutiful letters home, from memoirs often prefaced by such phrases as 'I can see myself now', from reports by those in whom they confided and from the life-like fiction of Thackeray and Dickens, we can attempt to conjure up the pleasures and pains of children setting out on their schooldays in Georgian times.

At the little boarding school to which Lord Salisbury sent his young sons, Lords Robert and Eustace Cecil, the Rev Francis Faithfull of Hatfield tried to apply his lordship's severe maxim. He required his young charges to rise at six o'clock, fast until ten, work for seven hours a day, ride without saddles, sleep on mattresses on the floor, avoid wearing greatcoats and eat green apples as a purgative. Those who failed in these endeavours were beaten with shaving straps. Robert (who later inherited his father's title and became prime minister) remembered his three years at this school as 'an existence among devils'. Respite came at the age of nine, when he was sent to another clerical school, this time in Devon. Although he was now much further away from Hatfield House (the family home), the boy benefited from kinder treatment; the Rev Henry Lyte, author of the hymn *Abide with Me*, took account of his delicate constitution and encouraged his interest in botany. But at the age of eleven Robert started at Eton. The clever child could cope with its intellectual demands but not with its ubiquitous bullies, who inflicted such tortures as burning his mouth with a candle. Eventually he sneaked to his father, telling him that he found the regime 'perfectly insupportable' and begging to be removed from 'this horrid place'. Thus ended a 'thoroughly miserable' school career which, in the opinion of his latest biographer, gave Cecil his life-long 'pessimism about human nature'. Years later he would dodge into a side alley if he saw a school contemporary approaching him in the street.[12]

It was not unusual for a child to be taken away from a school if he could manage to communicate his misery. When William Thackeray arrived at Mr and Mrs Arthur's highly recommended school in Southampton in 1817, he could barely write, and his letters to 'My dearest of all dear Mamas' (who was in India) were probably penned by the schoolmaster himself. They record that he enjoyed his lessons in geography, Latin and ciphering, saying nothing of the cold, the bad dinners and the awful caning which he recalled in later years. But the relations with whom he lived must have understood his plight, for he wrote in 1818 that he was 'very glad' not to be going back to the Arthurs.[13] Instead, he attended a school run by his great-uncle, Dr Turner, in Chiswick Mall, 'a stately old brick house' which makes an appearance as Miss Pinkerton's Academy in *Vanity Fair*.[14] It was an improvement. But before long young William tried to run away, fearing punishment for a caricature he had drawn of Dr Turner; he did not get further than the Hammersmith High Road, where he was frightened by the traffic. Perhaps Thackeray used this memory in his story 'Dr Birch and His Young Friends', in which a boy successfully absconds after a row with the 'croaking, scolding, bullying' Miss Birch, whom the narrator witnesses 'eating jam with a spoon out of Master Wiggins' trunk in the box-room'.[15] He settled down after this but did little work and was pronounced an ignoramus – 'The boy knows nothing' – when he arrived aged ten at Charterhouse, where a senior boy greeted him with the words: 'Come and frig me.' William never developed much 'gratitude or affection for that respectable seminary near Smithfield', where the headmaster wielded 'a forest of birch rods'. But he enjoyed such local diversions as Bartholomew Fair.[16]

It sometimes took extreme measures to convey a desperate child's message to parents and teachers. Samuel Wilberforce, son of the abolitionist campaigner and later Bishop of Winchester, so disliked the Rev Marsh's school at Nuneham Courtney that he devised a novel method of getting himself expelled in 1817.

> He ran into the road before the cottage, then traversed by a score or two London coaches a day, threw himself flat on the ground, in the very track of the coaches, and announced his intention of remaining there till he was sent home. After he remained there several hours the tutor struck his colours and Samuel was sent home.

He was transferred to the Rev Hodson's school at Stanstead Park, where he apparently indulged in no more suicidal behaviour.[17]

Physical, as well as psychological, ill health could cause a boy to be removed from a school. The mother of Edward Bulwer (later Lord Lytton) was so shocked by his appearance after two weeks of merciless bullying at Dr Ruddock's school in Fulham that she took him away immediately.[18] Some boys lasted longer. Henry Manning, Archbishop of Westminster, recalled that he had been at the Rev Davies' school in Streatham for about two years before he fell ill and was 'fetched home' in 1820. Despite the 'trail of immorality' he found at this school, Manning seems to have embarked on the religious course which led to his becoming a cardinal in the Roman Catholic Church. His main recollection was 'of walking about in the playground trying to think what there was before the world was made'. He spent a long time getting well at home before proceeding to a school in Totteridge run by the Rev Abel Lendon, an austere figure who inspired 'a wholesome fear' in his pupils. The 'dormitories were well watched' at this school, where there was 'more moral purity, refinement and civilisation'.[19]

Henry Coke did not last many years at Temple Grove in the 1830s under the tutelage of Dr Pinckney, the model for the 'sycophantic Doctor of Divinity' satirized by Benjamin Disraeli, whose brother had attended that 'fashionable school preparatory to Eton'.[20] After being taken to the magnificent villa in East Sheen by a family friend from his Norfolk home, Holkham Hall, Henry was 'half starved ... exceedingly dirty ... systematically bullied ... flogged and caned as though the master's pleasure was in inverse pleasure to ours'. Coke's account of the three gradations of caning, of meals preceded by doughy pudding 'to save the butcher's bill' and of the complete lack of baths,[21] is borne out by his contemporary, Major-General Sir Archibald Anson. A further torture which Anson described was the twice-yearly visit of the dentist who 'pulled teeth out causing as much pain as possible', an ordeal from which he was excused by his father.[22]

After three years of 'gerund-grinding', Henry Coke was removed from the school without getting the place at Eton to which Temple Grove was normally the 'atrium'. This was because his cheeks remained pallid despite, or because of, regular doses of sulphur and treacle. After a period of convalescence in France, he entered the Naval Academy at Gosport. Here he got the year's 'hard training' that apparently equipped him, aged twelve, for night watches aboard HMS *Blonde* bound for the Opium War in China, when he was 'blinded with snow, drenched by the seas, frozen with cold, home sick and sea sick beyond description'.[23] Coke was later to leave the navy and resume his education by studying on his own to get into Cambridge University, whence he proceeded into politics. Meanwhile, Anson had progressed to a school on Woolwich Common, where boys were prepared for the neighbouring Royal Military Academy with the help of unmerciful thrashings 'all over the body'. Thus he was equipped for a distinguished army career in the Far East. Temple Grove had already earned its reputation as a 'cradle of empire'.[24]

No political, religious, naval or military future lies before old-fashioned little Paul Dombey. He spends one long term at Doctor Blimber's 'great hot-house' in Brighton, where 'the studies went round like a mighty wheel and the young gentlemen were always stretched upon it', before the breakdown in his health leads to his death at the age of seven.[25] Dickens's exposure of Doctor Blimber's 'forcing system and its fruits' is much more good-natured than his more famous portrayal of Mr Squeers's Dotheboys Hall – to which Henry Coke, among many others, compared his prep school.[26] Both schools were drawn from life. Dickens himself claimed that 'Mr Squeers and his school are faint and feeble pictures of an existing reality.'[27] And his friend and biographer, John Forster, knew the original of Doctor Blimber's daughter and assistant, Miss Cornelia Blimber, who is portrayed as 'spectacled and analytic but not unkind'. To be sure, she gives Paul a hard time as she tries to bring him on in Latin grammar, ancient history and arithmetic. But when he collapses under the strain she and Doctor Blimber, as well as Mr Feeder BA, release him from his books and treat him gently. What Dickens does with incomparable empathy in *Dombey and Son* is to look at the school through a child's eyes. Confused by his lessons, Paul wanders around the joyless house, listening to the ticking of the great clock in the hall:

> He was intimate with all the paper-hanging in the house; saw things that no one else saw in the patterns; found out miniature tigers and lions running up the bedroom walls, and squinting faces leering in the squares and diamonds of the floor-cloth.

Once the holidays approach, however, the lions and tigers become 'quite tame and frolicsome' and the faces peep out at him 'with less wicked eyes'.[28]

Just as, in real life, schools varied in their severity, so they did in academic competence. This is hardly surprising for, as a German visitor to England pointed out in 1791: 'Every person, man or woman, is at liberty to set up a boarding-school.' In his view English parents took more care in selecting a dog trainer or a horse breaker than they took in choosing a good school for their children.[29] Many schoolmasters undoubtedly resembled Thackeray's Dr Birch, who got up his Classics with translations 'or what the boys call cribs', and could easily be caught out by 'elder wags' who asked him for help with 'hard bits of Herodotus or Thucydides'.[30] One former pupil of an expensive Mitcham academy told his father that the Rev Roberts could not instil anything more than the 'the rudiments of the dead languages'.[31] Headmasters often used barely educated ushers (teaching assistants) to implement an unimaginative system of education similar to that pioneered by the Rev Thomas Lancaster at Wimbledon School and endured by Arthur Schopenhauer for a term in 1793: 'Everything – teaching, punishment and everything to do with the children – is done mechanically in accordance with given rules, regardless of age, character and ability.'[32] Still, most boys managed, like Tom Brown, to imbibe a fair amount of Latin and Greek, even if it was sometimes unhelpful to them. Manning had to begin all over again when he went to Harrow because the Westminster Greek grammar he had been made to learn at Totteridge was not used there. At the age of nine, Henry Coke could repeat, parrot-fashion, several hundred lines of Virgil's *Aeneid*. But he soon forgot it. Like many other Georgian children, he paid for this learning dearly and with 'many tears'.[33]

There were, of course, more humane pedagogues than Temple Grove's Dr Pinckney. Cardinal John Henry Newman related to a friend an affectionate memory of Dr Nicholas, who found the seven-year-old crying by himself after his parents' first visit to Ealing School. When the doctor proposed taking John to the big room to join the other boys, the child objected because his tears would have been observed and would cause derision:

> 'O sir! They will say such things! I can't help crying.' On his master making light of it: 'O sir! But they will; they will say all sorts of things,' and, taking the master's hand, 'Come and see for yourself!' and led him into the crowded room, where, of course, under the circumstances, there was no teasing.

This memory, as revealing of the pupils' normal behaviour as it is of Dr Nicholas, tells us rather more than Newman's early diaries. These record, for instance, that on 25 May 1810 he 'got into Ovid and Greek' and that on the same date two years later he 'began Homer'. Luckily for his literary development he had enough free time at Ealing to read the novels of Sir Walter Scott and to write his own verses – though his schoolfellows 'have left on record that they never, or scarcely ever, saw him taking part in any game'. So attached did young John become to Dr Nicholas that he persuaded his parents not to send him to Winchester; he then progressed so well at Ealing that he went up to Trinity College, Oxford when he was only fifteen.[34]

It was at Oxford that Newman met Richard Hurrell Froude (as well as other future leaders of the Oxford Movement). Froude, too, had been fortunate in his headmaster, the Rev George Coleridge (nephew of the poet) of the Free School, Ottery St Mary. Belying his nickname 'Coldrage', the clergyman was kind to Hurrell (who was known by his second name) and his brother Robert, when his friend Archdeacon Froude of Dartington sent them there in 1812. The boys sometimes needed such comfort as Coleridge could give after they had been 'rapped' by the Classics master, who once beat Robert senseless and was 'far more severe' with Hurrell than with other pupils from whom he expected less. There was also a certain amount of bullying, in which Hurrell joined, rebuking himself afterwards in his journal. But the brothers also had fun with boats, wooden swords and apple feasts and were delighted when their mother sent them a 'very rich cake'.[35] Thus was Froude prepared for Eton, which he entered at thirteen, an age at which he was just about able to cope with harsh public school conditions.

The same could not be said of his youngest brother, the future historian James Anthony Froude, who never forgot the *'infandum dolorem'* (unspeakable anguish) he endured at Westminster from the age of eleven. Before that, however, Anthony (known, like his brother, by his second name) had been very happy at Buckfastleigh School, five miles away from Dartington Rectory. The school inflicted the usual 'vigorous and frequent application of the cane' – the birch being reserved 'only for theft or lying or other disgraceful offences'. But Anthony himself was probably not caned a great deal since he was 'tolerably accomplished' at Latin and had 'a special aptitude for Greek', which he studied under the enthusiastic tutelage of the headmaster's son.

> He flung himself into the combats of Gods and men with as much eagerness as if he had been one of the warriors. He found in the small me a partner in his enthusiasm. I was put into a Homer class by myself, and before I was eleven I had read all the *Iliad* and the *Odyssey* twice over.

There was not much bullying at Buckfastleigh and Anthony found that, despite being prevented by a hernia from fighting and 'taking a part in the rough games of the playing field', he was popular with the other boys. Perhaps the goodwill was increased by the frequent cakes and baskets of fruit which arrived from Dartington Rectory. In other respects, however, home was less congenial than school, for his mother had died and Archdeacon Froude was hard on his youngest son, making him 'work without pause or relief' in the holidays. Moreover, his brothers taunted him for being 'sawney' or sentimental.[36]

Anthony further charged that his father sent him to Westminster early just so that he could soon be relieved of 'further cost'. This may be unfair for, as we have seen, it was not unusual at that time for a clever child to be advanced in this way. But it does seem to be true that his father and brothers insisted on his entering the scholars' Foundation, 'with forty lads all living in one chamber', rather than one of the more 'gentlemanlike' boarding houses. Apparently they 'considered that a little roughing it would do me good and cure me of nonsense'. Anthony relates that for three and a half years he was beaten, starved, frozen and bullied in this 'den of wild animals'. Then, falling behind with the work, he was removed by his disappointed father.[37]

Anthony's stories of the older boys setting his legs on fire to make him dance, holding cigars to his face and making him drunk on brandy punch were similar to those told about many other public schools of this time. After all, Squire Brown warned Tom that at Rugby he would see 'a great many cruel blackguard things'. And, as Thomas Hughes knew from his own experience in the 1830s, bullying, fighting and beer-drinking continued at the school even under Dr Arnold's reformed regime. In his memoir of his brother George, who was at Rugby with him, Hughes describes the 'kings of the close' as 'a rough and hard set of task-masters, who fagged us for whole afternoons and were much too ready with the cane'. He relates a particularly prolonged torment, whereby the younger boys had to spend their half-day holidays digging the sixth-formers' garden plots with the use only of sticks.[38] No doubt they were beaten if they flagged in this labour, for Dr Arnold did not subscribe to the Romantics' notion that children came into the world 'trailing clouds of glory' and had Heaven lying about them in their infancy.[39] More inclined towards the Evangelical concept of unredeemed children of Satan, he believed in the 'essential inferiority in a boy as compared to a man'. This apparently justified 'the exercise of authority implied in personal chastisement' by pubescent prefects as well as by mature masters.[40]

As the poet William Cowper concluded, 'great schools suit best the sturdy and the rough'.[41] So it was that some junior public school pupils fared better than delicate boys like Robert Cecil or Anthony Froude. Two aristocratic Whig prime ministers had as much mettle in their youth as Tom Brown himself. The handsome nine-year-old William Lamb (Lord Melbourne) positively flourished in Eton's 'uproarious barbarity'. And plucky Harry Temple (Lord Palmerston) resisted the Harrovian vices of 'swearing and getting drunk' – as he later resisted foreign 'injustice and wrong'.[42] When they reached the top of the school, such sturdy young gentlemen were likely in their turn to subject vulnerable little boys to 'every misery and every indignity which seventeen years of age can inflict'.[43] Anthony Trollope, for example, was the complete victim: a seven-year-old char-ity boy with a 'disreputably dirty' appearance and comical name was fair game as he ran between Harrow School and his impoverished home at Orley Farm. In addition, Trollope admitted, he lacked 'that juvenile manhood which enables some boys to hold up their heads even among the distresses which such a position is sure to produce'. He fared a little better after he was moved to Arthur Drury's private academy at Sunbury, until an unfortunate incident plunged him again into disgrace. Anthony was among four boys punished for a nameless crime, probably some form of sexual experimentation, of which he was 'as innocent as a babe'. Fifty years later he could not forget the injustice: 'It burns me now as though it were yesterday. What lily-livered curs those boys must have been not to have told the truth – at any rate as far as I was concerned!' Later, at his father's old school, Winchester, the 'big, awkward and ugly' boy was to be bullied by his own brother and made 'a Pariah' after his college bills stopped being paid. The only consolation for such an unhappy childhood 'is that life afterwards can only get better' – as it did for Trollope once he found early success as a novelist.[44]

The experiences of three other lads suggest that Trollope might have been happier at Christ's Hospital, an ancient foundation which still fulfilled the terms of its endowment by educating, housing and clothing many sons of indigent gentlemen. It had even set up a school in rural Hertfordshire at which boys were prepared for the bleak austerity of the large London academy. Contemporaries at both schools in the 1780s were Charles Lamb, whose parents 'were in a humble station', and Samuel Taylor Coleridge, the youngest of a Devonshire clergyman's fourteen children; ten years later came Leigh Hunt, son of a tutor in the household of Lord Chandos. All were described as delicate but all had sufficient spirit to cope with the school's 'antique peculiarities' and to draw from it an intellectual training which eventually sustained their literary careers.[45]

From the age of seven or eight they suffered the normal hardships of a Georgian boys' school: a scanty diet by which 'appetites were *damped*, never satisfied' and the 'excessive subordination' of younger boys to monitors who had the authority to beat them with leather thongs for talking in the dormitories.[46] Indeed, these rigours were severe enough to cause some boys to run away, despite knowing that they would be confined in a dungeon and (if they tried again) publicly scourged and expelled. Otherwise, there seems to have been little bullying. Lamb was not ridiculed for his speech infirmity or for his inability to take part in boisterous sport and Hunt got away with refusing to fag. None of them resented submission to a religious routine in which they 'rivalled the monks' – though, as Hunt wryly observed, 'the effect was certainly not what was intended'.

The three boys mastered their Greek and Latin grammar, administered in the upper school by the 'passionate and capricious' Rev James Boyer. They all had tales to tell of his tyrannical methods but seem at the same time to have respected him. In a fit of impatience at Hunt's stammering, Boyer knocked one of his teeth out 'with the back of a Homer'. But the incident worked to Hunt's benefit. Boyer was so shocked by the amount of blood shed that he became positively paternal and 'it was felt that I had got an advantage over him'.[47] Lamb recalls Boyer's whipping a boy and reading parliamentary debates at the same time, 'a paragraph and a lash between'.[48] The ungainly Coleridge, who always got an extra cut from Boyer because he was 'such an ugly fellow', was flogged when he rashly admitted that he was attracted to atheism by reading Voltaire's *Philosophical Dictionary* – and he even felt that the punishment was justified.

Despite this academic tyranny, the boys had enough freedom to profit from their London surroundings. Hunt bought poetry from second-hand bookshops; Coleridge rushed from school to borrow two books at a time from a circulating library in Cheapside until he had read everything in it; and Lamb enjoyed excursions to the river, in which the boys swam like otters, and to the Tower where they saw lions. Lamb had an additional boon. The proximity of the school to his family home in the Inner Temple meant that he received supplies of hot loaf and roast veal and that on every half-holiday 'he passed from cloister to cloister'. 'Here was his home, here was his recreation.'[49]

Coleridge, by contrast, was far from his Devon home and had no acquaintances with whom he could spend free afternoons or vacations. He started at the school when he was nine and paid his first visit to Ottery St Mary at the age of twelve. After that stay Boyer found the homesick boy crying and administered comfort in his own terms:

> Boy! the school is your father! Boy! the school is your mother! Boy! the school is your brother! the school is your sister! the school is your first cousin, and your second cousin, and all the rest of your relations! Let's have no more crying![50]

But the pupil's plight was not eased until his last three years, when he was befriended by the Evans family, who treated him like a son. Coleridge never complained of those lonely years, which are described not by him but by Lamb, who wrote an essay in the voice of his less fortunate friend. Yet such a long exile inevitably left scars. Coleridge was dogged all his life by 'psychosomatic illness' (a term he himself coined), by an acute 'hunger for friendship and understanding' and by an inferiority complex.[51] Perhaps this was sublimated in his poetry. In 'Frost at Midnight' he recalls being lulled to sleep by thoughts of his 'sweet birth-place, and the old church-tower' which then formed the substance of his dreams. But the next morning, as he sat in class:

> Awed by the stern preceptor's face, mine eye
> Fixed with mock study on my swimming book:
> Save if the door half opened, and I snatched
> A hasty glance, and still my heart leaped up,
> For still I hoped to see the stranger's face,
> Townsman, or aunt, or sister more beloved,
> My play-mate when we both were dressed alike![52]

Coleridge was far from being the only boarding school pupil haunted by the ghosts of home.

The 'turn for romance', which Lamb thought characteristic of Blue Coat boys, may well have dimmed their more unpleasant memories. Certainly he, Coleridge and Hunt blessed their alma mater even after they became part of the radical, free-thinking circle of their day. Coleridge, who became a Grecian (or prefect) at the top of the school before proceeding to Cambridge, said that he had learnt from Boyer the severe logic of Poetry. Hunt and Lamb were prevented by their stammering from becoming Grecians and did not go to university. Nevertheless, Lamb applauded an institution which enabled its alumni to 'hold up their heads in the world' and Hunt was grateful for 'a well-trained and cheerful boyhood' within its 'old cloisters'. The three old boys met regularly at gatherings of 'dreamers and thinkers' in Lamb's Inner Temple house, where the furniture may have been 'old-fashioned and worn' but the talk was astonishingly like that of modern intellectuals.[53]

Meanwhile, at more exclusive Georgian schools, boys stood a good chance of getting in with the future Establishment. At the Rev Roberts's school (which charged £200 a year) Edward and Philip Pusey, of Pusey House in the village of Pusey, enjoyed the companionship of the Stanley brothers (the future Lords Derby and Carlisle). Less outstanding pupils, such as Thomas Acland and the sons of George Barlow, the Governor of Madras who started life as a silk mercer, sometimes felt 'crushed' when the irascible Roberts complained that they were all 'dunces but the Stanleys and the Puseys'.[54] After moving on to Eton, eleven-year-old Edward Pusey was in the same form as many other eminent Victorians: a prime minister, a Lord Lieutenant of Ireland, a Colonial Secretary, a Treasurer of the Royal Household, a Speaker of the House of Commons and three ambassadors.[55] Pusey himself became a distinguished theologian, a leading light in the Oxford

Movement and Regius Professor of Divinity at Oxford University.

Other great and famous men felt that being sent away to school at a very young age had given them little benefit. Alfred Tennyson's only legacy from Louth Grammar School was the memory of one Latin phrase, 'sonus desilientis aquae' (the sound of falling waters). He had opted for school when offered the choice between that and going to sea, but he hated it from the time he arrived, aged eight. He related to his son an enduring memory of 'sitting on the stone steps of the school on a cold winter's morning and crying bitterly after a big lad had brutally cuffed him on the head because he was a new boy'. Three more years under the sway of the Rev Waite, 'a tempestuous flogging master of the old stamp', did not make Alfred any fonder of the school, which he could not bring himself to revisit when it granted a holiday in his honour many years later.[56] One of his biographers, Harold Nicolson, judged that it left the poet with 'an almost morbid horror of the hostility of his fellow-creatures and . . . a no less morbid love of the admiration of the chosen few'.[57] Alfred returned home at the age of eleven to his father's rectory, where he composed epic poems and recited them loudly in the fields. He acquired enough classical proficiency under the rector's tuition to gain a place at Trinity College, Cambridge, whence he quickly made his mark and eventually became Poet Laureate.

Can one generalize from these experiences? What harvest did the typical young Georgian gentleman reap from his preparatory education? Did he grow up all the stronger and better for the rough treatment he so often received? Or was Sydney Smith right in his conviction that making a boy miserable 'produces those effects upon the temper and disposition which unjust suffering always does produce' and that he would be a better man if treated 'with a wise and rational indulgence'?[58] Did rote learning of dead languages give a child vital intellectual discipline? Or did he acquire merely 'the ignorance of the learned', as argued by the radical journalist, William Hazlitt, spitefully using the example of Tory MP, George Canning, son of an actress: 'the least respectable character among modern politicians was the cleverest boy at Eton.' Hazlitt thought a pupil should have more opportunity to 'feel the circulation of his blood and the motion of his heart'.[59] Did it help a boy's future career, a friend asked William Cowper, to be at school from an early age with 'great men in embryo'? Or were such connections 'liable to extinction' once the boys became men? To these debates, in which parents endlessly engaged, the experiences of their children have provided no easy or sweeping conclusions. But one thing is surely clear: school terms of four to five months and long coach journeys necessitating vacations spent away from home placed a heavy and sometimes insupportable burden on a young child – even if, like Tom Brown, he enjoyed the adventure of 'a dark ride on the top of the Tally-ho'.[60] Lacking 'the solicitous care of both his parents,' a boy ran the risk of becoming, as Cowper said, 'a stranger in his father's house'.[61]

Children themselves often understood this danger better than their parents or teachers. The Yule family archive reveals the differing viewpoints. Major and Mrs William Yule, having retired from India to Edinburgh, sent their twelve-year-old son George to Redland Hill Academy near Bristol in 1826. Dr John Swete, the headmaster, assured the parents that their son's health and spirits 'have been uninterrupted' and that he was 'very happy with us'. It is true that George's letters (which were not inspected by Dr Swete) mentioned no beating or bullying – they simply complained, in typical schoolboy fashion, about 'too many lessons and so little play that I can scarcely get any dinner'. But George became increasingly anxious about the long separation from home. He often asked his parents why they had not written; he could not think of anything to say to his younger brother Robert 'except to take care of the pony and the cat'; he wished he was at home to celebrate the King's birthday, imagining Bob 'firing the cannon'. On 20 December he wrote: 'Most of the boys are gone and the rest will go today except the five that stay here.' With these companions George walked, played and painted books over Christmas.[62] At least he had a better time than Dickens's Ebenezer Scrooge, the only child left in the 'chilly bareness' of his school 'when all the other boys had gone home for the jolly holidays'. Scrooge weeps in pity for 'his poor forgotten self' shown him by the Ghost of Christmas Past, 'reading near a feeble fire', his only cheer the visions conjured up by *The Arabian Nights* and *Robinson Crusoe*.[63]

George Yule was joined by his brother Robert in September 1827, when their mother prayed for God's support in her own grief at losing two sons. George's letters could not have been much comfort:

8 September: I don't think Bobby likes the school very well and neither do I. . . . All the boys are going home in the winter holidays and mamma do let us come home. I can't help crying when I think of it.

15 September: We have only got one letter from you yet. You see we write regularly every Saturday. . . . Do tell us whether we are to go home in winter. There won't be a single boy here and we will be so dull by ourselves.

The letters continued into 1828, during which both boys were concerned about the baby sister they had never seen. 'I wish,' wrote Robert, 'I was at home to teach baby to talk. You must teach her to say Doddy [Georgy] and Bobby.' By the summer George had been prepared for Haileybury, the Hertfordshire school which trained boys for entry to the Indian Civil Service, with 'long lessons in three languages we know scarcely anything of'. Loyal to the family of which he had seen so little, he promised that he would maintain 'a good character' despite the distractions of other lads getting drunk, breaking windows and kicking in doors. Certainly he would be equipped for the further exile which was eventually to await him (as well as Robert and their younger brother Henry) in India.[64]

Schoolboy letters are not usually as frank as those of the Yule brothers. More often, as Thomas Hughes said of his brother George, a boy would 'write home of everything . . . except what he knew would only give pain, and be quite useless'.[65] Schoolmasters encouraged a sententious epistolary style, such as that used in the juvenile letters of Walter Hook from his school in Tiverton. He did not mention frivolous matters such as saving up his spare pence for buns and loaves to alleviate his hunger. But he did tell his mother the shocking tale of a boy who had twice sold borrowed watches to fund flights from school: 'You will with me pity that wicked boy, Henry George Salter, who is now publicly expelled from this school: and his master blotted his name from the Register.'[66] Ten-year-old Charles Barlow wrote an entire letter in Latin addressed (ungrammatically) to *Meus Care Pater* and two weeks later listed all the classical texts he was studying.[67] Such epistles, observed Mrs Gaskell in *Cranford*, were more in the nature of 'show-letters' like those written home by her character, Peter Marmaduke Arley Jenkyns, and treasured by his sister Matty:

They were of a highly mental description, giving an account of his studies and his intellectual hopes of various kinds, with an occasional quotation from the classics; but, now and then, the animal nature broke out in such a little sentence as this, evidently written in a trembling hurry, after the letter had been inspected; 'Mother dear, do send me a cake, and put plenty of citron in.'

Later samples from Miss Matty's bundle reduce her to tears, as she reads Peter's stilted expressions of penitence for his many scrapes and a 'badly-written, badly-sealed, badly-directed, blotted note' promising 'I will be good, darling mother.'[68]

It is rare for a child's cry from the past to echo so clearly outside fiction. But it can be heard in the correspondence of the historian Thomas Babington Macaulay, collected in Trinity College, Cambridge. For Macaulay had the emotional and intellectual sophistication to express feelings which 'inoffensive boys' like George and Robert Yule struggled to convey and which many other children dared not disclose. Macaulay's biographer and nephew, George Otto Trevelyan, describes Macaulay's 'quiet and most happy childhood' in Clapham, incessantly reading 'on a rug before the fire and a piece of bread and butter in his hand', creeping unwillingly to Mr Greaves's day school and exploring the 'delightful wilderness' of the Common.[69] His father, Zachary Macaulay, considered sending his gifted son, who was already writing history, heroic poems and hymns at the age of eight, as a day boy to Westminster, but decided in 1813 on a private school run by a clergyman of his own Evangelical persuasion. The Rev Matthew Preston's academy at Little Shelford, near Cambridge, was not rough by the standards of its time, though Preston, according to his precocious pupil, sometimes 'kept the Sabbath by being in a bad temper'.[70] But generally, Thomas reported, Mr Preston was very kind to him, lending him books and taking him for walks 'every now and then'. There was, it is true, some bullying – even by pupils from the holiest of homes. One new boy was mocked by William Wilberforce (oldest son of the reformer) for having a cockney accent. Luckily, Macaulay got into the good books of the 'very clever, very droll, and very impudent' Wilberforce: 'a favourite with most of the big boys, he has often begged me off from a beating.' He also appreciated his own 'delightful, snug, little chamber', in which he could read and write to his heart's delight, as well as occasional visits to Cambridge, where he was entertained by the Dean of Queens' College.[71]

In spite of all these advantages, Thomas's letters to his mother reveal the acute homesickness he felt from the time he left home at the unusually late age of twelve. He never felt more gloomy in his life than when he departed from Clapham in the Cambridge Stage; he waited anxiously every day for the postman; he dreamed of home almost every night; he begged in vain to be allowed to come home for his birthday; he counted 'the weeks and days and hours' of the four months which were to pass before the holidays; he planned the presents he would bring for his brothers and sisters, 'a couple of rabbits for Selina and Jane, and something for John and Henry and Fanny and Hannah and pretty little Margaret'; he relished his holidays amid the 'fireside pleasures' of home.[72]

It was after his return to the school from the first summer holiday that Thomas felt most depressed. Trevelyan thought it would be cruel to include the letter he wrote home on 12 August 1813, but it is worth quoting at length here:

> I cannot bear the thoughts of remaining so long from home. I do not know how to comfort myself, or what to do. There is nobody here to pity me or to comfort me, and if I were to say I was sorry at being from home, I should be called a baby. When I am with the rest I am obliged to look pleasant, and to laugh at Wilberforce's jokes, when I can hardly hide the tears in my eyes. So I have nothing to do but to sit and cry in my room, and think of home and wish for the holidays. I am ten times more uneasy than I was last year. I did not mean to complain, but indeed I cannot help it.

Although this desperate plea was addressed to his mother, it was Zachary Macaulay who replied. He urged his son to 'Pray to God . . . that he would enable you to give up cheerfully your own selfish preferences when these stand in the way of duty.' Perhaps this Evangelical reproof had its effect, for subsequent letters present a more cheerful front. But even after the school moved to Aspenden in Hertfordshire when he was thirteen, Thomas still felt his 'maladie de Clapham', which was relieved only by writing in letters to those he loved best 'what I think and wish and feel without any more restraint than if I were talking to them'.[73] Similarly, his only comfort during a physical illness he suffered at Aspenden was his mother's coming to nurse him: 'How well I remember with what an ecstasy of joy I saw that face approaching me, in the middle of people that did not care if I died that night except for the trouble of burying me.'[74] Through this remarkable correspondence Macaulay preserved the loving relationship with his family which was to sustain him during his busy political and literary life. He did not marry or have his own children but, as his nephew relates: 'It is impossible to exaggerate the pleasure Macaulay took in [his nephews and nieces], or the delight which he gave them.'[75]

Another Victorian who was remembered (in this case by a daughter) as a 'delightful play-fellow and the most perfect sympathiser' with children was

Charles Darwin.[76] He had been more fortunate in his schooldays than Macaulay. In 1818, at the age of nine, he was sent to 'Dr Butler's great school in Shrewsbury' which was very close to his home. In his *Autobiography* Darwin evokes the advantage of this proximity.

I boarded at this school, so that I had the great advantage of living the life of a true schoolboy; but as the distance was hardly more than a mile to my home, I very often ran there in the longer intervals between the callings over and before the locking up at night. This, I think, was in many ways advantageous to me by keeping up home affections and interests. I remember in the early part of my school life that I often had to run very quickly to be in time, and from being a fleet runner was generally successful; but when in doubt I prayed earnestly to God to help me, and I well remember that I attributed my success to the prayers and not to my quick running, and marvelled how generally I was aided.

It is true that the child was bored by Shrewsbury's 'strictly classical' curriculum and rote-learning methods, concluding that 'the school as a means of education to me was simply a blank'. He preferred to browse in a borrowed copy of *Wonders of the World*, which gave him 'a wish to travel in remote countries' and, at home with his brother, to conduct chemical experiments which earned him the nickname 'Gas'. He was also able to continue the hobbies he had developed while still at day school: observing rare insects, shooting birds, collecting birds' eggs and classifying minerals, activities that were all, in the opinion of Dr Butler, entirely 'useless'.

Darwin continued with such pursuits throughout his education. Shooting was his main diversion as he vainly studied for his father's profession of medicine at Edinburgh and collecting beetles his greatest interest when he was sent to prepare for holy orders at Cambridge. It was only when a chance meeting gave him the opportunity to set off on the voyage of the *Beagle* as a naturalist in 1831 that Darwin received his 'first real training or education'. He was later to attribute his scientific success to his passionate early 'desire to understand or explain whatever I observed' rather than to the 'wretched' classical drilling which worked only the memory.[77] This is perhaps too harsh a judgement of Georgian education but there is no doubt that Charles Darwin's juvenile bug-hunting played a part in forming the intellect that produced *The Origin of the Species*. In that age of adventure a boy could still follow his own path. This would not be so easy in the more organized preparatory school system which developed in Victorian times. Shades of the prison-house began to close upon the growing boy.

2

'The Only Way to Bring up Boys'
Victorian Prep Schools

Many narratives about the busy Victorian middle classes are woven into William Frith's popular painting *The Railway Station* (1862). In particular, it illustrates their increasing tendency to send young offspring away to school. In the centre of the picture Frith and his wife Isabella bid farewell to two of their sons who are about to depart for their Somerset prep school on the convenient new line. Isabella Frith embraces the younger boy who clutches a cricket bat, while the artist rests his hand on the shoulder of the more stoical older lad. Right up to the time of Harry Potter's search for platform nine and three-quarters at King's Cross, railway stations have been a continuous and often emotionally charged feature of the prep school story.

Britain's railways had grown apace since 1830, when Tennyson (with his famous failure to understand the new engineering) had travelled along 'the ringing grooves of change' on the pioneering Liverpool to Manchester line. By the time Frith portrayed Paddington Station, London was linked to nearly every town in Britain. There were 10,000 miles of track – and about the same number of private schools. No doubt many of these were 'fly-by-night establishments intended primarily for the lower orders',[1] but a good number were described by Lord Taunton's Schools Inquiry Commission of 1868 as 'preparatory schools for the second and first grade' in society. As old and newly founded public schools adopted the common practice noted in that same inquiry of not taking pupils until they were thirteen, the network of feeder schools grew to produce suitably qualified pupils.[2] Famous names such as Summer Fields (known as Summerfield until 1891), Rose Hill and Orley Farm joined the ranks of Temple Grove and Twyford. At the same time some of the more efficient old private academies, like Cheam and Eagle House, confined themselves to the preparatory age group. It was in this period, too, that choir schools like those of Magdalen College, Oxford, and King's College, Cambridge, became 'highly attractive' establishments, preparing choristers for life after their voices had broken.[3]

The ideal prep school met three criteria: rustication, separation and preparation.[4] In other words it was an isolated rural establishment where boys aged
between seven and thirteen were grounded in the Classics and fitted with the
character required for entrance to the public schools. These arrangements suited
nouveau riche parents who sought a gentlemanly education for their sons, as
James Bryce commented in the Taunton Report:

> When a Lancashire merchant or manufacturer sends his sons away from home, he desires
> as often as not to send them a long way off, partly that they may lose their northern
> tongue, partly that they may form new acquaintances, and be quite away from home
> influences.[5]

Thus in George Eliot's *The Mill on the Floss*, Mr Tulliver of Dorlcote Mill is
prepared to lay out £100 a year so that his son Tom might become 'a bit of a
scholard' and a 'smartish' business man with a 'big watch-chain' – even if it
means that Mrs Tulliver will not be able to 'wash him and mend him' once he
goes to King's Lorton.[6] At a rather more exalted level the distinguished barrister
Baliol Brett (later Lord Esher) was anxious that his son Reginald's school friends
should be 'nice, good, gentlemanly fellows' with whom he would spend the rest
of his public life.[7]

The dispositions of the Guest family illustrate the new lines of educational
development. Sir Josiah John Guest MP, owner of the world's largest iron foundry
and chairman of the Taff Valley railway company, who had himself attended day
schools, sent his three sons through the prep/public school system. As his wife,
Charlotte, contemplated their departure, she wrote in her journal in September
1845: 'It seems a sad prospect but everybody says it is the only way to bring up
boys; and what is to be done? How can I, a poor weak woman, judge against all
the world?' In fact, Lady Guest put off the dreaded day. The oldest son, Ivor, was
already thirteen in 1848 when he was sent to a prep school in Mitcham. It proved
unsuitable, for his pious mother found out that there was a great deal of swearing, which was not confined to the boys. 'Now as the master is a clergyman,' she
wrote, 'the offence is aggravated in his case and, deeply as I feel the disadvantage
of change, I do not think it possible to let Ivor go on exposed to such bad influ-
ences and so surrounded by temptations.' After taking advice from other parents
and from the headmaster of Harrow (the public school for which the boys were

destined) the Guests journeyed by train to several prospective schools before selecting one at Totteridge. So impressed were they with its headmaster, the Rev George Renaud, a son-in-law of 'the celebrated Mr Faithfull, the Hatfield schoolmaster' and ex-tutor to Lord Rosebery, that they enrolled both Ivor (later Baron Wimborne) and his ten-year-old brother, Merthyr. Lady Guest's journal does not reveal whether Renaud's regime was any less rough than that of his father-in-law in the 1830s.[8]

The Guests were by no means the only Victorians to harbour doubts about the religious and moral worth of boys' boarding schools in the wake of Thomas Arnold's example of godliness and good learning. Evangelical women, such as Sarah Ellis and Mary Sewell, urged mothers to play a greater role in the rearing of sons, 'mischievous, disorderly and troublesome' though they could be. Schools were all very well for the children of 'weak and injudicious mothers' or fathers 'whose conduct and conversation are such as to render the atmosphere of home ungenial to the growth of religious feeling'. Mrs Ellis, who had no children of her own, found it extraordinary that in normal circumstances 'a fond mother should prefer sending her children away from home to pursue their education entirely under the care of strangers'. She feared that boys would learn at school 'the lesson of domination and the lesson of abject compliance with tyranny', both injurious to 'the dispositions of men'.[9] Rather than such lessons, urged Mary Sewell, boys needed 'the affections trained and developed to make them good domestic men', a concept to which boys' schools were antagonistic. (Mrs Sewell had no sons on whom to test her theories but she was the mother of Anna Sewell, author of *Black Beauty*.)[10] Religious fathers could be equally cautious. Philip Gosse, a devout Plymouth Brother, was so protective of his son's soul that Edmund was not allowed to associate with any other children until he was ten. When Philip did dispatch him, aged thirteen, to a boarding school run by an elderly Brethren couple, he stipulated that the boy should spend Saturday and Sunday nights at home. Little did he realize, writes his son, that 'the piety of the establishment . . . resided mainly in the prospectus'.[11]

Philip Gosse's reluctance to send his only son away may well have been inspired by his deep love for the boy as well as by his religious faith. Other fathers were more openly moved by affection. Alfred Tennyson, who had not forgotten his unhappy days at Louth Grammar School, wanted to make the lives of his own children 'as beautiful and as happy as possible'. He and his wife Emily kept their sons, Hallam and Lionel, at home for so long that friends said they were 'growing up in a hot house' and needed to 'expand and harden in the world'.[12] Sir James Stephen, a civil servant in the Colonial Office (whose strenuous efforts to impose his own Evangelical moral imperatives on his political bosses caused him to be known as Mr Over-Secretary) refused to send his sons away to prep school. He explained the reasons in his diary:

> Would parents care for their children, or husbands for their wives, after a long and indefi-
> nite separation? How much of our most intense passion . . . is but the cherished warmth
> of habits artificial, accidental, perishable? . . . My own boys, God bless them, have I trust
> had pleasant early days, and may have pleasant retrospects.

So much did he cherish the 'confidence and regard' of Fitzjames and Leslie that he would not consent to their being anything but day boys at Eton with all its 'impurities, profaneness, gluttony and rioting'.[13]

Charles Darwin expressed similar reservations in letters to his second cousin, William Fox, whom he admired and envied for educating his own boys at home. Darwin despised 'the old stereotyped stupid classical learning' and hated 'the whole system of breaking through the affections of the family by separating the boys so early in life'. He kept his sons at home for their initial education but did not have 'the courage to break through the trammels' and 'after many doubts' sent his oldest son, William, to Rugby in 1852. Darwin was never happy about this decision and thought of Willy whenever there were 'detestable cold gales and much rain, which always give much *ennui* to children away from their homes'. (At the same time he realized that there were worse fates for children and gave his support to the campaign against the use of climbing boys: 'It makes one shudder to fancy one of one's own children at seven years old being forced up a chimney.') For his four younger sons he sought 'some less classical school' which would allow more 'reasoning and observation to come into play'. Thus, after their preparatory years at home, during which their father encouraged but did not impose his own interests, George, Francis, Leonard and Horace were sent in turn to a Clapham school run by Charles Pritchard FRS. All went on to pursue scientific careers, while William became a banker.

For all his qualms Darwin saw certain merits in a boarding education: 'I dare not run the risk of a youth being exposed to the temptations of the world without having undergone the milder ordeal of a great school.'[14] He thus spoke for most middle-class Victorian parents, among whom home education of sons was increasingly rare. School was supposed to prepare a boy for the world by teaching him 'to rub shoulders with his peers, to experience competition, and to bend to public authority'.[15] Character counted for more than the Classics, as Darwin himself conceded: 'A boy who has learnt to stick at Latin and conquer its difficulties, ought to be able to stick at any labour.' Edward Granville Browne, an unhappy product of the boarding school system, remembered hearing similar words voiced by its adult defenders: 'A boy does not go to school to learn Latin and Greek, but to learn to confront disagreeable tasks with equanimity, to do what is distasteful to him with cheerfulness.' Browne could find no answer to this argument since he had indeed learnt 'what the word disagreeable means' during his years of 'the most tedious monotony ... and the most acute misery' at Glenalmond and Eton before developing a passion for Oriental languages at Cambridge.[16]

Another critic of what he called 'the barrack system' of schooling was the radical journalist Frederic Harrison. The son of a prosperous stockbroker, he had been educated in the 1840s at the private day school attached to King's College, London, from which he won a scholarship to Wadham College, Oxford. Frederic found learning 'a delight' because his school, unlike a prep school, did not have 'to cram the scholars to the regulation pattern so that they may win prizes at the particular public school to which they are attached'. He agreed with defenders of boarding process that it produced 'a certain manliness and man-of-the-worldness' and taught boys to behave as 'gentlemen' – at any rate towards their social equals. But they did not learn to be 'either generous or just to those poorer than themselves'.[17]

These educational debates were usually conducted at an Olympian level, over the heads of children. In making their choices adults tended to assume (as did Darwin) that schools were 'not so wicked' as they had been and some historians take this on trust. Harold Perkin, for instance, suggests that the Mamma portrayed in Frith's painting 'need not worry' because the schools which had been made so much more accessible by the railway were no longer 'the nurseries of vice and idleness of the old society'.[18] Was this really the case or was Lady Guest right to shudder at the 'sorrow and temptation' to be endured by her sons as well as by thousands of other boarding school pupils during the first four decades of Queen Victoria's long reign?

A closer look at Frith's painting reveals reluctant tears trickling down the cheeks of his older son. The moment of parting was nearly always painful although some children managed not to cry at the station. For Edward in Kenneth Grahame's *The Golden Age* (who is really an amalgam of the author and his older brother Willie), the trick was to hold on to his hat: 'He recollected the hat he was wearing – a hard bowler, the first of that sort he had ever owned. He took it off, examined it, and felt it over. Something about it seemed to give him strength and he was a man once more.' As the train moved off, his siblings saw that Edward's small white face bore a 'first-quality grin', stoutly maintained until 'a curve swept him from our sight, and he was borne away in the dying rumble . . . out into the busy world of rubs and knocks and competition'. But, for all his juvenile stoicism, the writer developed a hatred of railway termini, those 'shrieking, sulphurous houses of damnation . . . [where] the very spirit of worry and unrest is embodied'.

Further tests awaited a boy once he arrived in the 'barrack-like school' and 'arid, cheerless classrooms' evoked by Grahame.[19] Would he be able to hold back the tears or would he succumb to the 'heart-breaking sobs' which shook the future playwright Herman Merivale, when he found himself alone in the garden of the school he calls Little Dotheboys? In his memoir he admits, 'It was weak of me to cry; unmanly, the school-mistress that very night informed me with a glare through spectacles. But I was only eight.'[20] Or would homesickness involve an actual desire to be sick? This was what worried young George (later Lord) Curzon as he watched the white horse and carriage drive away 'my mother who was dearer to me than anyone in the world'.[21] Many such anxieties and experiences are evoked with vivid immediacy in a large collection of unpublished letters from Cecil, Charles and Kenneth Monro, three brothers who boarded at Eagle House in Hammersmith during the 1840s. Using the unrestrained language characteristic of early Victorian times, they wrote regularly to their parents, a lawyer in the Court of Chancery, and his wife, who lived a short train journey away at Barnet in Hertfordshire.

As soon as Cecil and Charles (aged eleven and nine) arrived at Eagle House in February 1845 they faced the inevitable cross-questioning which greeted new boys. They were asked whether they were related to 'the fellow who fought the duel'. He was Lieutenant Monro, who killed his brother-in-law in 1843, in one of the last duels fought in England. The brothers, who were not in fact related to the Lieutenant, can only have gained glory for being associated with the event, which naturally fascinated their fellows. 'One afterwards asked me whether I had fought it myself,' reported Cecil.[22]

In subsequent letters the Monro boys described their daily routine, making no complaint about the spartan conditions at Eagle House where, according to a historian, 'urination was performed in a leaden trough around the ablutions room which had leaden bowls for washing but no hot water.'[23] These unhygienic arrangements may have contributed to the frequent outbreaks of ringworm which afflicted the pupils. But the brothers grumbled only about the cold, for it gave them bad chilblains which kept them awake at night and multiplied despite Matron's embrocation. They were quite happy with the food, especially with 'a kind of pudding called stickjaw very like plum pudding' and with the roast mutton or beef for dinner – though they were glad when they could buy a penny orange from the cakeman. They had to admit that not all the boys were of the same opinion. Cecil described to young Kenney, who was still at home, one boy's theory of how the school tea was made: 'First what remains of the masters' tea they boil up with a great deal of water and a pint of milk and then they heap ever so much sand which they call sugar and pour that out for us to drink. And he says that the butter is dripping but I forgot what the bread is.'[24]

Cecil and Charley had more serious preoccupations. From the beginning they were anxious about their position in class and whether they would win prizes. Particularly worrying was the process called 'standing up' when they had to recite 500 lines of verse by heart. As time went on, they often complained of having so much work that they could do little else: 'I certainly don't know what Mr Wickham [the headmaster, Rev E. C. Wickham] calls playtime' or 'I cannot write a very nice long letter because we have to get ready some Euclid, not having had near time to learn it in school time.' At the age of twelve, Cecil seems to have been at his wits' end when Wickham told him that he could exert himself more: 'It is about as great a mistake as ever was made, for I work harder than I ever have before and quite as hard as I can, but still I cannot get up in my class.'[25]

Dutiful boys that they were, Monro major and minor kept out of trouble. But they often reported cases of other boys being caned or birched for offences such as buying from 'a cakeman who came without Mr Wickham's leave', making a noise in the dormitory or 'stealing three pears and a few medlars out of Mr Wickham's study'. Sometimes they had a more dramatic tale to tell. When Miller was to be caned for bullying, 'he kicked and fought' so much that he had to be held down by two other masters; he was subsequently expelled and went on to military college. And there were two escapes during their time at Eagle House. An Irish boy, who had been caned twice in one day, ran away after making 'preparations for his journey by stuffing three or four pieces of bread and butter into his pockets'. He was pursued by the fencing master and two policemen and brought back after a few days but 'he wasn't caned as we thought he would be'. Six months later Charley reported that a boy named Shawl 'cut' before games and was spotted on an omnibus by another pupil who had gone to London to have a tooth extracted. Shawl came back the next day and also 'got nothing'.[26]

Of course the brothers paid a price for being so studious. Boys would laugh at them for learning their lines and for not playing well at cricket club. Both of them suffered also from bad dreams, especially when under pressure from work. By and large, however, they did not 'find school a very disagreeable place'. They managed to keep on the right side of the Rev Wickham: 'I have not been flogged yet,' wrote Cecil to Kenney, 'neither has Charley and we don't mean to be.' They got some pleasure from the periodic crazes which swept through the school: making crossbows, painted masks or little boats, skipping, rearing silkworms and learning shorthand. They particularly enjoyed marbles and often requested agates from home until the headmaster decreed that marbles should not be played 'in earnest, but only in fun because he said it was like playing for money for agates cost two or three pence'. They also appreciated the new Sunday book club, in which devout boys read 'books proper for Sunday, such as *The Early English Church*' rather than the story books preferred by most pupils.[27]

But the greatest consolation Cecil and Charles had during sixteen-week terms was the thought of home. They clearly loved writing to their parents and little brother, 'pretty Ken': 'it seems as if I was talking to you at home'. (They tried to store the letters they received in a box but kept losing the key, which doubtless explains why only one side of the correspondence survives.) Often they counted the weeks and days to go before the holidays began, planning which train they would take. They were delighted when Mr Monro made surprise visits, taking them on walks around the neighbourhood which included the local cake shop – 'you may guess what we did there'. Above all, they were glad of each other's company, making sure that they sat together at tea and breakfast, writing joint letters and reading *Evenings at Home* together. All this sounds utterly genuine, expressed as it is in normal schoolboy language with occasional use of private family terms. One of Cecil's letters to his mother ends with a farewell appropriate to the new railway age: 'Hampers full of love, as many as the train will carry to you, Papa and Kenney. PS The reason I tell you how much love we send is that if the train is late you will know why.'[28]

The box full of Kenneth's letters in the London Metropolitan Archive reveals a startling difference between his experience and that of his brothers. By the time he arrived at Eagle House in 1847, Cecil had moved on to Harrow. Charles must still have been there for a while but is not mentioned, perhaps because the three-year age difference made contact difficult. From the start Kenneth sounds miserable, lapsing into baby language in his first letter home: 'Me is absolutely plagued out of me life me must either go away or die of vexation because I am beaten about from place to place and kicked and slapped and very often I feel absolutely unwell and sick.' He ends by urging his mother to remember her 'itty boy, Kenney'. His particular *bête noire* was a boy called Blore who stole his shoe horn and beat him with it when Kenneth refused to pick up his shoes. Masters tried to help by moving his desk but he was still tormented. Boys stole and destroyed his possessions and teased him when he received presents from home 'because Mamma loved her dear little Kenney so'. The little boy was shocked by such events as Blore being publicly birched for stealing 'a great many apples' and Campbell having the stick for using dirty words. But before long he too was getting the cane for misdemeanours like having his desk open at the wrong time and throwing books at dinner. Kenneth struggled to reach the high academic standard set at Eagle House but he gained only 'pretty middling' grades. 'Between work and boys' he often felt ill and unhappy, longing as his brothers had done for the holidays. But he managed to hold his own.[29]

In 1848, however, Wickham gave up the school and Dr Huntingford took it over. This must have proved unsatisfactory to the Monros as well as to other parents, for numbers generally declined and Kenneth was transferred to Elgin House School in Highgate. He clearly found the move difficult. He was very sick on the first night after being examined by Mr Dyne, the headmaster, and placed in the second form (which sounds rather low for a ten-year-old). Several letters to 'my own mother, nobody else's mother' report disturbing dreams and feeling ill at night but he concludes stoically: 'It teaches me when I think about it that all things of this world are very short of endurance.' To cheer the boy up

Mr Monro made a habit of calling at the school on his way into the City 'by the mail', although Kenneth was not always allowed to go out and see him.

It is clear that a crisis occurred in the summer of 1849. An undated letter, placed at the end of the archive but written on the paper and in the handwriting Kenneth was using earlier, expresses utter despair. He was suffering from cold sores, restlessness in bed and 'frightful dreams' and he seems to have been in some kind of trouble. The letter is a litany of wretchedness, incoherent, repetitious and tragic, echoing down the ages.

> I am so miserable. I am so hated. . . . I have no comforting thoughts. . . . What will become of me among sores, dreams and still more plaguing boys . . . School and happiness cannot agree together . . . me miserable miserable miserable miserable miserable miserable miserable miserable miserable miserable miserable miserable miserable miserable miserable . . . Even you impute everything naughty or silly in me. No one imputes a good thing to me. . . . I am in desperation. I feel ill. From one prison to another, from Mr Huntingford to here. Good bye. I am Kenney. You don't know me.

Soon after writing Kenneth seems to have run away, for on an envelope dated 18 July 1849 Mr Monro has written, 'Took Kenneth back to Highgate and he was very kindly received by Mr Dyne.' The boy's letter inside the envelope apologizes for causing his parents so much unhappiness and promises that they will soon hear a good account of him from Mr Dyne: 'I know that you will if I pray to God *and myself try also*.'[30]

Kenneth stayed the course at Highgate, although he continued to feel troubled. By the spring of 1850 he was able to report: 'I feel quite established. I dare say I am very effeminate and all the rest of it, but my bones feel very funny in bed.' He was strong enough to be able to console another boy who had been flogged for poor work and, in 1851, he was pleased when he was at last put into the fifth form, where he had certain privileges such as staying up for supper and going out walking freely. However, his two last letters to Charley betray his fundamental feelings about Elgin House. He thanked his brother for sending him a cricket bat but said he would not take it to school 'because bats do not subsist at piccaninny schools, where there is no place to put anything'. He was glad to be leaving the 'broken down place' and going to Harrow, where he hoped (vainly) to 'see you every day and talk to you and sleep in the same room with you every night'.[31]

After their time at Harrow, both the older Monro boys went on to read Classics at Cambridge while Kenneth joined the army. Cecil developed tuberculosis and had to give up reading for the Bar to spend much time in the south of France; he died when he was forty-nine. It is not clear what became of the middle brother who is often referred to as 'poor, dear Charley'. Kenneth also suffered from consumption, which galloped when he was posted to Nova Scotia and killed him at the age of twenty-four. Sadly, the brothers did not derive great benefit from their costly and arduous education. But they did leave an invaluable record of their emotional lives, which belies the assertion in a recent history of childhood that no schoolboy of this time 'poured out his feelings on paper'.[32] The experiences they recount so vividly can be compared with those of other Victorian children.

The variation in the Monro brothers' entrance age was not unusual at this time, when boys might start prep school at any age between seven and thirteen. Charlotte Guest's hesitation in dispatching Ivor was shared by other parents. Hallam and Lionel Tennyson were twelve and eleven respectively by the time they had their 'beautiful golden hair' cut in preparation for Mr Paul's school in Dorset. In 1865 their parents accompanied them on the journey across the water from their home on the Isle of Wight and then by train to Wimborne, where they parted. 'A sorrowful sight to us both,' wrote Emily Tennyson in her journal, 'our two boys, on the Bailie platform, alone, for the first time in their lives as our train left.'[33] Baliol Brett, who did not send his beloved Reginald to Cheam until he was eleven, worried that he had delayed too long: 'I hope you will do all you can to be high in your class. Because otherwise owing to your having gone too late to Mr Tabor's you will be somewhat behind fellows of your age.'[34]

At whatever age a boy started boarding school he would have to undergo initial ordeals such as those described by the Monros. Some, indeed, were much worse. The eager young Arthur Quiller-Couch arrived at Newton College only to be met with terrible threats from the son of a vicar. 'He would have my ankles strapped to a trapeze and be swung off, head downwards from the gymnasium bridge-ladder. He undertook to cut me down before I turned black in the face.' But before any of this could happen Arthur had fled into hiding for the rest of the day.[35]

Ian Hamilton coped 'right enough' with his unaccompanied journey in 1863 from the family estate in Argyllshire to Cheam School in Surrey, which must have been long and complicated even if he travelled on the Caledonian Railway from

Glasgow to London. But, as the future general recalled, 'The entry into Cheam at the end of it was, as far as my childhood was concerned, exactly like a dose of poison.' The new boy from the north had soon been 'kicked upon the seat of my beautiful new pants; had been asked all sorts of silly questions about my mother, who was dead; about my sisters, who did not exist; and generally . . . had been taken for a ride by the young plutocrats of England and put into my place as a rank outsider'. To the further question 'Are you up to snuff?' (an inquiry about his knowledge of sex), he had the sense to answer 'Rather.' But further torment followed when it was discovered that Ian, who had never before worn anything but a kilt, did not understand the mechanics of braces and had to remove his coat and waistcoat when going to the lavatory. He now became 'everybody's fag'.[36]

These sufferings corroborate those described in George Melly's novel of 1854, *School Experiences of a Fag*, which was based on the reports of others as well as his own experiences at 'Elm-House School' very early in Queen Victoria's reign.[37] After his arrival by mail coach in 'the watering-place of Weston', the ten-year-old is interviewed by the headmaster and found to be 'nowhere in the classics'. He is then taken to the school room where 'new boys always must show the stuff they're made of'. As the smallest of fifty boys he is thoroughly 'thrashed and bullied'. The next day the wretched child is sent into the town 'with fourpence-halfpenny to purchase three ounces of pigeon's milk and two pounds of strap oil'. General hilarity greets his return from the shop at which he has had his ears boxed. Eventually the persecution gets the boy down so much that he runs away.[38] The most common adult response to such trials was that directed at Herman Merivale: 'Never mind, dear, the lesson will do you good.'[39] As Merivale himself and Kenneth Monro discovered, that was not always the case.

As far as material conditions were concerned, the boys could scarcely be expected to take the same view as their parents. The latter might have been impressed by the grand mansions in which schools were often housed or by modern facilities such as those established at Cheam by the Rev R. S. Tabor: 'the very latest thing in swimming baths, a carpenter's shop fitted with turning lathes, new Eton fives courts, an ideal cricket ground and manservants'.[40] Boys were preoccupied with more humdrum matters. Thus Charles (later Lord) Hardinge remembers life at Cheam in the 1860s as spartan. The boys were underfed. Luncheon was usually pretty good because parents sometimes partook of it, but at breakfast and tea boys were given 'nothing but chunks of bread smothered with salt butter and tea ready mixed from a hot-water can'. Ian Hamilton resented this evening menu because 'the Tabor family at the high table paraded their buns and jams'.[41] Reginald Brett's problem with Cheam was that it was 'very full' so that (like Kenneth Monro) he had no locker in which to keep his things. Perhaps in response to his father's insistence that he should keep himself smart, with '*pretty hands* and *white teeth*', Regy also mentions that the boys had a bath only once a week, though 'they wash our face neck and feet every night'.[42] On the whole, however, schoolboy letters and memoirs do not deal with such boring matters, even though the sanitary arrangements were sometimes bad enough to cause outbreaks of 'low fever'. Gilbert Bourne's memoir suggests that at Helidon School these were paratyphoidal in nature.[43]

Much more common were worries about work as boys struggled to gain entry to the best public schools. The pressure could come not only from headmasters keen to build up the reputation of their own establishments, but from anxious parents such as Baliol Brett. Reginald knew that he would have to 'work very hard to get a prize because the boys in this class are more forward than I'. When twenty-four boys went down with measles in 1863, he reckoned he stood a 'chance of getting the prize' because his rivals would fall behind in their work. Then he got measles too and 'lost a great many marks by being laid up'. He was obviously quite ill, for in his first letter after getting up he apologized for its being 'very badly written because my hand shakes very much'. Eventually the homesick child was 'very sorry' to report that Whitmore, and not he, had won the prize; the blotches on this letter suggest that Reginald shed tears as he wrote it.[44]

Not all boys reported on their own progress as conscientiously as Cecil Monro and Reginald Brett. But headmasters' reports told their own story. John Oxley Parker, a land agent, was not happy in 1863 to hear that his ten-year-old son Christopher 'would do better with more attention at your desk'. A stern paternal letter went off to Christopher, who was at school in Worthing: 'Now this is the old story of "playing at lessons" [and] the sooner you get rid of it the better.'[45] If the father was himself a headmaster, the response could be more fearsome. The Rev Edward White Benson, headmaster of Wellington College, was most displeased in 1870 with the first report he received on his oldest son, Martin, from his friend and fellow headmaster, the Rev Ottiwell Waterfield of Temple Grove: 'You must *never* let me see such a poor report again. .... What is the use of sending our boy to be *taught* if he is so silly as not to give attention to the Teaching?' Two years later Martin's work had improved so much that he was top of his class and in 1874 he gained the highest scholarship to Winchester. Here he was scorned by other pupils for his diligence but plagued with paternal calls that he should 'not flag with the goal just in sight'. In this case, the father would bitterly regret making such high intellectual demands. Martin died of meningitis while still at Winchester and the Rev Benson feared that his brain had been over-taxed. His middle son, Arthur, reckoned that this heartbreaking experience gave his father 'a horror of any sort of pressure and a tender desire to subordinate everything to our happiness.'[46]

A headmaster had so much power for good or ill that even the mildest could severely affect the lives of his charges. He was after all, as Arthur Benson himself said, 'the irresponsible lord of the little domain who is judge and executioner alike'.[47] The Monros had respected the Rev Wickham (though the boys never expressed any positive liking for him) and other families clearly regretted his retirement from Eagle House. But reactions to a particular headmaster often varied in surprising ways. Opinions of the Rev Tabor ranged widely among his pupils at Cheam, the most expensive preparatory school of its time. Reginald Brett said that he was very nice, better than his wife who administered doses of nasty black medicine and 'who doesn't speak much'. Charles Hardinge pronounced the pair of them 'very unpopular' and found Mr Tabor 'one of the greatest snobs I ever met'.[48] Ian Hamilton had a soft spot for the 'colossal' Mrs Tabor, finding that her occasional goodnight kisses 'did me good' and that Sunday evening parties in her drawing room 'kept me alive'. For her husband, however, he felt 'sheer terror'. He remembered being summoned to the headmaster's study soon after his arrival at Cheam. As Tabor interrogated him, after a preliminary prayer for the help of the Almighty, about the blaspheming habits of the other boys the face of the clergyman changed into 'that of a werewolf'. But despite being pinched, shaken, struck and made to stand for a long time with arms extended, the child did not betray the schoolfellows, of whom he was equally frightened. He was released and sent to bed without dinner, after being told that he had 'made a bad start at Cheam'.

Ian's spirits descended to an even lower ebb than Kenneth Monro's. Later on in the term, while on a visit to his uncle's nearby home, he was overcome by 'an intolerable feeling of utter friendlessness and [terror] of my enemies in the dormitory' and considered throwing himself in the river. He concluded when looking back on this crisis: 'Now I know how and why some boys do it.' Life at Cheam improved only after his aunt Emily Basset sent a grand coach with two powdered footman to collect him for an exeat to her home in Berkeley Square: 'From that exact date onwards I became Someone.' But, although Tabor did not lay a finger on him after this incident, Ian continued to live in fear both of him and of the 'systematic and cruel bullying', which the headmaster did not curb.[49]

Modern historians sometimes make light of such recollections, dismissing them as 'inaccurate information by ill-informed old boys'. Leinster-Mackay goes so far as to blame Arthur Benson, who nursed unhappy memories of his prep school headmaster, for having been the wrong sort of boy.[50] After joining his brother Martin at Temple Grove in 1872, Arthur 'never found the least difficulty in any of the work' and was generally top of his class. Nor was he bullied or 'made fun of in any way'. His problem was the tall, bearded Rev Waterfield, whom he feared more than any other human being he ever met. In a later essay, Benson did not deny his 'splendid presence', 'real instinct for leadership', 'strong educational interests' and the 'patience and sympathy' he showed when he was in a good humour. But what Arthur Benson could never forgive was that he was 'too severe, punished a good deal, believed in caning and flogging' and thus terrified the boys (and also the masters) under his control. As a result the boy retreated into himself 'like a creature that had lost its way in the wilderness'. He read as much as possible in order to forget his surroundings and to keep out of Waterfield's way.[51] The youngest Benson boy, Edward, who joined the school in 1878, was also inspired 'with hellish terror' but was rewarded with more of 'the sweet fruits of hero-worship' than his brothers had been. Thus he was able to conclude that Waterfield was 'the best private schoolmaster who ever lived'.[52]

Another view of Temple Grove in the same decade comes from the pen of young Archie Campbell, son of Sir George Campbell of the Indian Civil Service. He reported to his parents that he liked the masters better than the boys in his house, who were all older than he was. He concluded philosophically that this 'is not exactly pleasant but it all goes in with school life'. Archie was probably aware that a master would read his letter but he did venture to enclose a sketch of a boy being beaten by the bearded Waterfield, explaining that he had not yet suffered this fate, 'but I daresay I shall'. Further representations of this imposing figure were made by two of nine Grenfell brothers who attended Temple Grove; he is shown towering over a row of other caricatured masters.[53]

Such severe and autocratic behaviour was, of course, common among

Victorian schoolmasters and fathers. But it is not enough to conclude that a man such as Waterfield or Edward White Benson was 'simply a mirror of his time'[54] without remembering the children whom he intimidated and sometimes damaged. One of the few prep school diaries preserved from this time shows George Corrance frightened and bruised by the frequent 'jaws' and canings meted out by Dr Proctor at a Brighton school in 1845: 'Dr in a great wax: got caned.' On one occasion George was made to 'stand on a form for three hours'.[55] Nor should we forget the more humane parents and teachers of the age, exemplified in Mr Monro's morning calls on Kenneth. When Lord Salisbury became a father, he believed that children should be both seen and heard and allowed the younger Cecils to run riot in Hatfield House. As it happens, the heirs of the Rev Faithfull, the plague of Lord Salisbury's youth, also had new ideas about rearing children. His namesake and son, who was also a clergyman, doted on his children and took the greatest interest in their games, according to his daughter Mary. After the death of Faithfull senior in 1854, his widow had moved the Hatfield school to nearby Hoddesdon, where it was renamed The Grange and run by an enlightened son-in-law, the Rev C. G. Chittenden. Mary Faithfull, who was allowed to attend her uncle's prep school, calls Chittenden 'one of the best teachers I have ever known' and commends him for his 'extraordinary patience and steady purpose'. Clearly, she was inspired by his example for she went on to become headmistress of Cheltenham Ladies' College.[56]

Another pupil who benefited from Chittenden's methods was Arthur Balfour, Lord Salisbury's nephew and another future prime minister. He remembered that the 'ordinary school routine had often to be seriously relaxed' to accommodate his poor health. When Arthur took an afternoon rest on doctor's advice, Chittenden would play the organ softly in the Hall below to soothe his nerves, an indulgence the elder Faithfull would never have countenanced.[57] There was, however, a harsher side to The Grange, which neither the girl nor the delicate boy had to endure. Lord Frederic Hamilton remembered that any boy who allowed his mind to wander 'promptly made the acquaintance of the "Spatter", a broad leathern strap [which] hurt exceedingly' when used on a boy's hand.[58] Other former pupils testify to the free use of this disciplinary device for any infringement of the rules. But they also appreciated the kindness of both Chittenden and his wife 'when they unbent out of hours'.[59] Perhaps the two glasses of beer the boys were served at dinner also helped.

Kindness could make all the difference, as nine-year-old Arthur Conan Doyle discovered. His unaccompanied railway journey from Edinburgh to a prep school near Preston in 1868 was not a happy one, even though he was leaving what his biographer calls 'a dysfunctional family'. At its head was a drunken and depressed Irish father who could not provide for his wife and three children.[60] Arthur's uncles had feared for his future and offered to pay for him to go to Stonyhurst, an establishment originally founded in St Omer in 1593 to educate exiled English Roman Catholics. Doyle's memoir recalled that he 'felt very lonesome and wept bitterly upon the way' to Hodder House, the prep school attached to Stonyhurst. It was not an auspicious start to his two years there, which were unbroken 'save for six weeks each summer'. But he found that he could hold his own 'both in brain and strength' among the other boys. He was also lucky enough to find himself 'under the care of a kindly principal, one Father Cassidy, who was more human than most Jesuits are' and sometimes dished out chocolates to the boys. The creator of Sherlock Holmes always preserved warm memories of the priest's 'gentle ways' and especially of his story-telling which, along with that of his mother, probably shaped his future. He even got used to spending Christmas at school, cheered by generous boxes of festive fare from home, by skating on the river and by ghost stories around the fire.

Arthur's would have been a different story if he had been launched immediately into Stonyhurst's tough orthodox regime – as indeed he is in Julian Barnes's novel *Arthur and George*, which does not mention Hodder's gentle initiation. When he did progress to the upper school at the age of eleven he reacted defiantly to its discipline enforced with strikes of the 'tolley' (a rubber instrument): 'To take twice nine upon a cold day was about the extremity of human endurance.'[61] Arthur's loving letters to his mother did not mention these beatings except once when he quoted a poem he wrote soon after arriving. This describes a homesick student lying on his narrow bed:

> He thought of the birch's stinging stroke
> And he thought with fear on the morrow
> He wriggled and mumbled and nearly awoke
> And again he sighed with sorrow.

Normally, he took care to write of more cheerful matters like his prized stamp collection, jolly cricket matches and train journeys when he and other boys 'let off crackers and romped'. Another solace to the young Doyle was his Catholicism. When he took his first Communion he told his mother how happy he was 'to receive the Creator into my breast': 'I shall never though I live a 100 years, I shall never forget that day.'[62]

Such fervent expressions of faith do not often crop up in boys' letters despite parental entreaties that they should be good and godly. Of course many boys may have uttered private pleas to God like Tom Tulliver's 'to make me always remember my Latin . . . and make Mr Stelling say I shan't do Euclid any more.'[63] And one sad new boy sent his mother a prayer from Temple Grove:

> Dearest Mother, this is awful
> Come and take me home at once,
> For Jesus Christ's sake, Amen.[64]

Reginald Brett once wrote to his father about a great missionary meeting at Cheam, when the Bishops of Mauritius and Ripon 'told us of the heathen and beautiful stories about them'.[65] Otherwise he was silent on religious matters. Nor does Martin Benson's correspondence bear out his father's idea of him as an exceptionally pious boy. He was simply 'a boy amongst boys', who was keen on conkers and got up to such mischief as wilfully cutting a table-cloth. Later on Benson senior chided the boy about his literary tastes: 'Novel-reading is a great cause of dreaminess.' Indeed he was very concerned in general about the 'flood of yellow novels, translations from Dumas etc, which pour in upon us from the railway stations'.[66]

Well might he worry. Few boys at Eagle House followed the Monro brothers' example of perusing *The Early English Church* or *The Christian Year*. Most school-boys preferred an adventure story which did indeed stimulate the imagination. At the age of eleven, Edmund Gosse was given a copy of *Tom Cringle's Log*, a nautical tale set in the Napoleonic Wars: 'It was like giving a glass of brandy neat to some one who had never been weaned from a milk diet.' He thought that this reading 'did more than anything else . . . to give fortitude to my individuality' – in other words, Edmund began to question his father's faith.[67] Other boys escaped from the monotonous routine of school into the exciting worlds conjured up by popular writers like Captain Marryat, James Fenimore Cooper, Captain Mayne

Reid and R. M. Ballantyne. Arthur Conan Doyle was delighted to find fifty new books in Hodder's library in 1869 and soon his heart and soul were 'out on the prairies and the oceans'. He wrote, 'It was all more real than the reality.'[68]

Reading could have a more practical application. Thus Stanley Baldwin's mother gave her son advice which would bear fruit long after he left Hawtrey's: 'Don't forget to ask for your *Illustrated London News*, and then you will know what is going on in the great world outside.'[69] For Edward Benson at Temple Grove even more down-to-earth literature provided an immediate escape route. He and a like-minded friend procured illustrated catalogues from the makers of model steam engines and spent many hours sketching their favourites. Edward worshipped the *Flying Dutchman*, which went from Paddington to Swindon 'without a stop and ran on a broad gauge'. He also devoted much thought to his model locomotive, the *Dart*, trying to devise a scheme by which it could 'generate a more abundant supply of steam'.[70] His was typical of the crazes which swept all prep schools, as they did Eagle House. Even the unhappy Ian Hamilton enjoyed glorious battles with chestnuts at Cheam. A few years earlier at the same school, the spirited young aristocrat Lord Randolph Churchill had joined in everything with 'a large magnificence'. When gardens were being designed Randolph was determined that his should be better than anyone else's. He got a local plumber to erect a large zinc tray and piping for a water display. 'When a sufficiently large crowd had been attracted Randolph turned on the water and two fountains played upon the rockery he had built around their bases.' His son, Winston, quotes a contemporary's vivid memory of the 'showy four-in-hand which Randolph "tooled" around the playground' with four young noblemen acting as horses.[71]

Lord Randolph also excelled in sport at Cheam, where the standard of games was high in the opinion of Lord Hardinge. This was true of a few other prep schools at this time. At Aldin House in Slough (also known as Hawtrey's) 'cricket was played under ideal conditions' in the 1870s, according to Lord Hawke. He attributed his future cricketing success at Eton to the prep school's 'fine coach' (and future headmaster), Edward Hawtrey, known as 'The Beetle'. Hawke went on to play and select for England, caring passionately about the game which he considered 'a moral lesson in itself', taught in a classroom consisting of 'God's air and sunshine'.[72] Not all pupils were so high-minded. Another future England cricketer, Alfred Lyttelton, did not much like Connaught House in Brighton but from the beginning he was determined to 'play well enough to be put in the first eleven'. His letters tell of his scores in school matches. But they do not reveal a story remembered by a former pupil of a neighbouring establishment. In a match between the second elevens of the two schools, both cheated by including members of their first teams. Alfred, whose determined hitting made 57 not out, 'revelled in the fraud'.[73]

In general, though, school sport had not yet assumed the importance it acquired towards the end of the century. Alfred Lunn describes games at Orley Farm (which is called Trollope House in his 1913 novel *The Harrovians*) as a relaxation where 'the supremacy of muscle was far less pronounced'.[74] This is borne out in letters like those of the Monro brothers for whom cricket seemed to be an optional activity. Gilbert Bourne was glad that boys in his day could 'develop our own individualities without interference'. He and his friends at Helidon 'were keen naturalists and had our private and malodorous zoological collections'. They competed not in cricket averages but in finding the best ammonites in the local quarry.[75] The young Roger Fry pursued similar interests at Sunninghill, Ascot. It helped him when he felt 'flat' and 'dull' (by which he meant homesick) to gather plant specimens from the countryside or from his own garden plot to send to his parents, who were keen botanists. He also kept a couple of snakes and was disappointed when his favourite one escaped.[76]

Boys had freedom to roam far from their school playing fields in those days. Arthur Benson, 'a poor and diffident performer in games', which were not strictly organized at Temple Grove, would 'moon about for hours in the grounds alone' and walk at will in Richmond Park. His destination would often be Richmond village, where he could stock up on supplies of tuck.[77] Kenneth Grahame at St Edward's, Oxford (which was still an all-age school), took advantage of his liberty to wander in the fields and explore the 'cool secluded reaches of the Thames'.[78] Perhaps these excursions helped to inspire *The Wind in the Willows* in which Mole abandons his chores, escapes from his burrow, and rambles busily 'along the hedgerows, across the copses, finding everywhere birds building, flowers budding, leaves thrusting', until he becomes entranced by the river with its 'glints and gleams and sparkles, rustle and swirl, chatter and bubble'.[79]

The Victorian children who emerged from the toils and triumphs, excitement and ennui of prep school had mixed emotions both at the time and in retrospect. William (later Admiral) Goodenough felt that his years at Temple Grove had left 'little mark' but he blessed its *'esprit de corps'* which served him well when he went to sea at the age of fourteen.[80] Lord Hardinge, on the other hand, left Cheam so 'weedy, thin and overgrown' that he failed his medical examination for the navy and went on to Harrow before embarking on a diplomatic career. He had not relished his time at Cheam. Nevertheless he judged that the school had turned out 'clean-minded boys with a high sense of honour and duty', who would 'lead in every walk of life and leaven the whole mass of the people'.[81] Perhaps this kind of ascendancy is what Kenneth Grahame had in mind when he voiced the apprehensions of Edward's sisters at the return of a 'swaggering Captain, fresh from the Spanish Main', who would 'in the same half-hour dismember a doll and shatter a hallowed belief'.[82]

Ian Hamilton did not leave Cheam with a swagger for the relentless work, the scanty sleep and food, and the 'poisonous' moral atmosphere had made him 'lanky and languid', with a hacking cough and in his mouth a 'strange faded earthy taste'. But in other ways he did resemble Edward, in his own opinion at least. Pain had made him callous and thick-skinned; thus he was 'keen as mustard to escape into any sorts of wildness' at Wellington, where he became 'something of a rebel' despite 'a succession of beatings given by a future Archbishop of Canterbury', the ubiquitous Edward White Benson. 'Cheam', he concludes, 'did a lot of harm to my character'.[83]

For some former prep school pupils, the great consolation was that life got better afterwards. Edward Browne was thankful that he unlearned, once he became a Persian scholar, the lesson of his early school life, 'to be a pessimist, a misanthrope, and a cynic'.[84] And Herman Merivale thanked heaven that his school was preparatory 'for a life that was not to be'. His own life, he later wrote, 'has not been a dull one, or an unhappy one, after all'.[85] Even so, George Eliot was unusually discerning in her view that 'we should not pooh-pooh the griefs of children'. As she observes in *The Mill on the Floss*, that wonderful evocation of juvenile trials, every bitter moment in childhood leaves a lasting trace which blends 'irrecoverably with the firmer textures of our youth and manhood'.[86] The future admirals, generals, statesmen, bishops, judges and colonial administrators, so proudly listed in the annals of schools like Cheam, Eagle House and Temple Grove,[87] might carry through life not only the manly attributes which won them public acclaim but also less obvious psychological scars.

'Three Stumps, One Wicket'
Late Victorian and Edwardian Heyday

In June 1899, a thirteen-year-old pupil of Clifton Junior School made the highest score ever recorded in cricket. To rapturous applause Arthur Collins hit 628 not out in a house match, watched by eminent Old Cliftonians including Major Douglas Haig and the patriot-poet Henry Newbolt. Arthur had been born in India where his father had served as a judge, and the boy was now an orphan. Both his parents had died in Burma, a country recently annexed to the British Empire. A reserved lad, he did not relish being hailed as a hero in the press (including *The Boy's Own Paper*) and never liked to be reminded of his famous innings. But further glory awaited him at Woolwich Royal Military College, which he represented in football and rugby as well as cricket. His career in the army took him to back to India as a subaltern and then to the Western Front as soon as war broke out in 1914. His imperial origins, sporting prowess, self-effacing modesty and military career – even his chivalric Christian name – made Collins the model prep school product of his age.[1]

By this time Britain had acquired the largest empire in history, covering nearly a quarter of the globe and encompassing great swathes of Africa and Asia. At home, prep and public schools proliferated to produce more 'rulers capable of extracting the voluntary compliance of the ruled' and to house the children of these far-flung colonial administrators – so that they acted as 'the cradle and crèche of Empire'.[2] The ideal training for imperial service was the 'Roman Rule' of a school like Clifton which, according to Newbolt, inculcated the 'virtues of leadership, courage and independence'. It also encouraged 'the sacrifice of selfish interests to the ideal of fellowship and the future of the race'. Historians point out more practical lessons. Separation from their families prepared boys for 'long, lonely and chaste years in remote parts' while spartan regimes educated them for 'the sort of "frontier" life led in the colonies'.[3] And the hierarchical system taught them how to exercise an authority 'crowned with legitimacy'.[4]

The demand for prep schools grew all the more rapidly because most public schools now set entrance and scholarship examinations which required boys to be crammed with the correct information. The new elementary schools, established by the Education Act of 1870 and supported out of local taxes, could not be expected to train boys in Latin and Greek grammar. Nor could they equip them to explain (as applicants to Cheltenham College had to do) the Miltonian allusion: 'Call him up who left half told the story of Cambuscan bold.'[5] Private establishments aimed to do just that and flourished as a result. As an official Report on Preparatory Schools observed in 1900, 'the intense desire of parents to do the best for their children' led to a 'vast exodus of boys from their homes'.[6] Or, as James Barrie put it more romantically: 'On attaining the age of eight, or thereabout, the children fly away from the Gardens, and never come back. . . . The boys have gone to Pilkington's.' (Barrie was referring to his young friends, the Llewellyn Davies brothers, going off to a prep school near Kensington Gardens run by Mr Wilkinson, the model for Captain Hook in Peter Pan.)[7] Prep school headmasters now began to hold regular meetings to discuss the curriculum required by what became the Common Entrance exam. In 1892 they formed an Association of Headmasters in Preparatory Schools (AHPS), forerunner of the current IAPS (Incorporated Association of Preparatory Schools).

Significantly, the question discussed at the first of their gatherings, chaired by the fearsome Rev Tabor, was whether boys under fifteen should be allowed to use full-size cricket balls. The debate reflected the new cult of athleticism that developed to reflect and promote the increasingly competitive spirit of the age. Manliness was overtaking godliness as an ideal, which expressed itself in a passion for organized games. By the 1880s the games ethic had become 'dominant across the public school system'[8] and the 1900 Report found a similar state of affairs in prep schools. Football and cricket were usually compulsory, with lesser sports like hockey, rounders, boxing, golf, racquets, paperchasing, bicycling, swimming and athletics also on offer. Boys' letters of this period often contain long descriptions of inter-school fixtures, of exciting paperchases and of special expeditions to such events as the Eton-Harrow cricket match. The government report gave its approval to the development of sport on the utilitarian grounds that it provided 'wholesome recreative occupation' for the 'herd artificially collected' in boarding schools. It also attributed to school sport the peculiarly English tendency 'to be willing to sink the personal in the public interest'.[9] These were the sentiments enshrined in Newbolt's famous poem, 'Vitaï Lampada': from batting amid 'the breathless hush of the Close' to battling on desert sands 'sodden red' with the blood of the square that broke, the schoolboy hero would selflessly 'Play up! play up! and play the game!' Or, as the headmaster of Wolborough Hill more simply observed: 'The boy who learns to play for his side at school will do good work for his country as a man.' Another prep school headmaster, the Rev E. L. Browne of St Andrew's, Eastbourne, regularly used sporting similes in his sermons from the chapel pulpit. He once explained the Trinity as 'three stumps, one wicket'.[10]

It was this same headmaster who, at Victoria Station, discouraged an anxious mother from coming to visit her son in his first two weeks at the school with the words: 'If you had a puppy, would you cut off its tail an inch at a time or do it all at once?' When asked by other parents how their boy was getting on, Browne would report only on the progress of his batting technique.[11] Games were symbolic of the way in which headmasters at the turn of the nineteenth century created highly self-regarding closed communities. Letters home were usually rationed, especially in the early days. It was better, a headmaster's wife explained, to wait until boys had 'got over the first feeling of soreness and are ready to write letters that will give pleasure to their parents'.[12] A pupil at another school apologized for not writing to his father more often because 'the Head seems to consider it is not good to write many letters, in which I do not agree'.[13] In addition, most schools discouraged exeats, on the grounds that 'they have an unsettling effect on the boy and also that they are a means of introducing infectious illness into the school'.[14] With their own strong ethos, boarding schools were, as Robert Graves said, more 'disassociated from home life' than they had ever been.[15]

Parents would tend to believe what they were told, that 'humanity, health, moral and physical, happiness and industry' now prevailed in schools.[16] This opinion was voiced in an article for the 1900 report by Arthur C. Benson, now a housemaster at Eton. Ironically, the very historian who dismissed Benson's memories of Temple Grove as unreliable, Leinster-Mackay, accepts it as gospel. Clearly he considers Benson's schoolmasterly judgement more trustworthy than his juvenile reactions.[17] But, since teachers were biased and parents ill-informed about school conditions and since inspectors did not interview pupils, the only way to find out about the experiences of these children is through their own accounts. Letters, if uncensored by teachers, tell part of the story. But in many cases, as Maurice Baring said, 'The truth about any individual boy is not known … until he is grown up.'[18] Since Baring and all others who went to school before the First World War are now dead, we must seek that truth in what they left behind.

In fact, Benson himself expressed mixed views on the state of prep schools. He recognized that 'disciplinary difficulties' had not entirely disappeared – in other words, there was still 'a good deal of severity, even of incidental corporal punishment'. He also regretted that the 'extravagant view of athletic distinction' pushed intellectual honours 'far into the background' and made it hard for a boy to pursue other interests. There was a danger, as the main body of the Report also suggested, of pupils emerging 'as uniform as the buttons of the regulation tunic'.[19] Another critic of the 'extravagant value set on games' was Frederic Harrison. He gave examples of pupils whose health had been damaged by being forced to play football or go on long runs when not fully fit and concluded that the cult amounted to 'a national disease'.[20]

Some parents thought that the boarding system itself was at the root of the trouble. A group in Liverpool, feeling that it was 'unnatural and undesirable' for children between eight and thirteen, set up Greenbank, a prep school for day pupils. One of these was Henry Willink, who gained a good scholarship to Eton even though he had not been groomed for the exam as meticulously as those who became his public school friends. What is more, as Willink explains in his unpublished memoir, he found during the 'testing and toughening years' of the First World War that he had learned as thoroughly as his fellows the lesson that 'Service came very definitely before Self'.[21] For John Neville Keynes the advantage of day schooling was that he could observe when his son, John Maynard, was 'quite overdone' by being kept behind to write out his mistakes at St Faith's, Cambridge, instead of being allowed to complete this task at home. The boy was also being knocked about and bullied by an older boarder. Unknown to his son, Keynes asked the headmaster, Ralph Goodchild, to make sure that nothing of this kind happened again. Later on, he removed Maynard from school for a time because he felt that too much pressure was being applied to the clever child. Neither this interruption nor the lack of evening supervision prevented Maynard from gaining a top scholarship to Eton in 1896 and becoming the foremost economist of his day.[22]

Many parents, of course, could not afford to send their offspring to boarding school. John Buchan, eldest son of a Presbyterian minister, grew up in the 1880s on the Fife coast, where 'the wood, sea and hill were the intimacies of my childhood'. Attending a series of Scottish day schools, he lived in the atmosphere of home and mixed 'on terms of comradeship and utter equality with children from every kind of queer background'. It was, he confessed, an idle boyhood but he acquired for himself a 'real intellectual interest in the Latin and Greek classics', which he studied further at Glasgow and Oxford universities.[23] He thus achieved the academic distinction and later the imperial preferment which were desired goals of a prep/public school education.

Buchan was also the author of stories which thrilled future generations of school children. In 1910–11 young readers of *The Captain* (a magazine started in 1899), followed his serialized 'Tale of Adventure in the Transvaal'. In it, the Black General, 'a Kaffir missionary who uses his religious calling as a cloak for fomenting discontent among the native population of South Africa', is worsted by 'sturdy young Scotsman' David Crawfurd. Both *The Captain* and *The Boy's Own Paper* dwelt on such exploits in far-flung outposts of the Empire, real as well as imaginary. During the Boer War (1899–1902) *BOP* readers were urged to follow events on a map of South Africa and even, by means of a game advertised for the purpose, to 'defeat the Boers in your own home'. Another *BOP* contributor, Conan Doyle, felt obliged to set an example to his young fans by volunteering to do medical work with the troops in South Africa. Two aristocratic young friends at Summer Fields, Edward Horner and Julian Grenfell, got drunk on the spirit of jingoism and pronounced themselves 'very excited about the war'. When the siege of British troops and civilians at Mafeking was relieved in May 1900 they had 'awful fun' at the school's celebrations. In July 1900, *The Captain* carried a letter postmarked Cape Town from the hero of Mafeking himself, General Baden-Powell. He was pleased to know that 'the boys of England are watching us and learning from us so that when their turn comes to do their duty for their country they will know how to do it'.[24]

In addition, prep school readers of these stirring journals were encouraged to collect stamps, heraldic crests and pictures of battleships, to follow public school cricket, football and racquets or to go on fishing expeditions, bicycle spins and summer camps. They might even become magicians, ventriloquists or detectives. Life in these pages is portrayed as good, traditional, wholesome English fun. The question is whether it is true to the actual experience of prep school pupils in late Victorian and Edwardian times. Or was the real boy, as Leonard Woolf suggested, very different from 'the usual picture presented to us by adults'?[25]

Some boys clearly thrived in the muscular Christian ethos. Even Robert Graves, who arrived at Copthorne in a depressed state after attending four other prep schools, learnt 'to keep a straight bat at cricket and to have a high moral sense' at this 'typically good school in Sussex'. His younger brothers also flourished there in the early 1900s. Charles Graves made his first cricket century as well as playing hockey and football for the school and learning to box from a Cambridge boxing blue. He felt that he could never be 'sufficiently grateful for having been sent to Copthorne'. The next brother, John, became 'head-boy with athletic distinctions' and later returned to teach at Copthorne.[26] The cricketing records of Horris Hill show that 'not a match was lost' when Douglas Jardine led its first eleven during his glorious last-year (1914). Neighbouring schools like Summer Fields found it hard to contend with his 'great command' as a batsman and as a bowler.[27] Similar cricketing distinction awaited Jardine at Winchester and at New College, Oxford. But his privileged educational background was not an asset when he captained England against Australia in the 1920s and 30s. Australian spectators were outraged not only by his team's controversial bodyline bowling but also by his sporting an Oxford University Harlequin cap, a 'symbol of class and imperialism to a sensitive society'.[28] Another cricketer to learn his art at prep school was 'Crusoe' Robertson-Glasgow, who described his dormitory as 'a man's first club, with a self-appointed committee and a few difficult members'. It was one of these who taught him the additional skills of belching, spitting and making ink bombs.[29]

Robertson-Glasgow's memoir also admits to some early 'bad moments', such as those endured at much the same time by Dickie Mountbatten (Prince Louis of Battenberg) at Lockers Park. But the cheerful young prince soon settled down even though he was nicknamed Batterpudding and taunted for his title. It must have helped him to receive loving letters from his mother containing the promise: 'If you needed me much, I would come to you from anywhere.' Lady Mountbatten also assured her son that there was no disgrace in being 'swished'. Generally Dickie got on well with the 'decent, kindly and conventional' headmaster, Percy Christopherson, who praised his 'high standard of industry and keen enthusiasm in work and games'. Despite these efforts he had an undistinguished school career though eventually, in 1912, he was elected captain of the second cricket team – the 'little-little'. The promotion prompted a letter from his adored father, who was soon to be appointed First Sea Lord: 'This is the beginning of what you will have to do in the Navy – always looking after others who are younger and know less.' Later the young prince went on to hone these leadership skills at the Royal Naval College, Osborne.

In truth, Dickie Mountbatten was, in the words of his biographer, 'an ordinary little boy'.[30] He was not a schoolboy hero like Douglas Jardine at Horris Hill or the still more golden Rupert Brooke at Hillbrow. In an autograph album, which is now in his archive at King's College, Cambridge, the young Brooke defined his idea of happiness as being at 'the top of the tree in everything'. He listed his favourite amusements – cricket, tennis, football and reading. Both the aspiration and the interests are illustrated in his diary for 1899–1900 – which also reveals a passion for the contemporary craze of stamp collecting. We see the eleven-year-old striving for inclusion in the first cricket team, excited when he has to be fitted out with the necessary white flannels, proud of his batting and bowling scores and fed up when matches are cancelled – 'It's rather rot!' He is also competitive in academic work, vying for top marks in Latin with his classmate, James Strachey (Lytton's younger brother). But James, who described himself as '*quite* hopeless at games' could only look on with admiration at the sporting prowess of his friend. As a young man he was to become unhappily infatuated with the poet.[31] This was just the sort of development which worried Arthur Benson, who considered that 'the hero-worship which surrounds a very successful athlete is in itself a grave danger, if he is prone to sensual faults'.[32]

Meanwhile, another future soldier-poet, Siegfried Sassoon, had a more mundane sporting problem. When he was sent at the late age of fourteen to The New Beacon, Sevenoaks, his mother had provided him with plenty of starched Eton-collars but no shirts. This embarrassing deficiency became apparent at the first cricket practice when he was unable to remove his coat despite the warm weather. Luckily, Matron was able to supply some shirts and he now became 'a more or less ordinary boy'. Despite the inauspicious start, Siegfried enjoyed being at school and was eager to catch up after an 'over-prolonged and somewhat segregated childhood'. His memoir conjures up happy times such as when a master read *Moonfleet* aloud 'while boys crackled chestnuts noisily'. But Sassoon was keenest of all on cricket at which, he says modestly, he 'did quite well'. Luckily no one suspected that he wrote poetry, although his nickname 'The Onion' suggests that some boys detected odd layers beneath the skin.[33]

The fact that Sassoon got into Marlborough after just a year at The New

Beacon testifies to the school's efficiency as well as to his own intellectual ability. Entry to public school was not always so easy. Leopold Amery, the son of an officer in the Indian Forestry Department, spent his early years in Gorakhpur, where he was lulled to sleep by the 'weird increasing moan' of the infant Ganges. These words come from a haunting poem his father wrote in 1882 on Leo's departure for England with his Hungarian mother, expressing the pain felt by imperial parents when parting from their children. In fact, the Amerys' marriage did not survive the separation, so that Leo and his brothers were brought up in Sussex by their mother. She could not afford to send them to a pukka prep school but (after taking them to Germany for two terms) settled for York House in Folkestone, which was still an all-age school. She had intended them to be day boys but the headmaster, the Rev Edward Heel, persuaded Mrs Amery to let them board so that he could concentrate on preparing Leo for the Harrow scholarship exam. He explained that there was 'fierce competition for most scholarships [with] ten boys for every vacancy'.[34]

Leo Amery's unpublished letters to his mother bear out his memory that he was happy at York House under the 'kindly' Rev Heel and 'his buxom wife': 'We had plenty of games, long walks round the countryside, swimming in summer and not too much work.' The boy often wrote home in German, perhaps as a means of intimate communication. In fact, the letters contain nothing critical of the school – though Heel's employment of what he called 'wholesome severity' is suggested in Leo's small drawing of him instructing pupils with a book in one hand and a cane in the other. He also penned many expressive drawings of the Devil in his childhood letters, which may suggest some disturbance in his mind. Mr Heel's own anxieties about the difficulty of getting into public school were realized when Leo failed to reach the high standard of Latin required in the Harrow scholarship exam. After extra coaching sessions, however, he passed into Harrow, where he had 'a much wider range of general knowledge than most boys of my age'.[35] One of those contemporaries was Winston Churchill, whose prep school trials appear later in this chapter. Amery himself went on to a successful political career marked by a special attachment to India and the Empire.

A more modern and efficient prep school than York House was Lambrook, near Ascot, attended at the turn of the century by the three sons of the Liberal politician and future prime minister, H. H. Asquith. It was equipped with the latest luxuries, a heated indoor swimming pool, a proper gymnasium and a carpentry workshop. The headmaster, E. D. Mansfield, author of Latin and Greek grammars and thrice chairman of the AHPS, was known for his progressive ideas; he allowed boys who had done well to go to the Ascot races. This is not to say that Lambrook was 'ahead of its time', as has recently been suggested, in providing organized sport and a range of spare-time activities. The oldest and youngest Asquith brothers certainly made full use of what the school had to offer. Both Raymond ('The Captain') and Arthur ('Oc') became skipper of games and won scholarships to Winchester. The memoir and letters of Herbert ('Beb') reveal more hesitant progress. He arrived at the school soon after the death of his mother from typhoid and was immediately made to fight another small boy: 'I had no grievance against him, nor he against me, and we had never met before until we faced one another on the edge of the gravelled playground to make sport for the others.' This enforced pugilism was, like other Lambrook activities, quite common in its day. After this ordeal Beb got along 'merrily', according to Mansfield, but he himself did not look back at the school with enthusiasm. He never took sport as seriously as his brothers and was not ashamed to tell his father about a paperchase in which he and a few other chaps went off to paddle in a stream instead of trying their best to come first. But he clearly learnt some lessons in aggression. Another letter home proudly recounts a 'decent' lark in which he and Marsden ('an awfully kiddy little chap') deliberately got in the way of four 'high bicycles coming down the hill abreast', with the result that they all fell down in a heap. At the end of his prep school career Beb sat the Winchester papers in a particularly competitive year; he did not win a scholarship but went there to join Raymond, who had been sending him slices of ham to supplement Lambrook's monotonous diet.[36]

Most prep schools took care to keep their pupils busy. This is apparent from the unpublished correspondence of historian Arthur Bryant in the Liddell Hart Military Archive at King's College London. Bryant's regular letters to his parents (signed 'Boy') show him as an ideal Edwardian schoolboy, taking part whole-heartedly in everything at Pelham House, Folkestone, between 1908 and 1911 – but never learning to spell correctly. After an initial period of being 'terribly homesick always befor breakfast' he played many a 'ripping game of footer' and golf, gained his cricket colours, read copiously from the school library, edited a newspaper, made lots of chums, acted in plays, attended slide-shows and competed for position in class with his 'ainchient rival'. Even at this early stage Arthur took a particularly keen interest in all things military. He was 'mad on toy soldiers', spotted aeroplanes, collected postcards of battleships and observed the Atlantic Fleet (including HMS *Dreadnought*) on manoeuvres. He also recorded details of a neighbouring army camp and made up his mind to go into the army. He revelled in drum-beating sagas such as *With Roberts to Pretoria* and *How England Saved Europe*, which made him 'awfully swell over Napoleon's history'. He clearly had access to newspapers from which he learned in 1911, for example, that 'the Scotch Guards who won the great battle of Stepney against hordes of anikists have gone to Egypt'. Most strikingly, he illustrated his letters and filled his sketchbooks with drawings of land and sea battles, generals and admirals, uniforms and flags. He seems, in fact, to have developed almost from the cradle the uncritically patriotic view of the past which was to inform his popular historical writing as an adult.[37]

A different view of Arthur Bryant comes out in the reports and letters written by the headmaster, Mr Haskall, and his wife, who seem to have been a benevolent couple. In 1908 Mrs Haskall commiserated with the anxious Mrs Bryant about Arthur's initial homesickness, saying that she had 'been through all the same trouble' with her own son. Her reassurance embodied current thinking about the value of a prep school education:

> Arthur will always be highly strung, but with care it will mean strength of character, and if we have to suffer for our boys we are rewarded by pride in them and their pluck and self-control.

The next year Mrs Haskall reported that Arthur was 'fat and brown', that he was 'nearly always laughing' and that his appetite amazed her. But the headmaster was worried by his 'nervous fidgety state', which resulted in 'silliness', dreaminess in class and work spoilt by 'blottiness, erasures and omissions'. He recommended that the boy should be '*vegetable*' in the holidays so that his 'ragged nerves' could settle down. To the end of his prep school career, Arthur's reports referred to 'the tense condition of his nerves', although he was a 'fairly good school monitor'.[38] All this suggests a rather less well-adjusted boy than the one conveyed in his own letters. Despite this – and his spelling which had not improved much by 1911 – Bryant gained admission to Harrow. At least he had more grasp of English than Francis and Riversdale Grenfell, twins who trod in the footsteps of their seven brothers at Temple Grove, playing cricket and football for the school in their turn. John Buchan's biography of the pair recounts such 'original and ingenious spelling' as a weather report on a rainy day when 'it pordanpord'. Both boys followed their brothers to Eton where they continued to show 'little interest in their books'.[39]

There must have been many such sturdy little boys who got on with life in the 400 or so prep schools of this period. Their daily round is well conveyed in the unpublished diary kept in his last term at Summer Fields (May–July 1882) by Robert Arrowsmith. Laconically he records several playground fights as well as more approved activities like 'tip and run' or 'chivy' (a chasing game), cricket matches, drilling (sometimes with rifles), weather conditions ranging from stormy to 'jolly and fine', adding to his moth collection with a cinnabar and 'three monkey faces' and Sunday attendance at church and missionary meetings. He gets into trouble for 'attacking Eustace', 'making a row before prayers' and going to his room without leave, but suffers no more serious punishment than writing lines or being kept in. This leniency is surprising in view of his almost daily list of 'a good many fellows' being 'licked' (caned) for unspecified offences, and may reflect Robert's good class performance ('first in Latin third in Greek'). Further entries concern letters to and from home and a mid-term visit by his parents, who were probably able to do the journey between Oxford and their vicarage near Coventry in a day.[40]

Sufficient contact with his family could be a great help to a boy. It might mean starting to board at a later age than seven or eight, like Arthur Rhys Davids, the son of a university professor, who attended local day schools until going to Summer Fields in 1909 when he was twelve. Here he was not shy of thanking his sister for her 'booful letter' and he was able to assure her that 'nobody reads your letters here'. He soon 'got the measure of all his opponents in every subject', the headmaster reported, and distinguished himself by finding 'his way on to the Eton list from the third class'.[41] Geographical proximity could also be a comfort, as it was to Rudyard Kipling's son, John. Kipling had chosen the nearby St Aubyns, Rottingdean, partly to assuage his own misery at the parting – he remembered his exile from the parental home in India. But the diffident little boy was undoubtedly cheered by the prospect of 'speeding home in the motor' for his 'blissfully happy' holidays at Bateman's.[42] The presence of his cousin, Oliver Baldwin, also helped John to feel at home. Every other Sunday the boys would walk down the road to visit their great-aunt, Georgiana Burne-Jones, who kept a cupboard full of intriguing toys such as 'birds that turned and chirped when you wound them up'.[43] The cousins were more fortunate than their schoolfellow, Bob Boothby, who was about as far as it was possible to be from his Edinburgh home. The child pined desperately for his parents, begging them to take him away from St Aubyns and ending one letter with the plea: 'Oh *come, come, come, come.*'[44] Other factors fostering prep school boys' happiness, as copious evidence confirms, were sporting proficiency, satisfactory academic ability, useful family connections, a kind headmaster and unquestioning acceptance of the school's values.

A child who lacked all or some of these advantages could spend miserable years confined in an uncongenial institution. Many saw the schools as penitentiaries with spacious grounds instead of prison yards, a wide horizon instead of a little tent of blue. For Willie (Somerset) Maugham, a ten-year-old stammering orphan who arrived at King's School Canterbury in 1885, 'the high brick wall in front of the school gave it the look of a prison'.[45] Gerald Tyrwhitt-Wilson (later Lord Berners) was filled with an 'aching desire for home' as he gazed from the barren classrooms of Elmley, with their 'cheerless smell of fresh paint and furniture polish', at swallows hovering over the cricket ground: 'My soul breathed out a message to the swallows for them to bear homeward.'[46]

Particularly insecure were boys who found it hard to meet the academic demands required by the school. In July 1895, ten-year-old Eric Brown at The Rookery, Headington, must have wondered how to reply to the latest paternal cross-examination. He knew he was supposed to be a credit to his father (a retired colonel in the Indian Army) and his older brothers, Frank and Claude, and that he should set an example to his younger brothers, Wynward, Kit and Llewyn. But what was Eric to say in response to his father's interrogation?

1   What games are you playing in the field?
2   Are you quite well?
3   What can you do in gymnastics?
4   How far have you read of *Dick o' the Fens* or any other story book?
5   Have you had any fines in the past week and what for?
6   What are you doing in Latin?
7   What are you doing in French?

8   What do you like best of all your lessons?
9   Read over Mother's and my letters and answer all the questions we have asked.

Eric must also have suspected that his latest school report was not too good. And he was right. In Classics there was 'still a sad want of life about his work'; his History papers were 'far from satisfactory'; his reading was 'still poor' and he had had thirteen fines in the half-term. He might not have known that the headmaster had written to Colonel Brown, wishing that he could see Eric 'really putting some heart in it' and also advising that the boy's hearing should be tested.

No reply to Colonel Brown's nine questions appears among the family's unsorted papers at the Centre for South Asian Studies in Cambridge. Perhaps Eric did not attempt one; after all, he had recently told his father that he liked 'geomatry the best', that cricket was 'being plaid now', that he found 'French the most difficult', that he had not 'been able to ceap quite clear of fines', that he was 'reading at page 90 something in *Dick o' the Fens*' and that he had a 'rather bad cold and cough'. In his letter of 21 July, he hoped to please his parents by telling them that he was going to collect stamps 'because when I grow up they might become rear and very valuable' and that he supported the Conservatives who had just gained a majority in the election. When he returned to The Rookery after the summer holidays in September 1895, Eric promised that 'with God's healp' he would try to do his lessons well and to get no fines. In fact, Colonel Brown died later that year and Eric was moved to Hildersham House, where he 'put his shoulder to the wheel', took entrance papers for Rugby in French, Mathematics, English and Geography (but not apparently in Latin) and was glad to announce in July 1898: 'I *have* passed after all.' Reports from Rugby also found Eric 'backward' and 'too slow all round', but he got into the Army Class Lists and followed in his father's footsteps to India. In later correspondence with his only sister, Jess, he confided that he had been miserable at school and had not got on well with his parents at that time. Letters to Mrs Brown disapproving of Jess taking up 'this suffragette business' and referring to 'the revolting habits and outlook of the Indians' suggest that Eric had not abandoned his prep school Conservatism.[47]

Another 'rather backward' boy features in the unpublished papers of the 3rd Earl of Morley, a Liberal peer who served under Gladstone. His eldest son, Edmund, Viscount Boringdon, went to Wixenford School in 1888 and was clearly expected to follow his father to Eton and Oxford. The headmaster, Edward

Arnold, realized that this was a tall order because the ten-year-old was delicate and had lost 'a year of early training'. Further reports that he was very thin, lacked 'go' and seemed 'unable to rouse himself to any mental effort' indicate that the boy was still not physically strong. They also suggest a condition which could not be diagnosed at the time: Edmund was clearly dyslexic. Arnold gives the example that he wrote 'ej' instead of 'je' in French and the boy's own letters are a thin alphabet soup. Sometimes he even got his own name wrong, signing himself 'Broingdon'. The school's efforts, as well as the family title, gained Edmund a low place at Eton in 1891 but he did not fare well there. He was 'a gentle and good boy' but even the attentions of A. C. Benson could not bring him on. The headmaster's report confirms his dyslexia: 'Spelling ludicrous; even in words of one syllable the order of letters is often reversed.' After two years, culminating in a nasty attack of scarlet fever, Boringdon's public school career came to an end.[48]

At the other extreme, being a 'swot' could make a boy a misfit. The brilliant ten-year-old William Beveridge, arriving as 'a little skeleton' at Kent House, Eastbourne, after a bout of typhoid in India, had at first to be protected from bullies by his forceful mother. He never became an athlete but he did join in jolly activities like 'spoof-golf and cockalorum'. He also made friends with Morgan Forster, a delicate child who had not found many soulmates at Kent House: 'The worst of school is that you have nothing and nobody to love, if only I had somebody.' Morgan had tried but failed to win popularity by such exploits as jumping in at the deep end of the pool even though he couldn't swim.[49] Both boys went on to rather sporty schools (Forster to Tonbridge and Beveridge to Charterhouse) at which they were unhappy. They might have been better off at St Paul's (preceded by its prep school, Colet Court), where G. K. Chesterton found too many 'swots' for his liking. He also remarked that there were 'a great many Jews', whom he described as 'foreigners that were not called foreigners'.[50]

Leonard Woolf, a pupil at Arlington House in Brighton, came into both of Chesterton's categories. But he was very good at games, which were treated with the greatest seriousness at the school. Under the stylish tutelage of Mr Woolley, he learned to play cricket and football so well that he could get away with being a 'swot' in lessons, which were not taken at all seriously. Normally, 'anyone seen to be good at lessons or rudimentarily intelligent was suspect both to masters and boys'. Equally irregular was anything other than the Conservative politics espoused by the 'nice and generous' headmaster, Mr Burman. Leonard decided to become a supporter of Mr Gladstone (whom Burman continually abused as 'the author of all evil') after seeing the Liberal leader drive by in an open carriage, not looking at all like a 'criminal anarchist and traitor'. In addition Leonard thoroughly disliked the 'extraordinarily dirty-minded' tone set by a group of boys at the top of the school. This nastiness (the nature of which he does not spell out) was eradicated by his older brother, Herbert, and by Leonard himself when they became school captains in their turn. By the time he left the atmosphere was 'more appropriate to fifty fairly happy small boys'.[51]

On the other hand, a homesick little boy like Wilfred Bion, who was left at an unnamed prep school while his parents were in India, found consolation in masturbation – '"wiggling" of whatever variety was the only redeeming thing in our lives.' A psychiatrist in later life, Bion concluded that boarding schools used games as a substitute for sex. Actually he was good at sport as well as sex, which helped him to survive a lonely and segregated childhood – but he was never happy.[52] Generally sex does not loom very large in memoirs of prep school life and still less is it the subject matter of boys' letters home. Indeed, it is probably safe to assume that most of these pre-pubertal boys were as innocent as the contemporaries of Alec Waugh at Fernden prep school during the early 1900s. When lectured by the headmaster about the dangers that awaited them at public school, they had 'no idea what he was talking about'. Nevertheless, Alec took part in a practice which had an unwitting but very definite sexual basis. Boys would belabour their 'bared posteriors on bath nights with knotted boot laces and hairbrushes', discuss their experiences in the changing room and then be surprised to find themselves with erections. How widespread such pastimes were it is difficult to know. Waugh was exceptionally frank about these matters both in his memoir and his novel *The Loom of Youth* (1917), which shocked contemporaries by its portrayal of homosexual passions in a public school, though it reads tamely today. Incidentally, his letters home, which told of 'cold baths, canes and milk-pudding', were enough to put his younger brother, Evelyn, off the whole idea of boarding school.

Alec Waugh described his prep school years as 'not unhappy', although he had reservations about the headmaster. For years afterwards he heard the echo of Norman Brownrigg 'harrying me from dawn to dusk'. And he could never again eat sago after being made to eat up a bowl into which he had vomited.[53] But for some children the headmaster was the *bête noire* of their schooldays. Lord Berners (as he always calls himself) concedes that at Elmley in the 1890s the education was sound, the food was tolerable and there was fun to be had on occasions like the annual Box Hill picnic. To be sure, he disliked 'the eternal obsession of games' and often 'longed to be allowed to indulge in other pursuits, such as the study of natural history, reading, drawing, music or even riding'. But he salvaged his athletic reputation by developing some skill in running, jumping and hurdling 'where one was more or less an individual'. He even managed to escape the Third Form 'torture chamber', which the masters discovered and suppressed before he could become a victim. He concludes that 'the only really serious drawback to the school' was its headmaster, Mr Gambril, 'the Angel of Death stalking through a plague-stricken city'. Berners describes in graphic circumstantial detail his 'stock of tortures', both physical and mental, his uncontrollable temper and the charm 'specially reserved for parents'. To his own parents the boy said nothing: 'My complaints would probably have been discredited at the time and merely led to further punishment.' When the child's depression was noticed at school he was prescribed a tonic: 'Its bitter taste was a daily complement to the bitterness of my heart.'[54]

Nine-year-old Winston Churchill also 'fell into a low state of health' after two miserable years at his first prep school, St George's, Ascot. His letters home reveal that one cause of his unhappiness was the infrequency of visits from his busy parents. Along with rows of hugs and large kisses (visible only in the originals) he included constant pleas. One letter to his mother conveys nothing except the need for his family:

> I am wondering when you are coming to see me? I hope you are coming to see me soon, dear. How is Jack [his brother]. You must send somebody to see me. I went out to diner last Sunday with the Alfred Churchills.

He begged for visits from his beloved Nanny Everest, which were sometimes allowed; in July 1884, for instance, he reported that 'she enjoyed herself very much'. On other occasions he complained of his parents' not writing to him very often: 'I have only had one letter from you this term.' Otherwise Winston's school letters at this stage tell of nothing except events such as an outing to Hampton Court; cricket matches, for instance, do not seem to have caught his interest. Another clue to the child's unhappiness lies in the reports of his headmaster, H. W. Sneyd-Kynnersley. They contain strongly worded complaints about his poor work, feeble efforts, troublesome behaviour, late arrival at lessons and greediness at mealtimes. With unique schoolmasterly percipience Sneyd-Kynnersley even managed to discern that Winston had 'no ambition'.[55]

The adult Churchill gave two explanations for his lack of progress in work and games. One was that his 'reason, imagination and interest were not engaged' by lessons in which nothing was explained or related to real life. Famously (and perhaps apocryphally), he never understood, for instance, why he would ever have to address a table: 'O table'. But the main reason for his mental and physical decline was the anxiety and fear aroused by Sneyd-Kynnersley's practice of 'flogging with a birch in accordance with the Eton fashion'. Churchill describes the procedure by which delinquents were marshalled off from the assembled boys by the two head boys who held them down as they were 'flogged until they bled freely, while the rest sat quaking, listening to their screams'. Altogether, it was a great relief to Churchill when his parents decided that his precarious health required sea air and the proximity of the family doctor.[56] Lady Randolph's niece, Anita Leslie, gives another reason for the change – an 'outraged' Mrs Everest had shown her mistress the birch marks on Winston's bottom. Churchill later told Mrs Leslie that he would have 'broken down completely' if he had stayed at St George's, Ascot.[57]

Winston's new school, at the rather less grand address, 29 and 30 Brunswick Road, Brighton, was run by the Misses Thomson, who treated him kindly. They reported 'very satisfactory progress' and Winston pronounced himself very happy both in letters and in conversations with his parents – but his school career was hardly glorious. In 1884 he was stabbed with a paper knife during a dispute with the 'very passionate' boy sitting next to him in a drawing exam, an incident he does not mention in his autobiography.[58] In 1886 he nearly died of pneumonia, remaining weak and weepy for some time afterwards – the paper of a letter telling Nanny Everest that he 'could cry at everything' appears to be marked by tear stains.[59] He burst into tears again at an 1887 Brighton pantomime featuring a sketch of his father, who was hissed by a man in the audience on whom the twelve-year-old rounded with these words: 'Stop that row you snub nosed Radical'.[60] In the same year he 'found himself unable to answer a single question in the Latin paper' for the Harrow entrance exam.[61] Presumably the fame of Lord Randolph, whose autographs Winston sold to his school friends to augment his pocket money, helped to gain him a Harrow place despite this unimpressive performance.

Some years after Churchill left St George's, Maurice Baring heard 'dreadful stories' about his naughtiness which 'appeared to have surpassed everything'. It was said that after being flogged for taking sugar from the pantry 'he had taken the headmaster's sacred straw hat from where it hung over the door and kicked it to pieces'. Baring himself found his fellow pupils' lack of sympathy with Churchill priggish and attributed it to the fear instilled by the same headmaster: 'We lived in an atmosphere of complete uncertainty.' He reports that one boy was flogged for cutting off a piece of his hair and keeping it in a drawer. Maurice enjoyed certain aspects of St George's – crazes for collecting stamps and butterflies, competitions for the prettiest garden, Sneyd-Kynnersley's readings of *Treasure Island* and *The Pickwick Papers*. But he never 'seemed to do right in the eyes of the headmaster'. He resented being punished for 'want of patriotism, bad manners and vulgarity' when he and a friend climbed on to a wooden platform during a cricket match. Nor was he happy about Liberal politicians like Gladstone and Joseph Chamberlain being burnt in effigy on bonfire night. The future dramatist had his revenge when, at a new school set up by two masters from St George's, he took part in a theatrical performance making fun of Mr Sneyd-Kynnersley's ménage.[62]

Further testimony to this headmaster's 'sadistic' punishments comes in the unpublished school letters of the artist Roger Fry, who was one of his first pupils when the school opened as Sunninghill and was still there when it was renamed St George's because the saint's day fell on the head's birthday – 'a remarkably feeble reason'. By 1880 Roger was feeling less 'dull and flat' than he had done in his first three years. He was delighted to have got into the football team and he even made 26 runs in a cricket match – though he clearly took more pleasure in his painting lessons and in singing solos at the school concert. Previously something of a misfit and the butt of school bullies, he could now report that 'the fellows don't seem to dislike me at all'. He joined in with the general fun when an effigy of the Emir of Afghanistan (with whom Britain was in conflict) was stuffed with fireworks and blown up on bonfire night. And he could cope with being mocked as the only Liberal pupil during the election of 1880. But the headmaster's savage beatings upset him. Throughout his prep school career, Roger informed his parents whenever boys were flogged in the public manner described by Churchill. As a clever and well-behaved pupil, he was usually one of the two boys who had to witness the event. Only as an adult did he reveal that this had affected him in a manner which could not be described to his Quaker parents. In a private memoir he described these occasions with their 'precise and solemn' ritual and their bloody and sometimes excremental outcome. Fry was convinced that the floggings had deep sexual connotations both for Sneyd-Kynnersley and for him as an observer. Shockingly, in a passage censored by his first biographer, Virginia Woolf, he relates that after one flogging he had his first erection without having at that time 'the faintest idea of the function of the organ'. Perhaps, as a later biographer has judged, Fry was an excessively anxious boy 'pathetically attached to his mother'. 'Whatever the cause,' concludes Fry himself, 'my horror of these executions was certainly morbid and it has given me all my life a morbid horror of all violence between men.'[63]

In 1886 Sneyd-Kynnersley died suddenly of a heart attack at the age of thirty-eight, though there is no reason to link this with his energetic flagellation. Still less is there evidence to back up the bizarre stories of another former pupil, Sir Edmund Backhouse. In an 'obsessively obscene' secret memoir, the eminent sinologist asserts that the headmaster died while flogging a fellow pupil and that the boys took their revenge by having the broken rod inserted in his shroud 'like the ancient Egyptians who buried familiar objects with their dead'. In fact, Backhouse had left the school by the time Sneyd-Kynnersley met his death, which took place in Birmingham rather than Ascot. Thus the story tells us more about the pupil's feelings than about the headmaster's demise.[64]

It is not so easy to disprove the accounts of the soldier/spy, Richard Meinertzhagen, about his being subjected to physical abuse at Fonthill School in the 1890s. He did not publish his *Diary of a Black Sheep* until 1964 and he apparently destroyed the diaries on which it was based. He claims that one of the Radcliffe brothers who ran the school interfered with him sexually during clandestine nocturnal visits to his room and beat him sadistically three or four times a week. Eventually the boy smashed the cane over Walter Radcliffe's head before escaping to the home of an influential family friend who was so shocked at the marks on his back and legs that he remonstrated effectively with the school. The latest biography points out that there is no independent evidence for any of this and that Meinertzhagen certainly did lie about some aspects of his later life. But in view of the brutality known to occur in some boys' boarding schools in the late Victorian period, these stories ring all too true.[65]

Cruel methods were not universal. Lionel Helbert, a former Clerk to the House

of Commons who established West Downs in 1897, was clearly a most enlightened man 'who made a genuine effort to understand his pupils' – even when
they happened to be the young Oswald Mosley for whom childhood was 'just
a nuisance'. Mosley had unpleasant memories of the intense cold at the school,
which he found 'depressingly dull', but unmitigated respect for its headmaster's
'rare insight'.[66] Helbert did not eschew corporal punishment. On 3 November
1900, for example, he reported to a father that he had given his son 'a good lick-
ing' for 'showing a bit of cheek and open slackness' – but he intended to make
up for it by giving the boy 'an extra share of the fireworks'.[67]

A few prep school heads viewed the use of flogging (which had almost disappeared from the army and navy) with the same 'disgust and indignation' as
was felt by the Liberal politician, Joseph Chamberlain.[68] C. E. F. Stanford, who
founded St Aubyns in 1879, 'regarded the use of the birch as an outworn barba-
rism' and replaced it with a system of conduct marks. Even so, his favouritism,
fierce temper and unfaltering Conservatism aroused 'a violent spirit of rebellion'
in at least one pupil. John Strachey Barnes (another exile from India) wrote that
'it became a war between us with the gloves off'. Matters came to a head during
the 'astonishing flag-waving, patriotic jingoism' of the Boer War. On the day
Mafeking was relieved, John, a professed atheist at this stage, asked boys which
they would choose between their country and their God. When they opted for
country he told them: 'In that case your country is your God.' He was sent to Mr
Stanford, who actually had a cane in his hand but managed to reduce the boy to
a pulp by his invective alone. He extracted a promise that John would in future
keep his dangerous thoughts to himself.[69] Oliver Baldwin was subjected to similar
censure when he wrote a ghost story called 'The Hell-born Babe' which passed
rapidly around the boys. Reduced to tears by Stanford's accusations that he 'had
got the idea from the servants' he promised never to write such a thing again.[70]

On the other hand, the unhappy Bob Boothby was treated patiently by both
Mr and Mrs Stanford, despite being as sore a trial to them as he often was in later
life to fellow MPs. The Stanfords tried to distract the child from his homesickness, sometimes letting him have 'a good cry', and watched over him for fear
that he would run away. He repaid their kindness with such tricks as burying
all the gardening tools when he decided that working on allotments was 'cissy';
they were not discovered until a swimming pool was being dug many years
later, at which point he came clean. Boothby, who was never caned until he

went on to Eton, became an ardent opponent of corporal punishment at a time when that view was unfashionable, especially in the ranks of the Conservative party.[71]

Another awkward pupil of Stanford's was Charles Lister, the younger son of Lord Ribblesdale, a Liberal peer and the subject of John Singer Sargent's famous portrait depicting the archetypal aristocrat. Charles's early letters home are normal enough. He inquires about the stock of guinea pigs on the family estate at Gisburne, explains to his mother the meaning of cricket terms such as leg bye and expresses excitement when his brother Tommy goes to fight in the Transvaal with the 10th Hussars: 'I hope Tommy will win tons of medals and a Victoria Cross. I do hope he won't be shot by those brutes of Boers, treacherous cads that they are.' It is unlikely that Charles found John Barnes's jokes about the war very funny. His fears for his brother's safety were justified not during the Boer War but when Tommy was sent soon afterwards to fight the 'Mad Mullah' in British Somaliland. Captain Thomas Lister died after being shot and speared by Somali rebels in 1904. Meanwhile, Charles had developed unconventional views of his own. While still at St Aubyns, he began to develop the socialist principles which led to his later joining the Independent Labour Party. He became interested in an East End mission and 'property came in for serious censure'. Although Charles seems to have escaped the wrath of Mr Stanford, Lord Ribblesdale judged that 'this was not a cheerful phase' of his son's life.[72]

The safest course was for a child to respect the ethos of the school. Antonia White's Edwardian convent girl, Nanda Grey, comes to grief at the end of *Frost in May* because she has read 'unwholesome' books like Kenneth Grahame's *Dream Days*, asked 'awkward questions in the Christian doctrine class' and written a secret novel about 'brilliant, wicked, worldly' characters.[73] Even Dunhurst, the progressive co-educational prep school established in 1905 as an offshoot of Bedales, was not quite as 'simple and free and happy' as it appeared to Helen Thomas when she first visited it in 1906. She and her husband, the poet Edward Thomas, enrolled their son and later a daughter as day pupils, but Helen was disappointed to find when she went to teach there herself that its 'conventions were as rigid and intolerant' as those of other schools – the staff just happened to be wear 'Socialist, Vegetarian, Humanitarian' labels.[74]

Most prep schools were still dominated by Conservative Christian beef-eaters. At The Grange, Folkestone, Harold Nicolson was labelled a 'freak' for expressing sympathy for the Boers and rejoicing at the reprieve of Captain Dreyfus. Such 'pro-Jewish principles, anti-militarism and pacifist tendencies' would not do.[75] The pressure towards conformity strengthened in the years before the First World War. In 1910 the headmaster of The New Beacon, convinced that there would soon be European conflict, wrote to the headmasters of all leading public schools urging them to prepare their pupils for military service. In fact, politicians, military leaders and imperialist writers like Kipling and Conan Doyle's brother-in-law, Ernest Hornung, were already spreading this message. In Lent Term 1913, for example, the magazine of Highfield prep school reported an illustrated talk by Lieutenant Knox on the Navy League and the headmaster's promise that a school branch would be established 'if the keenness shown during the lecture was maintained'. Another article regretted that 'certain boys who shall be nameless' found their drilling exercises rather a bore – but matters improved by the next edition when the squads were 'keener, smarter and their marching excellent'.[76] In this atmosphere public schools might look askance at a prep school candidate who questioned the patriotism of the day.

'God keeps our score,' warned Hornung, 'and He does not tell us what we have made until we are out.'[77] Taking their cue from God, the Olympians, as Grahame labelled adults in authority, did not brook questions and made decisions without giving a 'hint of the thunderbolts they are silently forging'. When the Elephant's Child in the *Just So Stories* 'asked questions about everything that he saw, or heard, or felt, or smelt, or touched, all his uncles and aunts spanked him.'[78] Thus, few former prep school pupils queried the call to war in 1914. Of the forty or so cricketing heroes, swots, stamp collectors, dunces, rebels and 'ordinary little boys' mentioned in this chapter, twenty-four enlisted in the army or in the new Royal Flying Corps. Most of those disqualified by age or unfitness worked in mobilization, propaganda, intelligence or medical units. One, James Strachey, fought instead for the right to declare himself a conscientious objector. Hornung's son, Oscar, was one of the eager volunteers from Eton. Writing cheery letters to his parents in 1914 and using sporting similes of the kind that sprang instinctively to the lips of his contemporaries, the young officer compared 'this game to the old House Ties – only the odds aren't so against us here and we've more to back us up!' He described hand grenades as 'glorious things, *just* the size and weight of a *Cricket Ball*!' It would not be long, he thought, before they beat the 'Teuton Batsman' and could return to the pavilion before rain created a sticky wicket or darkness brought an appeal against the light.[79] And so, in the breathless hush preceding a battle on the Western Front,

> . . . the voice of a schoolboy rallies the ranks,
> 'Play up! play up! and play the game!'

4

'Too Young to Gird on the Sword'
The First World War

At Christmas 1914, the 'Old Fag' (as the editor of *The Captain* called himself) reminded readers that the boys' magazine had been 'born midst the disturbances of war'. He drew attention to the 'list in many a school of the heroes who fell on the veldt' during the South African conflict. He went on to lament that 'the lists may be longer still, alas! when the toll of this war is taken' but added the consoling thought that 'every name will be written in letters of glory'.[1] By the time this was written, Captain Arthur Collins, the renowned schoolboy batsman, had already been killed at the first battle of Ypres while signalling for more men to protect the flank of his trench. His body was never found in what Sassoon described as 'the sullen swamp' of that incessant battlefield but his name is recorded '*in maiorem dei gloriam*' on the Menin Gate in Ypres.

The Great War was to see many more deaths of 'young heroes who but a season or so ago were familiar and respected figures in our schools and on our playing fields'. Of those prep school pupils who appeared in the last chapter, George Llewellyn Davies, Edward Horner, Julian Grenfell (and his brother Billy), Francis and Riversdale Grenfell (of a different family), John Kipling, Wynyard Brown, Raymond Asquith and Oscar Hornung were killed on the Western Front; Charles Lister and Rupert Brooke died at or on their way to Gallipoli; and Arthur Rhys Davids fell in aerial combat, which he described as 'the greatest game of all'.[2] Meanwhile, *The Captain* maintained, 'those too young to gird on the sword have also been keenly doing their bit to keep the flag a-flying' in every 'school of note in the land'.[3]

This patriotic message was reinforced by countless school magazines. *Summer Fields Magazine*, for instance, included a poem in its edition of April 1915 about those

> Who rushed from School and College, boys light-hearted,
> To quit themselves as men mid shot and shell.

Other editions carried a twelve-year-old pupil's verse entitled 'The Kaiser's Boast' and the famous poem in which Julian Grenfell wrote of the joy of battle, 'when the burning moment breaks,/And all things else are out of mind'. In 1915 Grenfell's name was included in the magazine's sombre roll of slain Summerfieldians. By 1918 it had to devote over seven pages to its Roll of Honour, which included 139 fatalities as well as long lists of those wounded. Among the soldiers killed were sons of Dr Williams and the Rev Alington, the school's wartime headmasters. Young Geoffrey Alington had taught there himself and pupils sent their Latin translations out to him 'somewhere in France' until his death in 1916.[4] Elsewhere in Oxford, as John Betjeman's verse autobiography recalls,

> Before the hymn the Skipper would announce
> The latest names of those who'd lost their lives
> For King and Country and the Dragon School.

And his 'gruff old voice' would be full of tears 'when a particular favourite had been killed'. All over the country schools had to make similar announcements, sometimes accompanied by the tolling of the chapel bell.

The pupils would look solemn on such occasions but, says Betjeman, this was because they knew that 'There'd be no extra holiday today.' Actually there is ample evidence that prep school children took the war seriously and did their bit in various ways, which may or may not have been useful. Dragon School pupils took up knitting needles to create 'shapeless gloves from string/ for men in mine-sweepers'.[5] The golfer, Henry Longhurst, remembered similar efforts at St Cyprian's, Eastbourne, where he and others 'knitted furiously for soldiers at the front', graduating from scarves to socks and balaclavas.[6] Even girls could join in. From the kindergarten of Walthamstow Hall, a boarding school for the daughters of missionaries, ten-year-old Phyllis Wilkins told her parents about knitting grey scarves and entertaining wounded soldiers.[7] Philip Bryant, who had followed Arthur to Pelham House, wrote of putting on a concert for troops in a Folkestone hospital: 'They will enjoy it so much because they are the soldiers who are too badly wounded to go out to tea and have any treats.' At the same time he gave a shilling of his pocket money, as did boys at many other schools, to a fund providing soldiers and sailors with tobacco at Christmas 'for they say there is nothing they want more.'[8] (In 1917 those servicemen would include Arthur, who joined the ranks of RFC.) The juvenile collecting mania was also harnessed to the war effort. Evelyn Waugh, a day pupil at Heath Mount, Hampstead, raised money for the Red Cross by collecting and selling jam jars and he cut up linoleum to be used as soles for wounded soldiers' slippers.

Waugh's day-boy status was a consequence of the war. Fearing financial ruin, his father had kept him on at Heath Mount rather than sending him to Fernden in his brother's footsteps. Evelyn was glad not to suffer 'the sharp separation common to boys of my sort'. 'We day boys,' he considered 'were always aware of the presence of parents, near, benevolent and, in the last resort, authoritative.' In the holidays, when there was no abatement of the war effort, Evelyn was thrilled when a friend's father found them work as messengers at the War Office, where his ambition was 'to serve Lord Kitchener'.[9] Other boys too played their part through family rather than school. Antony Knebworth, a pupil at West Downs, begged to be allowed to act 'as a messenger or helper or anything next hols' in his father's office at the Admiralty.[10] In the event he worked at the soldiers' hospital run by his mother, Lady Lytton. The novelist Henry Green (né Yorke) had a similar opportunity, since his family home was used as an officers' convalescent hospital. During his holidays from The New Beacon he would hear 'fantastic tales', especially from airmen, as well as the nightly screams of those traumatized by the fighting. Even so, the eleven-year-old Henry did not grasp the realities of war. It was only later that he realized what the servicemen had really faced: 'I remember thinking there could be nothing so bad as when one's holidays from school were over. . . . I had forgotten the men told by three doctors [the Medical Board] when they were fit to go back again to die.'[11]

Another way in which boys made themselves useful outside school was through the Boy Scouts, established by Baden-Powell in 1908. Just before the outbreak of war B-P offered the services of Cubs and Scouts to the government. The first task they were given was to watch telephone lines but soon they were keeping an eagle eye on other possible objects of sabotage such as reservoirs. They also lent a hand in Red Cross centres and public offices as well as being deployed by the Admiralty in 'coast-watching'.[12] Evelyn Waugh joined the Hampstead Scout Patrol but found the proceedings rather dull – though he did enjoy a march to the Heath for a mock battle followed by tea and cakes.

Few prep schools had Scout troops at this time, perhaps because their separation from the community made it difficult for the boys to keep the fourth Scout

Law – to model themselves on Kipling's Kim by being 'a little friend of all the world'. But prep school children enjoyed Scouting when it was on offer, doubtless in part because it gave them an opportunity to make a nuisance of themselves by whistling and singing under all difficulties and endangering their elders' health and happiness by doing a good deed every day. Phyllis Wilkins even tried to set up a secret branch at Walthamstow Hall, telling her parents that she had not yet 'missed a day without doing a kind deed'.[13] The future scientist Frank Ramsey found that it was a way of making friends when his parents sent him away to Sandroyd at rather a late age, feeling that he needed more of an intellectual challenge than King's College Choir School could offer. Sandroyd had been one of the first prep schools to establish a troop and Frank immediately asked to join it. 'The uniform costs between 25 and 30 shillings and there is a term subscription of two shillings.' (The high cost of Scouting, incidentally, militated against its egalitarian aims.) Once he had joined he aimed to become 'a second class Scout before the end of term'. Frank's letters for the rest of his Sandroyd career have not been preserved; his father reports, however, that 'the fine woods around the school gave a splendid opportunity for all sorts of scouting' but that the camp to which Frank was looking forward in the summer of 1914 'was cancelled owing to the outbreak of war'.[14]

Outdoor activities also feature in Antony Knebworth's wartime letters from West Downs. Scouting seems to have helped him to recover from the acute depression he suffered following an attack of appendicitis. Despite the efforts of the sympathetic Lionel Helbert (who was to suffer a breakdown himself in 1917), his parents had to remove him from school in March 1914 after receiving what his father called 'pathetic little letters'. Lord Lytton's famous memoir of his son (written after his death in a flying accident at the age of thirty) quoted the boy's efforts 'to be brave' but omitted his most poignant expressions of despair. In his unpublished letters Antony described his life as 'sadness coldness sleepiness'; he looked forward to his parents' visit 'like a huntsman to the hunt'; he urged them to 'come quick' and he confided to his mother that he could not live without her. Antony was more cheerful when he returned to school in the summer of 1914 and after the outbreak of war he seemed to find a real sense of purpose. He wrote a poem called 'Europe's War', drew pictures of battles and warships and immersed himself in Scouting games on the downs. His wartime diary and letters bubble with excitement as he describes signalling by semaphore, shooting with air rifles, bicycle drills, route marches, flag reading, bugling and camping. Some of this was rather more militaristic than Scouting was supposed to be, according to B-P, but Antony found it all enormous fun:

> On Thursday we had a grand route march with the 5th Winchesters. . . . *It was gorgeous.* They had tea here and I was sent down to the town on my bicycle to buy them tobacco quite late.

One of his most thrilling moments occurred in February 1916, when he met Captain Rowland Phillips, a commissioner for all school troops, who told the boys 'some lovely yarns about the front'. The Captain talked so well 'that he makes you think you are in the trenches' – which is where Phillips was killed later in the year. Meanwhile, as Lord Lytton proudly recorded, Antony went on to become a patrol leader.[15]

All over the country children found similar ways to enjoy the war. In schools which ran branches of the Officer Training Corps (set up in the wake of the Boer War), many pupils found field days more fun than lessons. They simulated conflict in many ways, wearing makeshift uniforms, making wooden rifles and mimicking machine-gun fire. It was all too realistic for some parents, such as those of the future historian, Alan (A. J. P.) Taylor. Convinced pacifists by 1916, they objected to his being taken with the other pupils of Buxton College to view the trenches used for OTC training. Alan was promptly 'delivered from the evils' of his day school, which he enjoyed, and dispatched to The Downs, a Quaker prep school, which he described as 'a prison house'. When his uncle Harry visited him there after spending the war in gaol as a conscientious objector, he told Alan: 'You have had a tougher war than I had.'[16]

At least Mr and Mrs Taylor, now preoccupied with the Russian Revolution, had ensured that their son would not take part in activities such as those described in *St Edmund's School Chronicle*: 'No.1 machine-gun, under Corpl. Auden (junior) was posted on the left ahead of his elder brother and his patrol was connected with the centre by connecting files.'[17] Of course, Corpl. W. H. Auden (the future poet) might have preferred to spend his time at the Literary Society which he set up in the school. But most of his contemporaries lapped up adventure stories such as those contained in wartime editions of *The Captain*: 'When Tank meets Tank', 'With Haig on the Somme' (a long-running serial) or 'The Camouflage

Craze' (set in a prep school). No doubt they were also tempted by its advertise-ments for Meccano battleships, Fry's Cocoa – 'Blighty's Best' – and a game called 'Bombarding the Zeps'. And some were inspired to capture German spies. A group of boys at Summer Fields arrested an enemy agent who turned out to be a harmless 'elderly gentleman with pince-nez glasses'.[18]

Youngsters whose homes or schools were within range of Zeppelin attacks had additional adventures. The future artist Edward Burra, writing to his father from Northaw Place, Potters Bar, conveys the thrill and also the discomfort of such an event:

> The Zepp raid on the North of London was most exciting. We got up in our pyjamas about ten o'clock on Sunday evening and stayed from then onwards to about three o'clock on Monday morning with intervals in the cellar. The cellar here is most appall-ingly dirty and damp. This morning we went out and collected bits of aluminium and burnt silk [which] smells horrid. I am sending you and Ma some bits which I found in the garden path. I hope you will enjoy them very much indeed.[19]

As well as war relics, boys loved to collect and swap cigarette cards. Frank Ramsey said that he had 'tons' of them, featuring regimental flags and 'all soldiers and sail-ors do, like firing at balloons, dragging canoes through a river, and parading and climbing ropes and all that sort of thing'.[20] Christopher Isherwood, at school with Auden in Hindhead, was lucky enough to be near a Canadian encampment where the boys could cadge rare specimens for their collections. Isherwood described this pastime in his schoolboy diary and used it later in a short story, 'Gems of Belgian Architecture', which also illustrates the pupils' practice of 'gorse-bushing'. It tells of a boy wrongly suspected of stealing some prize cards who is thrown into the midst of 'a great juicy gorse-bush'. When he emerges with bloody cheeks and cut hands, his persecutors explain to Matron that he has had a fall.[21]

The war quite often inspired boys to use their creative talents. John Gielgud's eloquent letters from Hillside School, Godalming, described typical experiences such as hearing the casualty lists being read out (one included the headmaster's brother) and listening to 'a topping lecture' by a young man who had escaped from Germany. 'Fancy,' wrote Gielgud, 'they had to feed on raw turnips and pota-toes.' A keen artist whose hobby was designing stage sets for his toy theatre, he also sent home realistic sketches of battleships and aeroplanes. In addition, the school gave him scope to employ his acting talents; he progressed from the Mock Turtle and Humpty Dumpty to Shylock and Mark Anthony during his time there. In one way or another, he seems to have had 'the best fun going' at Hillside and only to have started to worry about the war and to feel dreadfully homesick after 1917 when he went to Westminster School, sited all too near potential Zeppelin targets. Then, saying that he was 'in extremis', he begged his parents (who lived in South Kensington) to let him attend daily. He promised to make his own bed and clean his boots in the absence of maids and added, 'I don't think the food question would be much of a bother, as I should always be out to lunch.'[22] In March 1918 he got his way and began to travel to and from school by underground, but he was still able to play an active part in Westminster's OTC. As Gielgud's case suggests, the conflict had more of an impact on older boys.

Earlier in the war Rex Whistler, who made a daily bus journey to Merton Court in Sidcup with his brother Denny, had begun to show his artistic talents with animated drawings of battles and torture scenes. According to their younger brother, Laurence: 'War with its rapturous indignations and fearful odds, its lovely bloodshed and daily solemnizing in grave grown-up conversation, was simply a new and more lasting excitement to them.' If the ten-year-old Rex took the distant death toll in his stride, he was grievously upset when Denny died in 1915 from a virulent type of measles contracted at school. They had been almost like twins and he had lost 'his close companion'. But when sent off to board at Gadebridge Park in 1916, Rex was able to win friends by responding to the other boys' requests for his drawings – which doubtless continued to depict military subjects. Laurence reports, on the basis of family sources, that Rex was bullied not by fellow pupils but by one of the joint headmasters for whom he developed a dread, only revealed after he left Gadebridge.[23]

School magazines, when they included contributions from pupils, also gave scope for creative activity. At St Cyprian's, eleven-year-old Eric Blair (the future George Orwell) wrote a poem in which he prayed for the 'strength of the lion' and 'the wisdom of Reynard the fox':

> And then I'll hurl troops at the Germans,
> And give them the hardest of knocks.[24]

Meanwhile, at The Grange, Crowborough, Tom Driberg (the only day boy) contributed a story in which two lads catch a German spy on the coast and are rewarded for their courage. As it happened, neither of these literary efforts was inspired by pure love of country. Eric knew that his poem would gain him favour with Mrs Wilkes (the headmaster's wife and the true ruler of the school, who was known to the boys as Flip). Driberg's vain hope was to escape the taunts of 'Kaiser Tom' levelled at him because of his Germanic surname.[25] He did not have the same luck as the hero of 'Baker the Hun', a story in *The Captain*; after being caught addressing a letter to his father, A. Beckhardt Esq, Baker is ragged as a 'beastly Hun' but saves his reputation by helping to dispose of an unexploded bomb with a triumphant shout: '*Would a German do that?*'[26]

It is clear from many of these examples that children were more preoccupied with their own affairs than with the war. The trenches and the guns, wrote Betjeman,

> Meant less to us than bicycles and gangs
> And marzipan and what there was for prep.[27]

Or, as Auden expressed it:

> The Great War had begun: but masters' scrutiny
>   And fists of big boys were the war to us;
> It was as harmless as the Indian Mutiny,
>   A beating from the Head was dangerous.[28]

So boys worried about such age-old matters as escaping the wrath of teachers and the taunts of bullies, making friends, getting enough food, coping with work and missing home – though sometimes these worries were accentuated by the war. Name-calling could become especially vicious in an atmosphere of spymania which put even dachshunds and Steinway pianos at risk. To avert hostility, families with Germanic surnames, including Battenbergs and Saxe-Coburg-Gothas, transformed themselves into true Britons. Evelyn Waugh noticed that several boys 'turned up with names suddenly anglicized' (Kaiser became Kingsley, for instance) but he claims that there was no persecution in cosmopolitan Hampstead.[29] Apparently less tolerant was neighbouring Highgate, where John Betjeman made his daily journeys to the Junior School before being sent to the Dragon. Even though his family had dropped a final 'n' from their surname to make it look more English, John's young enemies danced around him shouting:

Betjeman's a German spy –
Shoot him down and let him die.[30]

The writer John Lehmann had a similar memory of Summer Fields, where 'Ford *ma* would start chanting "Leh*mun* the *Hun*" at the most wounding moments.' Lehmann consoled himself with the thought that his father was editor of 'that spotlessly patriotic journal, *Punch*' and proudly started a similar magazine at the school. Despite the jeers and the fact that he nearly died there during the 'grim penultimate phase' of the war, Lehmann concluded that he was 'on the whole, very happy at Summer Fields'.[31] By contrast, his future friend Stephen Spender was desperately homesick at two prep schools, his misery compounded by the effects of the war. At the second of them, Charlcote, he and his brother were taunted as 'Huns' a year or so *after* the Armistice, once their contemporaries discovered that their mother's name was Schuster. Stephen eventually turned on his persecutors and in the ensuing fight a window was broken. As a result he was excluded from chapel on the grounds that he was not 'good enough to pray with the other boys'. The next morning the headmaster caned him.[32]

A hardship experienced by all wartime boarders was the deterioration in school food. Littleton Powys, headmaster of Sherborne prep school, remembered that it was 'none too easy' to keep the boys fed. His cook had to resort to the dishes described by one of his pupils, the poet Louis MacNeice: 'Shiny brawn full of hairs and apparent eyes called "Pig's Slosh" and a coarse yellow maize full of straws'.[33] According to Henry Longhurst, St Cyprian's served a similar 'liquefied orange-coloured maize pudding with the coarse husks floating on the top'. He and fellow pupil David Ogilvy also remembered the same 'burnt, tepid, lumpy porridge' of which Orwell complained in his celebrated essay about St Cyprian's. Indeed, Longhurst was so revolted by it that he was sick into his pewter bowl, only to be made to eat it up.[34]

Magazines urged boys to 'EAT LESS BREAD' and some schools imposed rations on this schoolboy staple. When Auden was spotted taking a second slice at teatime, the master in charge drew attention to his unpatriotic behaviour: 'Auden, I see, wants the Huns to win.'[35] Stephen Spender had worse to suffer in 1918 at Old School House, the prep school of Gresham's, where he was meant to be kept 'from children who were rough'. When it was discovered that he and some hungry companions had eaten four quarters of a slice of bread instead of the one that was allowed, the housemaster described them as food-hogs 'worse than Huns'. He then left them to be dealt with by the other boys in a manner recorded by Spender:

> They tied some rope, which they had found, round my hands and feet, and then pulled in different directions. After this I was flung down a hole at the back of the platform of the school dining-room, called the Kipper Hole because heads of kippers were thrown there.[36]

Many boys had memories of maize pudding, meagre bread supplies and sickly margarine but they were rarely as unhappy as Spender's. It is no wonder that his experiences at Gresham's and Charlcote put him off boarding school for good.

Britain just about kept starvation at bay but the submarine blockade had other damaging effects on school children. *The Captain* had to explain to readers that it had slimmed down because the raw material from which its paper was made came 'from across the North Sea'.[37] For the same reason *Summer Fields Magazine* had to stop printing full casualty lists in 1917. Of more immediate consequence was the fuel shortage which meant that school heating was especially deficient. Phyllis Wilkins reported to her parents that during the cold winter of 1916–17 'we have to go about the whole day in our sports coats' and that she and other girls had chilblains, bad coughs and colds. She then became so ill in that year's measles epidemic that she was unable to write any letters for a month, by which time her best friend had died of the illness complicated by pneumonia.[38] Most boys seemed to care less about physical privations but their health could nevertheless be affected. Chesty young Eric Blair was ground down by the disgustingly 'overcrowded, underfed, underwashed life' of a wartime prep school where 'in winter your nose ran continually [and] your fingers were too numb to button your shirt'.[39] Another delicate pupil was Edward Burra, who already had an arthritic condition when he started at Northaw Place. His sister considers that his nights spent in the damp cellar during Zeppelin raids 'contributed to the illness which ended his schooldays'. Edward was often confined to the sickbay and fell disastrously behind in his work before going down with anaemia and rheumatic fever. He was withdrawn from school and became increasingly crippled, though in the 1920s he was able to attend Chelsea Art School.[40]

When the virulent outbreak of measles caused 'serious loss of life' in boarding schools in 1917, the *Preparatory Schools Review* published an article by a doctor on 'The Prevention of the Spread of Epidemic Disease at Schools'.[41] He recommended gargling, nasal douching and steam spraying, which did nothing to save prep schools from the post-war pandemic of Spanish flu. Lionel Helbert of West Downs used every available safety measure. Edwin Duncan-Sandys, or 'Duncy' (the future Lord Duncan-Sandys), who was a pupil there in November 1918, told his mother about having to go into 'a sort of big fumigator' every day 'so as not to get the flu which is all over the place'.[42] Helbert took the controversial step of inoculating all his pupils, as he carefully explained to Captain Scott's widow who had recently entrusted her son to the school. Summer Fields also inoculated its boys, two of whom 'fainted and laid in the middle of the floor', reported John Churchill to his grandmother, Lady Randolph.[43] Despite this precaution (or even, some modern scientists would argue, because of it), the wave of illness 'knocked the whole school over' at Summer Fields and filled all the sick rooms at West Downs. Maurice Richardson recorded that Mowden was similarly affected, even though the headmaster's wife and sister 'were extremely conscientious about our health'. He remembered the boys' 'spartan convalescence' when 'we were all taken off work and told to sit about in sheltered seats in the March sun'.[44] Leila Brown, who arrived at Walthamstow Hall in 1918 at the age of seven, recalled the still more severe impact the pandemic had on that school. During the painful first months of separation from her family, she and her sister were ill and one pupil and a teacher died. The school's history confirms that about fifty girls contracted the flu and that 'no effort could save' Marjorie Milledge and Miss Sharpe.[45] There must have been deaths in other boarding schools, but their magazines chiefly lamented cancelled matches and temporary closures.

Schools more often had to close because so many of their teachers and domestic staff answered the call to war. In December 1914 Antony Knebworth told his parents about going 'to see Captain Bullery, Lieutenant Kirby [two masters at West Downs] and half a battalion of the 4th Hants off to India'.[46] Evelyn Waugh's diary for the same month tells the story of Mr Vernon's last day at school when the boys presented him with a watch and the headmaster made a farewell speech before the assembled 'blubbing' pupils:

> 'Boys' he said in a husky sort of voice I had never heard him use before, 'Mr Vernon has answered to his country's call. I know you all wish him a happy time and a safe return. Three Cheers for him!' . . . That was the last of Mr Vernon that any chaps saw. I feel rather sorry now as I used to rag him so.[47]

The Preparatory Schools Review of March 1916 listed 430 prep school masters serving in the Forces and urged their remaining colleagues to do 'everything in their power to secure exemption' from conscription. Most schools struggled on. Headmasters, like John Norman at The New Beacon, might take on much of the work themselves, 'teaching every subject, coaching every game' and (if Anthony Powell's memory is to be trusted) becoming more irascible in the process.[48] Others employed men who were too old or unfit for service. In addition, Littleton Powys recalled: 'Lady teachers came to our rescue and did their part loyally and well.'[49] It was the same story at progressive Dunhurst whose masters joined up, defying the spirit of Bedales which was pacifist even though 'the roll of honour in the school hall lengthened each day as old boys fell'. Helen Thomas felt that they disapproved when her husband enlisted in the Artists' Rifles to defend 'all we know and live by'. (Edward Thomas did not survive the war, during which he produced some of his best poetry.)[50] When, finally, Dunhurst's headmaster went off to work in a munitions factory, his wife was left in charge of an entirely female staff.

A verse of Auden's views recalled the 'varied lot' of teachers left at St Edmund's, some of whom had 'most peculiar features':

> Many were raggable, a few were waxy,
> One had to leave abruptly in a taxi.

The man in the taxi was Captain Reginald Gartside-Bagnall, who used to read the boys a play he had written and tell them his army tales, offering beer and biscuits to his favourites (including Auden). The Captain presumably solicited sexual favours in exchange, but Auden blessed the memory of a man who at least gave boys their 'earliest visions of the great wide world'.[51] Some boys also blessed the presence of women who could create a homely atmosphere. For six-year-old Peter Pears, whose parents were in India, The Grange in 1916 'took the place of home and I really didn't know a home better than that'. He liked the 'very nice Irish people', Frank and Mary Gresson, who ran it: 'They were fond of me and ... I was no trouble, I think.'[52]

That was not the case with Pears's dissident fellow pupil Tom Driberg, who found the Latin and French lessons which Frank Gresson taught (in the absence of younger masters) 'sheer tedium'. He also hated his 'sadistic' wrist-beating and the licence Gresson gave boys to mob a pupil who had broken the rules, 'kicking, tearing his clothes, anything they could think of'. This happened to Tom after he had drawn a caricature of a master on the blackboard. His subject may have been the pathetic Mr Rice, whose 'chronic snivelling catarrh' had disqualified him from war service: 'What we did to him was more savage than anything recorded in school stories.'[53] Peter Fleming (the travel writer Strix, and older brother of Ian), remembered behaving with equal cruelty towards another ineffectual schoolmaster brought in during the closing stages of the war. With Peter and his companions at Durnford School 'Mr Jackson never had a chance'. They wasted lessons by encouraging him to 'relate his memories of stirring times' in Singapore; they wedged a bloater under his mattress with stinky consequences; and they smuggled a three-foot-long grass snake into the classroom. When, after moving on to Eton, Peter heard that Jackson had died of influenza, he had 'an uneasy feeling that we hounded him into his grave'.[54]

Old Summerfieldians had fonder memories of wartime staff. Their school benefited from another category of replacements: undergraduates who were medically unfit for service but signed up as willing to take on the work of men who had been called up. One of these was Leonard (L. A. G.) Strong, who was later to follow a literary career. He was only twenty-one when he interrupted 'the reign of greybeards' at Summer Fields and the boys appreciated his less formal approach to teaching. Denys Buckley later recalled that Strong 'did more to humanize the relations between masters and pupils than anyone else' and conveyed 'that life as an adult could be interesting, indeed exciting and amusing'. For John Lehmann, Strong opened the door 'on to the strange and exciting world of modern poetry'. In the 1920s, when Strong returned to the school for ten more years after completing his degree, he became renowned for his 'history pictures', which used terrible schoolboy puns as aides-memoires – a horse with six spots represented the Emperor Maximilian because 'six noughts *makes a million*'.[55]

The least tangible effect of war on schoolchildren was the 'moral stress' of being told so often that 'the men in the trenches were having a worse time than ourselves'. Teachers were obviously following the advice of *The Preparatory Schools Review* that pupils should be reminded that 'relatives and friends are indeed sacrificing money, time, comfort, life itself'.[56] Girls were particularly susceptible to such pressure. Elizabeth Bowen could not imagine a girls' school without a war after being made to feel at Downe House the 'intolerable obligation of being fought for'. 'The war dwarfed us,' she wrote, 'and made us feel morally uncomfortable.'[57] Cyril Connolly recalled that at St Cyprian's, 'The example of brothers or cousins now in the trenches was produced to shame us.' But for him and his ten-year-old companions 'the war was skin-deep'. They could not fully understand the perils or the tragedy even when, for instance, 'Uncle Granville's only son [was] killed on the first day of the Gallipoli slaughter.'[58] Boys might take a gruesome interest in bereavement but they did not know how to react if it happened to them or to others. Peter Fleming, whose father was killed in 1917, felt that his loss was 'much too big for a boy of nine to cope with'.[59] Henry Green observed that fellow pupils 'shunned anyone afflicted by death' who would be 'left to himself because he ought to be'. This is what happened to him when his brother died at another school while Henry was at The New Beacon – although 'the old tyrant' of a headmaster was kind to him.[60]

Christopher Isherwood vividly conveys what it felt like to be an 'Orphan of a Dead Hero' at prep school. When his father was reported missing at Ypres in September 1915 he returned at the start of term with a black armband stitched on to his jacket. A taboo had been established among the boys: 'The band mustn't on any account be torn or even rumpled and therefore you couldn't be attacked as long as you were wearing your jacket with the band on it.' But what the boys could not comprehend was the 'concept of grief as a continuing state of mind'. So if any boy remembered his loss and shed a few tears over it he would have to cope with it by himself 'like an attack of hiccups'. Meanwhile the headmaster would remind Christopher of his 'obligation to be worthy of his Hero-Father at all times and in all ways'. In these circumstances it was easy for adults to make children feel guilty. Isherwood revolted against what he later called 'dishonest cant', preferring to cherish the memory of the father 'who had told him stories and drawn drawings for him and taught him the magic of make-believe'. Thus he created an 'Anti-Hero Father'.[61]

Sometimes, though, a more cheerful atmosphere prevailed even in a 'grim and grimy' wartime prep school. Cuthbert (T. C.) Worsley enjoyed the 'sudden treats' provided by the two young and enlightened headmasters of Llandaff Cathedral School. 'Any specially exciting war news was an excuse for a holiday, when the whole forty or fifty of us would be rounded up and taken off for a day's expedition into the surrounding countryside.' Cuthbert and his brother were popular because the outings were often occasioned by the deeds of their father, the Warden of Llandaff Theological College, who was currently engaged in 'highly distinguished' war service. It was only at home that the brothers felt 'an increasing sense of gloom and despair', when their mother entertained wounded officers from the hospital now housed in the College.[62] Louis MacNeice was another who preferred school to his home, which was motherless and strictly Presbyterian. Sherborne, he recalled, was 'gay enough' and the headmaster, who encouraged the boys to love nature as much as he did, always conveyed an 'assurance that all was well'. For his part, Littleton Powys valued 'the irresistible cheerfulness and high spirits' of his young companions while mourning the loss of others 'so full of promise'.[63]

Like a good few prep school products who grew up in the shadow of the Great War, Louis MacNeice went on to become part of the poetic generation of the 1930s. As his testimony shows, however, not all these left-wing intellectuals 'hated their places of education'.[64] His 'Autumn Journal' remembers with affection the beginning of a school year at Sherborne with its smell of 'changing-rooms – Lifebuoy soap and muddy flannels'.[65] Similarly, Worsley loved not only Llandaff but also the school which its two headmasters later purchased, the appropriately named Brightlands, where 'the foundations of a literary taste were laid'.[66] Stephen Spender felt nothing but relief when at last he was sent to University College School, a day school pervaded by 'the gentle spirit of the headmaster and most of the staff'.[67] Moreover, his recollections of his earlier schools cannot be dismissed as the typical 'whimpering and whingeing' of a man of letters.[68] Spender used his memoir to express the misery he felt at the age of nine but dared not communicate to his fellow pupils: 'The deep treachery of childhood infected the whole place,' he wrote of Gresham's, 'like a Fascist state where you discover every neighbour to be . . . an agent of the interests of the police.' The analogy is hardly apt but Spender insisted that he was not overstating how it felt to him at the time – nothing in his life was ever 'as bad as the beginning of term at the Old School House'. Like Anthony Powell at his own prep school, he would have been 'unwilling to live five minutes of it again'.[69]

Particular controversy has surrounded George Orwell's pungent account of St Cyprian's in his posthumously published essay 'Such, Such were the Joys'.[70] Clearly his complaints about the wartime food were justified – what is more, as David Ogilvy pointed out in his *Confessions of an Advertising Man*, Mr and Mrs Wilkes ate from a different menu. While not endorsing every gory detail, many contemporary accounts echo Orwell's description of a violent and spartan regime (which was not, of course peculiar to St Cyprian's). It is true that hardier boys, like Henry Longhurst and John Christie, relished sea bathing and compulsory long walks – Longhurst found the innovative casual uniform adopted at St Cyprian's ideal for such activities. But although such ex-pupils have criticized Orwell's account of the school, many readers of the essay must have been, like Cyril Connolly, transported back to the state of being a 'little boy in corduroy knickers and a green jersey' among 'the cramming and the starving and the smells' of St Cyprian's.[71]

But did Orwell cruelly caricature the formidable Flip who, by all accounts, 'dominated the school'?[72] Some of his schoolmates have leapt to her defence. Longhurst calls her 'the outstanding woman' of his life and Christie applauds her as 'an inspired teacher' from whom 'we learned about women'. Yet both, together with more hostile witnesses, acknowledged her volatile character. Longhurst remembered what it was like for 'one's whole existence to depend on whether one was "in favour" or otherwise', and Christie (who became a colonial administrator) likened his juvenile self to a primitive farmer anxiously scanning the sky 'for changes in the climate of Flip's grace and geniality'.[73] Certainly Mrs Wilkes brought boys on so well that a good number won the Harrow History Prize or scholarships to Eton. But, Connolly concluded, in the process she used 'too much physical violence and emotional blackmail'.[74] Ogilvy recalled being thrown to the floor for reading a speech in *The Comedy of Errors* with the wrong emphasis and being sent to bed without any supper for surmising that Napoleon was Dutch because his brother was King of Holland. Another boy went supperless for saying that Henry VI (who founded Eton) was a bad king. No wonder Orwell pined for home, 'which might be far from perfect, but at least was a place ruled by love rather than fear, where you did not have to be perpetually on your guard'.[75] Even those who question the accuracy of Orwell's essay concede that he was 'true to his feelings about the school'.[76] Like Kipling in 'Baa Baa, Black Sheep', he spoke for many another child of his time.

A further mitigating plea for Mrs Wilkes is that the extra duties of wartime worsened her temper. But, for all their woes and worries, prep schools were not ultimately weakened by the conflict. Indeed the reverse is true. Alongside its casualty lists, *Summer Fields Magazine* reported splendid terms and in 1917 it described the school as flourishing. Alaric Jacob, a pupil at St Cyprian's, observed that 'the latter years of the war were great ones for prep schools'. He attributed this to war profiteers like 'Mendelsohn, the postcard King and Tucker, the Plum and Apple Jam monarch', who wanted to educate their sons as young gentlemen.[77] Connolly gave a different explanation for the thriving state of St Cyprian's: 'its *raison d'être* [was] apparent in the lengthening Roll of Honour.' As pupil numbers rose in the wake of war, scores of new schools were founded to set more of 'young British manhood', as *The Captain* put it, 'on the road of imperishable glory'.[78] After the conflict the British Empire reached its geographical apogee and demanded the service of more young officers and officials. The glamorous football captain who tormented Connolly when he first went to Eton was killed in the 1920s while leading his men in defence of 'an untenable hillside' on the north-west frontier of India. Such, Connolly concluded with characteristic cynicism, was 'the reward of leadership, the destiny of character'.[79]

5

'All the Ghastly Smells of School'
The Inter-War Period

As Paul Pennyfeather enters Llanabba Castle to embark on a schoolmastering career after being sent down from Oxford on a false charge of indecent behaviour, 'all the ghastly smells of school' remind him of his alma mater on the South Downs. Evelyn Waugh's evocation of inter-war boarding schools in *Decline and Fall* (1928) is often fact posing as fiction. The historian Richard Cobb, for example, provides a pungent olfactory account of prep schools which lay in the 'massive masturbation reserve' of south-east England. He grew used to the pong at his own school, The Beacon. But he disliked visiting The Grange where the changing rooms had a 'peculiar, fuggy, *niffy* smell' and he found that all the neighbouring schools had 'a distinctive, unfamiliar, and therefore unpleasant smell'.[1]

Gavin Maxwell was more specific about the odours he encountered at Heddon Court, the first of his three prep schools: 'Stale tobacco fear smell of Mr Stallard's study where I was beaten; bare wood board and sour boy-sweat stink of gymnasium; ammonia smell of the urinals.'[2] As appears from the sixteen pipes counted by Pennyfeather in the staff common room, schools were permeated by the whiff of teachers' tobacco. For James Kenward this conjured up the 'pleasant, sunlit state' of prep school, where he relished the joy of passive smoking. After the headmaster's evening patrol, he records, 'boy after boy humps up from the beneath the bedclothes and stands, or kneels, or tiptoes about the dormitory breathing in incense'.[3] The historian Alistair Horne feels no such olfactory nostalgia. Indeed the reek of a certain strong Turkish brand has given him 'a sense of discomfort in the nether regions' ever since being beaten in the headmaster's study at Ludgrove.[4] In the light of Waugh's novel, this chapter examines the realities of prep school life in the 1920s and 1930s.

The farce was scarcely exaggerated. Even the Llanabba saga of a former master borrowing money from the boys and waking everyone up with his motorbike has its true-life equivalent. When Arthur Marshall's Latin master at Stirling Court ran short of cash, he confiscated pens, penknives and watches from the boys, pawned them in Gosport and 'then left by motor-bicycle at midnight with a chorus girl from the pierrot troop in *Hello Hampshire* on the pier'.[5] Because of the post-war shortage of young men, many schools still had to rely on unqualified or unsuitable masters rather like Pennyfeather's colleagues, Mr Prendergast, a clergyman who had lost his faith, and Captain Grimes, for whom the old school tie was always a lifeline out of the soup. The model for Captain Grimes was a teaching colleague of Waugh's at Arnold House, LLanddulas, who confessed over many drinks at the Queen's Hotel that he had been expelled from Wellington, forced to resign his commission in the army and left four schools precipitately either for being 'taken in sodomy' or for drunkenness. 'And yet,' marvelled Waugh, 'he goes on getting better and better jobs without difficulty.'[6] David Niven's teachers at a Worthing prep school just after the war do not seem to have been much more suitable; he decided that these 'sadistic perverts' had been 'dredged up from the bottom of the educational barrel at a time of acute manpower shortage'.[7]

The war continued to be a real presence in schools as it did in other walks of life. Food rationing continued for years – John Buchan's son, William, was still eating dried egg at the Dragon as late as 1925. Duncy Sandys fared better at West Downs, where he wrote on 23 May 1919: 'Today was the first time we had sausages and tost for breakfast on Sundays since the war.'[8] Weightier reminders were the plaques in chapels or local churches commemorating, with loving expressions of gratitude, boys and masters 'who very gladly laid down their lives for King and Country'. One which perfectly captured the sacrificial spirit of the time was that sculpted by Lady Kathleen Scott in 1920 for her son's school, West Downs. A slender, naked boy with his arm raised bears the inscription: 'Here am I, send me.'[9] An additional casualty of that school was its headmaster, Lionel Helbert, who died in 1919 after several nervous breakdowns caused, it was thought, by the stresses of war. Often, as at Highfield, rolls of honour quoted verses by war poets like Rupert Brooke or Laurence Binyon. After 1929 Highfield used another literary form of remembrance; every year the headmaster would read R. C. Sheriff's play *Journey's End*, taking all the parts himself and re-living the heroism of his old boys. 'Much was made of Armistice Day,' remembered Arthur Marshall. The boys of Stirling Court would march to take their places around the war memorial in time for the maroon to herald two minutes' silence: 'We removed our caps and bent our heads and looked thoughtful.' But boys did not always behave in the manner that was expected of them. On one occasion the silence was broken with 'wild and maniacal bellows of a sort of laughter' as a boy whose father and uncle had been killed had a fit of hysteria.[10]

The Great War was also a source of pervasive prep school myths. Llanabba boys erroneously attributed Grimes's artificial leg to the war. Roald Dahl and his contemporaries at St Peter's, Weston-super-Mare, blamed the short-tempered and violent behaviour of their Latin master, the demobilized Captain Hardcastle, on shell shock – even if 'we were not quite sure what that was'. Hardcastle's reputation as 'an officer and a gentleman' meant that his version of events was given greater credence than Roald's when the boy appealed to the headmaster against a false charge of cheating.[11] Another legendary officer was Captain Winn Johnstone-Wilson, one of Angus Wilson's older brothers, who founded Ashamstead at Seaford in 1923. His war wound was 'a source of wonder' to his pupils, to whom he sometimes revealed the impressive scars on his chest and back. Rumour had it that the bullet had passed through his body and killed the man behind him. In this case, too, the injury served as an explanation for an uncertain temper.

Apart from his hero status, Captain Johnstone-Wilson had no more head-masterly qualifications than Waugh's Dr Fagan. He had no degree or teacher training certificate – though he was a gifted story-teller and boys were thrilled when he took them up to the cliffs and, accompanied by the mournful cry of seagulls, described the retreat from Mons. Among the staff were his former batman and Captain Chudleigh from his regiment, as well as members of his family. His gentle wife nursed sick boys and mothered those whose parents were abroad. The teacher of English and French was his homosexual brother, 'Mister Pat', who sported spats, white gloves, tightly waved hair, a long cigarette-holder and a whiff of perfume. The one who would have fitted best into Waugh's novel was the Geography master, who illustrated his lessons with fantasies about his travelling adventures and borrowed money from the boys to pay his gambling debts.[12] With its relaxed discipline, religious tolerance and dormitories named after artists rather than imperial heroes, Ashampstead was an unconventional school for its time. It did not provide much of an education for clever young Angus, who would probably have gained a public school scholarship if he had gone to a more orthodox establishment. But he bore no grudge, for he was happier at this 'peculiarly individual' school than he would have been at one of those 'desolate and wooden-hearted institutions'. Angus was proud of having set 'a sophisticated tone', organizing acting games based on *The Scarlet Pimpernel* and persuading the young dancing mistress to teach boys the Charleston and the Black Bottom.

Ashampstead was one of the many prep schools which 'popped up almost overnight' in the post-war era, 'like mushrooms, or, if your recollections are unfriendly, poisonous toadstools'. Arthur Marshall explains how it was done. 'You just bought a sizable country house, thirty or so iron bedsteads, a few black-boards, engaged a few staff . . . and started in.'[13] The process is conjured up in J. B. Priestley's *The Good Companions*, published in 1929: after converting 'the desirable property' of Washbury Manor into a prep school, Mr Tarvin rarely has 'to complain that one of his little iron bedsteads was without its weight of boy'. This establishment, too, has 'little old smells that live in corners and large vague smells that drift about the corridors'. These disgust the young master Inigo Jollifant, before he gets the sack for drunkenly addressing the formidable Mrs Tarvin as a 'secret, black and midnight hag' and goes off to join a troupe of strolling actors.[14] Surprisingly often, schools moved from one stately home to another. George Faulkner, whose Falconbury School combined his own name with that of its first location at Bury St Edmunds, later upped sticks to Purley and then to Bexhill in search of more advantageous quarters. It was just as easy in this era to start a girls' private school, which would usually accept a five-to-fifteen age group. Dunottar, for instance, prospered after 1926 in a series of impressive Reigate mansions even though it had no library or laboratory, let alone qualified staff.

There was no compulsory school inspection at this time but it was important for proprietors to establish the correct ethos if they were to attract 'the very best families'. Llanabba's Dr Fagan boasted that his school was built on 'an ideal of service and fellowship'.[15] Stirling Court's headmaster impressed parents with 'a record of solid scholastic achievement'.[16] The visiting speaker at Falconbury's prize-giving in 1933 emphasized that the boys were 'being nurtured in a school which would make them what everyone is proud to be, namely an English gen-tleman'.[17] Behind the scenes it was sometimes a different story. Waugh himself sat his pupils 'in sullen rows all day long to learn grammatical definitions' and got drunk in the evenings as often as he could.[18] At Stirling Court the head 'was frequently awash with his country's national beverage' and turned a blind eye to 'a quite sensational amount of bullying'.[19] Exasperated Falconbury masters kicked desks so hard that the ink-wells spilt, pulled boys' hair and made them stand on chairs if they got things wrong. Still, maintains loyal Falconburian Johnny Bell, the school had some success in its aim of producing men who could stand on their own feet and hold down a responsible job.[20]

Just as anybody could start a prep school, so anybody could finish one – and in the 1930s that often happened. Numbers often fell as alarmingly as they did at Llanabba after 'Grimes gave the place a bad name'.[21] During the Depression, as Cobb recalls, Sir would sometimes announce in midterm that a boy had had to leave; the boys knew that 'his father had been hammered on the Stock Exchange'.[22] The declining birth rate and the keener competition of state education meant that prep school headmasters had to look to their laurels. Some simply economized by cutting down on entertainment and sports programmes. At Stirling Court 'there was no Speech Day and no Prize Giving, prizes coming in the form of five shilling postal-orders to spend as we saw fit'. Nor was there any formal Sports Day, 'which might have required a marquee and, for the adults, a jug or two of claret cup'.[23] The simpler uniforms recommended in the *Preparatory Schools Review* for this 'age of financial difficulty' probably appealed to boys as much as to struggling parents.[24] In the 1920s, the Dragon's open-necked shirts worn over dark blue shorts were considered cranky. Yet by the mid-thirties its smart Oxford rival, Summer Fields, had replaced its Eton suits with jerseys and plus-fours for everyday wear.

If Dahl and other old boys are to be believed, some schools cut down on food: 'It suited [the headmaster] to give the boys as little food as possible himself and to encourage the parents . . . to feed their offspring by parcel-post from home.'[25] But Robert Baker's parents could not send food supplies from their South Indian coffee plantation to Junior King's School, Canterbury. The headmaster 'ran a system of extras', supplying milk, butter, fruit and eggs to the boys. However, Mr Baker, himself a victim of the Depression, could not afford to pay for these items and Robert was 'permanently hungry'.[26] It was plainly pangs of hunger that prompted Bertie Wooster to make nocturnal raids on the ginger nut biscuits in the Rev Aubrey Upjohn's study at Malvern House. At Ashampstead pupils looked forward to the shared distribution of tuck, which luckily included large tins of Sharp's toffees sent to young Raynor Sharp. When things got really bad there, the boys had to help out by shooting rooks to put into pies. Somehow Johnstone-Wilson struggled through the thirties, taking in Jewish refugees from

Germany to bolster the rolls. But many heads were, like Dr Fagan, forced to close down or to amalgamate with other schools. For example, Eastbourne's complement of prep schools shrank from thirty in 1919 to five in 1946.

On the other hand, many headmasters avoided closure by improving their establishments. During the 1930s the Board of Education put increasing pressure on schools to apply for inspection and the proportion recognized as efficient rose from under a quarter to over a half. Some provided an outstanding academic education and bore little or no resemblance to Llanabba Castle. Among the improving schools was Highfield, which was bought in 1904 by W. R. Mills, also known as the Bug. Under his direction the school moved from Southampton to new buildings in Liphook, where it maintained a strongly Christian ethos and gained many scholarships to leading public schools. Among the means used to achieve these desirable ends were 'chilling diatribes' from the pulpit and the cane 'rigorously applied to classroom loafers or late-night revellers in the dormitories'. Anthony Chenevix-Trench, who went to Highfield in 1928, generally avoided chastisement by sedulously obeying the school rules. He gained laurels in the boxing ring and, under the Bug's hard tutoring, won a scholarship to Shrewsbury. Chenevix-Trench went on to become a schoolmaster himself, reaching the top of his profession as headmaster of Eton and retaining, according to his biographer, 'a fervent belief in the purifying effects of corporal punishment'.[27] Perhaps he derived this belief from Mills who, according to a less devoted Highfieldian, Ludovic Kennedy, got a real enjoyment from flagellation. On one occasion Ludovic defied the Bug by slithering to the floor and shouting 'No, no, no!' until the exasperated headmaster had to abandon the punishment.[28] Anthony Storr, who was 'bitterly unhappy' at Highfield, later became a psychiatrist and did much to explain the damaging effects of being beaten or of living in perpetual fear of the cane.[29] Meanwhile the school flourished under Mills's rule, which was to last for nearly fifty years.

Schools which did close down often had their premises taken over by old people's homes or mental hospitals. To avoid this fate, elderly or eccentric headmasters sometimes gave way to bright young men. In A. J. P. Taylor's last term, he sensed that The Downs was becoming a different and 'rather more agreeable' place, because the soft-hearted Quaker H. W. Jones and his overbearing, character-building wife were now running the school jointly with the efficient new owner, Geoffrey Hoyland, who was soon to take full charge.[30] Peter Scott was less confident about the future of West Downs after the death of Lionel Helbert. 'I'm rather pleased I'm leaving,' he wrote to his mother in 1923, 'because the school is going to pot.' Helbert, headmaster since 1897, always gave special treatment to this son of the national hero whose ill-fated Polar Expedition had been closely followed at the school in 1913. Peter was allowed to replace the school uniform with Aertex shirts and shorts and was not subjected to 'cramming for work or games'. Helbert's successor, Kenneth Tindall, was more orthodox in his approach and felt that Peter should play a greater part in the corporate life of the school. The intimidating Lady Scott expressed her concern that this regime was stunting Peter's growth: 'From being a really gorgeous specimen he has dwindled into a very ordinary little boy, both physically and mentally.' Undaunted, the headmaster replied with a classic justification for the preparatory school's role: 'You have the alternatives of letting Peter grow up into a healthy savage or training him rather gradually and perhaps painfully to civilisation.'[31] The pragmatic Tindall also abolished some of Helbert's more idiosyncratic traditions such as the Court of Honour, in which boys were arraigned before the whole school for offences like stealing or plagiarism. But he kept up the zealous health routines: daily taking of temperatures, experimental fibre diets and a most unusual ban on smoking among the staff. Furthermore, he continued the keen Scouting Patrols and maintained high Christian ideals. West Downs certainly did not go to pot under Tindall's forceful leadership. But it did not escape falling rolls during the thirties and some former pupils have said that 'the place seemed to lack heart'.[32]

Pupils at other schools also felt the effects of new regimes. Humphrey Lyttelton, who entered Sunningdale in 1930 under the 'bluff, rubicund, choleric old' Mr Crabtree, welcomed as his replacement the unconventional Mr Fox. Humphrey preferred Fox's readings of detective stories and limericks to Crabtree's 'terrifying impersonation of Fagin'.[33] Meanwhile, at Newlands,[34] Giles and Esmond Romilly saw out the archaic Mr Wheeler who had all the 'little eccentricities ... fatal to any schoolmaster'. He made way for an 'alarmingly efficient' member of the school's founding Chittenden family, who introduced a disciplinary system of green cards in place of Wheeler's 'paddywhack', invariably administered after the failure of pleas for order: 'I say, you fellows, do try to take a little more interest.'[35] The school flourished under the new regime and remained in Chittenden hands until recent years. At Temple Grove, by contrast, an old family lost control

in 1934 when the Rev H. W. Waterfield, cousin of the Victorian despot, was persuaded to retire after a stint lasting for over three decades. His place was taken
by Meston Batchelor, who steered the school to success in smart new premises
at Heron's Ghyll in Sussex. Out went the old iron bedsteads, which were used to
reinforce the concrete of a swimming pool. No doubt the boys appreciated this
amenity once they had done their stretch digging out the tank – the headmaster
acknowledged that it was 'slave labour'.[36]

Summer Fields was another family enterprise. By 1928 Cyril Williams and
Bobs Alington had taken over from their aged fathers (known as Doctor and
Bear) and three other relatively young masters joined them in a ruling partner-
ship of five. From the start, however, the sternly conservative Williams and the
mildly revolutionary Alington were at odds with each other. Matters came to a
head in 1937, when Williams announced that his position was too difficult and
that he must resign. In the event it was Alington who left (to become a schools
inspector) when his modern educational ideas proved unacceptable to the other
partners. Williams continued to preside over a school that still won many top
scholarships but suffered, nevertheless, from declining numbers. In 1964 Alington
took advantage of the school's centenary publication to explain the changes he
had wanted to implement: the stimulation of 'children's natural curiosity and
wonder' rather than a concentration on 'an unnatural world of abstraction'; positive rather than negative discipline; the fostering of self-confidence rather than a
sense of failure in those who could not come up to the mark. Nearly thirty years
on, he did not expect his readers to agree with him.[37]

Perhaps Bobs Alington would have been better suited to Dunhurst, where
the Montessori system was introduced by Mrs Fish, the headmistress appointed
in the 'dreary, difficult days at the end of the First World War'. This involved a
lighter, brighter environment, self-directed activity by the children and much
more music, art and games (including nude bathing). A special barn was built
for craft activities, a printing press was installed for the production of children's
works, and an orchestra was formed under the pioneering Arnold Dolmetsch,
who introduced the recorder to British schools. After visiting Dunhurst in 1920,
Dr Montessori herself found that 'each individual child seemed to be studied
and no child repressed'. Her system proved so popular that the school was full
throughout the 1930s, and in 1938 the inspectors were delighted with 'the confidence, concentration and happiness of the boys and girls at work'. Of course, Mrs

Fish had her critics. Among them was Dunhurst's founder, Russell Scott, whose son Alan was a pupil there and could never afterwards stand anything purple, the colour of Mrs Fish's stockings.[38]

The inter-war years provided fertile ground for new educational ideas. These were doubtless stimulated in part by the celebrated principles which President Woodrow Wilson brought to the Versailles Conference: self-determination, democracy, open discussion and the peaceful settlement of disputes. Wilson had not actually envisaged that these notions might apply to children any more than they would to African or Asian subject peoples. But some child psychologists, such as the American John Dewey, the English Susan Isaacs and Dr Montessori herself, did attach importance to the rights and liberties of children. 'The child is not a machine,' wrote Isaacs 'and we are not the omnipotent controllers of his destiny.' Many mistakes could be avoided, she thought, 'if only we could give little children the same degree of consideration as we naturally extend to adults.'[39] It is not surprising that in this climate of opinion, intelligent children began to express their own views.

These were often aired in school debates, usually on pretty safe topics. Thirteen-year-old Alan Turing (already a budding scientist) does not sound very excited in a letter to his parents about a debate at Hazelhurst on whether it was more interesting for a boy to keep pets or to cultivate a garden: 'I backed up the pets. The gardens won.'[40] Schools might sometimes allow discussion of more significant issues. When David McKenna became president of the Summer Fields Debating Society he suggested as possible subjects for debate 'Socialism, Should the Channel Tunnel be made, Universal Language and so on'.[41] Occasionally, too, boys had the opportunity to tackle questions more relevant to their everyday lives. In 1932, the year in which parliament rejected a bill to abolish corporal punishment in schools, the first meeting of Falconbury's Debating Society proposed 'That Corporal Punishment is necessary in schools'. Although the motion was 'well backed up by Mr Faulkner', the opposition 'won the day by three votes'.[42]

The Falconburian does not record the arguments used, but opponents might have referred to the increasing disinclination of magistrates to birch young offenders. Birching orders fell from 3,759 in 1918 to 365 in 1926 and there was an outcry when a fifteen-year-old boy was sentenced to twelve strokes for housebreaking in Leicester: 'The police could not even find a birch or, indeed, anyone who was used to using one.'[43] Needless to say, in spite of the decision of the debate, pupils continued to be beaten at Falconbury. As Roald Dahl's headmaster explained to his Norwegian mother when she complained about the marks on her son's bottom, this was how 'British schools were run'.[44] R. C. V. Lang, who succeeded the non-flagellant Stanford at St Aubyns in 1919, seems to have brought the school into line, even though as an assistant master he had 'accepted and improved on Mr Stanford's excellent theories'.[45] Wilfred and Brian Thesiger, untamed boys who had grown up amid the 'colour and savagery' of Abyssinia, were among his victims. They were thrashed with 'a steel-shafted riding whip until they bled', before an influential friend of their late father saw their scars and warned Lang that he would have him prosecuted if he ever beat the boys again. But, according to a near-contemporary of the brothers, 'Lang went on beating other boys as viciously as before'.[46] Peter Squire, once a pupil at Seafield, Bexhill, and later a don at Cambridge, was not alone in looking back on his prep school regime as a 'rule of fear'.[47]

There were a few instances where pupils acquired a little power to influence school policy. A. J. P. Taylor found the 'the winds of change . . . blowing even at The Downs'. Before retiring in 1919, Mr Jones set up a School Cabinet elected by the boys, 'ostensibly to advise him on the running of the school'. Alan was the most radical of the Cabinet's first five members and was able to take control when the other four got mumps. He and four 'loyal followers', whom he recruited to fill their places, abolished the penalties of beating and 'plain fare' (bread and water) and instigated the right of appeal against all staff sentences. But when it was time to vote for a new Cabinet, Mr Jones declared that Alan and his friends were 'unsuitable for election' and warned them that 'any further agitation would be severely punished'.[48] It was a bit like the exclusion of Germany from the League of Nations, which was central to the thesis of Taylor's famous book of 1961, *The Origins of the Second World War*.

Julian Amery had a little more success in implementing democracy at Summer Fields in 1930. The son of Cabinet minister Leo Amery and a budding politician himself (nicknamed Pompo by his schoolfellows for his self-important manner), Julian was founder and chairman of the Anti-Authority League. Nicholas Henderson, fellow pupil and future diplomat, explains that its 'main purpose was to challenge the right of the masters to tell us how to organize our spare time'.[49] Julian's own account does not record the topics discussed in meetings attended by a third of the school but he thought that the League had some impact on the authorities. To be sure, Cyril Williams 'hated all change, even change for the better', but some irksome minor regulations were repealed. What is more, the editorial in that July's *Summer Fields Magazine* (written by a master) proclaimed that in the 'heightened sensitiveness and humanity' following the Great War, preparatory schools were ruled by 'the principle that a boy should not be asked to do a thing without first being told the reason'.[50] At the same time Julian was warned 'rather like an agitator in the Colonies, that if I broke the rules, there would be serious trouble'.[51] (These warnings sound rather like those issued by Amery himself as Conservative Under-Secretary for the Colonies in the 1950s.) Meanwhile his parents advised him: 'Don't bother too much about "views" and ideas. Do your work and enjoy your games.'[52] Such instructions may have been deemed especially necessary because of the outrageous behaviour of Julian's older brother, John, at West Downs. He was apt to turn up for the school train smoking a cigarette and dressed in flamboyant garb that bore no relation to the school uniform.

Most prep school pupils toed the line, as they had always done, apart from ragging unfortunate masters like Waugh's Mr Prendergast. Finding 'all boys utterly intractable', he attributes his lack of success to the fact that he wears a wig. Waugh was not the only writer to find a rich vein of humour in this situation. A character who regularly appeared in *Punch* was 'A. J. Wentworth, B.A.', a hapless assistant master of Burgrove Preparatory School who is constantly side-tracked and ridiculed by Mason, 'a boy of ungovernable insolence'. During an explanation of the Theorem of Pythagoras, for instance, Mason queries whether it is likely for 'real-life triangles to have squares on their hypotenuses': 'It is this kind of attitude that makes a schoolmaster's task so unnecessarily difficult and wearing.'[53] In July 1939, after a great deal of such provocation, the wretched Wentworth throws a book at Mason and accidentally stuns another boy who happens to be asleep. Of course, his assault does not match that of Mr Prendergast who thrashes twenty-three Llanabba boys when under the influence of the champagne-cup served at Sports Day. And it is not in the same league as the murder of a pupil, which also takes place on a Sports Day, in the detective novel *A Question of Proof*, written in 1935 after the author, C. Day Lewis, had done a spell of teaching at Summer Fields. The killer turns out to be the French master whose classroom usually resembles a witches' sabbath, and the motive is revenge on the boy for 'a most vicious and unpardonable trick'.[54]

It is quite possible that the Romilly brothers indulged in such impudence at Newlands, though for future revolutionaries they seem to have been distinctly orthodox. Esmond recalled that he 'remained a Conservative' while at prep school – making up for it once he arrived at Wellington by helping his brother to set up a Communist cell before running away and spilling his story to the press. Indeed, each brother in his turn became head of school at Newlands, a 'position of power and importance' gained as a result of excellent academic work. Furthermore, Esmond won the tennis tournament and the boxing cup in his last term, during which his Scouting Patrol was awarded the Crispin Cup, leaving Newlands 'in a crescendo of triumph'.[55] The Romilly boys distinguished themselves almost as much as a pupil at Falconbury who, at Sports Day in 1930, won the Senior Gym Cup and the Victor Ludorum Trophy before emerging victorious from the boxing final: 'As long as we continue to get boys like Slattery,' reported *The Falconburian*, 'this great Empire will never be far behind in anything.'[56] Meanwhile, ordinary boys at the same school had little option but to conform. Johnny Bell worked hard to 'keep his place' in work and never made more than the second cricket eleven. Feeling rather 'cast off' from his family he was glad of the presence of his cousins, George and Rundle Brendon. George was rather a star and featured prominently in the magazine's lengthy football and cricket reports. But Johnny remembers that Rundle, who was 'slow' and lacked any sporting ability, was treated well at Falconbury. He 'just fitted in' and was allowed to develop at his own pace. It was a different story at his public school, Cranleigh, from which he had to be removed on the urgent advice of a child psychologist whom he saw alone. Rundle never spoke to anyone else about what had happened to him but it was probably some kind of bullying or sexual abuse.[57]

In this post-Freudian age it became more common for victimization or home-sickness to be recognized. When Roald Dahl got himself sent home to Wales from St Peter's, Weston-super-Mare, by faking appendicitis, the family doctor realized that what had really hit the child right in the stomach was his longing for family. Nevertheless, his considered medical advice was: 'Life is tough, and the sooner you learn how to cope with it the better for you.' After three days at home, Roald was sent back to school with his secret intact, promising not to try any more tricks. He kept his pledge but always took care to go to sleep facing in the direction of his home: 'It was a great comfort to do this.'[58] Other bids for freedom could shock schools into acknowledging misery. Alistair Horne's headmaster showed rare compassion when the boy was caught at Cockfosters tube station, putting his embezzled church collection money into the ticket machine during his Great Escape from Ludgrove. Alistair was surprised when he was not 'flogged unconscious or expelled in ignominy' – he even gained some respite from nightly bullying in the dormitory.[59] Another historian, Tom Pocock, also profited a little from his attempt to run away from West Downs and get back to his own bed 'from which I could see the frieze of sailing ships my father had painted on the wall'. Judged to be 'highly-strung', he was allowed extra parental visits at weekends and was never beaten by Mr Tindall. Realizing that 'escape was impossible', Tom decided to settle down and serve his time.[60]

This proved more than Gavin Maxwell could manage at his second school, St Cyprian's. He stuck it out for nearly two years, always feeling the 'odd-man-out' and dreading the displeasure of the chain-smoking Flip, who accused him of being a 'desperate nonentity'. Eventually, he began to have nightmares from which he would wake up screaming. Overcome by shame, misery and loneliness, he wrote his mother two frantic letters. Scrambling over the roof at night and climbing down the fire escape, he posted them in a pillar box outside the school gates. The second letter ended with this heart-rending appeal: 'For God's sake take me away from this awful place.' Lady Maxwell at once had Gavin brought back to his beloved House of Elrig. There he recovered before being sent to a third school, Hurst Court. In yet another study 'filled with dense blue pipe-smoke', his charismatic new headmaster, Dr Vaughan-Evans, inspired Gavin with the confidence that this time things would go right. And so they did.[61]

Most children did not resort to such drastic measures, but some managed to find an adult who would listen and respond to their worries. At West Downs Lionel Helbert, who had tried to help Antony Knebworth out of his depression in 1913, took a similarly paternal interest in young Duncy Sandys. He was, Helbert told his mother, 'a very highly-strung, sensitive boy, who makes one feel as if one wanted to eat him, when he comes in for a talk!' Realizing that there was some difficulty in the parents' marriage, the headmaster advised that Duncy ought not to be 'over-pressed at this stage'.[62] Helbert also showed considerable patience with the misdemeanours of Peter Scott, who was clearly not used to any constraints on his behaviour after his free upbringing at home. When Peter was found to be bullying a weaker boy, Helbert allowed him to give a talk on his favourite reptile in the hope that this would 'take the place of hammering Tennant's head'. In spite of such attentions, Peter became very homesick towards the end of the summer term of 1919, perhaps as a result of having the flu. He wrote desperate letters to his mother, asking her not to tell Mr Helbert what he had said:

OH MUM DO TAKE ME HOME, HOME, HOME SWEET HOME THERE'S NO PLACE LIKE HOME . . . Get me away from this confounded domatery if you can. I adore you presious.

In response, Lady Scott took her son on an extended trip to Italy. The break seemed to do the trick as Peter flourished after his return to school in March 1920, even though Helbert had died by the time. But the Geography master was not too pleased about the prolonged absence: 'He cannot very well shine in class if he goes off on voyages of his own.'[63]

Another boy who could count on his mother's sympathy was Julian Amery. He quotes in his memoir the forlorn letter he wrote her soon after arriving at Summer Fields at the age of nine: 'Write me a letter every day, if you can. I have seen the lavatories. They are most awful with no plugs. Most of the boys are bullies and kick.' He might have added that the lavatories had no doors and that he had already been involved in a fight with a boy who called him a 'rotten lit-tle cry-baby'. Writing with painstaking legibility and signing herself Vickie, Mrs Amery sent a solicitous reply:

Always say what you want to. . . . Mrs Williams says that you may use the indoor lavatory. . . . Bless you dear. I will write you a short letter every day if I can. I think of you every day and often.[64]

Such attentions probably helped her son to survive the bullying before he learnt to defend himself with what a contemporary called the 'fury of his tongue, the length of his nails and the lowness of his punches'.[65]

John Harvey-Jones had no such support at Tormore, the Kentish school he entered after being brought up in the Indian state of 'palaces and tiger-shoots' where his father served as a colonial administrator. At the age of seven, the future troubleshooter of British business could find no way of dealing with his tormentors and SOS calls to his parents 'seemed to be confined to oblivion for all the response I received'. Even when they did come back from India on leave after several years, the Harvey-Joneses delayed visiting their desolate son, whom they found underweight, shy and nervous.[66]

When Winston Churchill's son, Randolph, encountered bullying in his early days at Sandroyd, he put his trust in the forces of law and order as he had been brought up to do. But he found that reporting the aggressors to the headmaster 'proved no more effective than did the denunciations of a similar nature to the League of Nations'. There was nothing for it but to form his own counter-gang (including Terence Rattigan), which eventually got the better of the bullies.[67] Randolph's dutiful letters to his father reveal nothing of all this, reporting instead his rather unimpressive class ratings, his swimming and boxing exploits and the books he has read: 'I have just finished the "Time Machine". I think that it is a lovely book.'[68] They certainly make no mention of a 'disagreeable experience', when a young master took Randolph to his room, undid his trousers and got him to 'manipulate his organ'. Churchill senior would never have known of this incident if the children's nanny had not overheard the 'puzzled and worried' Randolph telling his sister Diana about it in the summer holidays and reported it to her employer. Having verified the facts with his son, Winston Churchill drove straight to the school, where he established that the master had already been dismissed on other grounds. There was no question in this household of a child's voice not being heard: 'I don't think I had ever seen him so angry before or since,' reports Randolph.[69]

It is not clear whether the young master in question went on from Sandroyd to another teaching post. After all, as Waugh concluded in the case of his own disreputable colleague: 'Headmasters were loath to admit that they had ever harboured such a villain and passed him on silently and swiftly.'[70] Other cases of sexual abuse which were brushed under the carpet in this way have come to light in subsequent memoirs. Richard Rhodes James, who later taught at Haileybury, suffered at the hands of 'Mr W.' at Stratton Park and concludes: 'In those days prep schools were an underworld in which too much was hidden.'[71] Despite these episodes of what would now be called paedophilia, Rhodes James says that Stratton Park nourished him and Randolph Churchill's final report from Sandroyd pronounced him 'full of the cheerfulness and gaiety of life'.[72]

Most prep school pupils found something to keep their spirits up – which often took the form of food. Parkfield's cricket teas of 'special buns coated with white or pink icing' (as savoured by George Melly) were obviously as scrumptious as the lavish refreshments at Llanabba's Sports Day.[73] For Tony Orchard, captain of boxing at Bickley Hall, the best thing about competitions against the West Ham Boys' Club was the tea provided for their underprivileged guests. After being hammered in the ring, 'we all sat down in the dining hall with our opponents to huge plates of bangers and mash'.[74] It is no accident that the best food was associated with sporting events. These were still the highlights of the school year and, as ever, one of the greatest thrills for a boy was to win his cricket or football colours.

But there were other ways of keeping happy and fit. Over a hundred prep schools now had Scout troops, though these sometimes meant more to the masters than to the boys. George Perkin remembers tears streaming down the cheeks of his bachelor headmaster at Caldicott as he conducted Scouting investitures resembling marriage ceremonies on the steps in front of the chapel altar – much to the boys' embarrassment. He also devised adventurous new rituals for a chosen few when they were on camp in North Wales, housed in a real American Indian tepee. Dressed in grass skirts, they would perform the 'Swazee Wallah' dance around the fire at midnight before processing through the woods with paraffin flares.[75] The headmaster clearly derived as much pleasure from such evening entertainments as did his hero, Baden-Powell. At Brownsea Island B-P was observed as he stood in the flickering light of the fire, 'full of the joy of life, now grave now gay, answering all manner of questions, imitating the call of birds, showing how to stalk a wild animal, flashing out a little story, dancing and singing around the fire, pointing a moral'.[76] No doubt many of the boys enjoyed themselves too, though perhaps few imitated B-P's habit, when on camping expeditions, of taking a bath in dew-covered grass.

Alternative outdoor activities were now provided by the Woodcraft Folk, who claimed 'kinship with every living thing'.[77] Under the influence of this movement, formed by Leslie Paul in 1925, many boys spent joyful hours in the open air engaged in nature study, and were duly taunted by their more athletic contemporaries as 'bug-hunters'. At prep schools all over the country, children collected birds' eggs, identified wild flowers, watched caterpillars turn into hawk-moths, bred mice or alarmed Matron by housing snakes and lizards in the dormitory. Sometimes nature study became part of the curriculum, though this didn't suit everybody. A. J. P. Taylor tried tadpoles, newts, lichen and a wild flower list but found that 'the whole affair was a nightmare'.[78] On the other hand, some well-known naturalists began learning about wildlife when they were very young, receiving varying amounts of encouragement from their schools, which might award prizes for the best collections. At Hildersham House, Broadstairs, Thomas Hennell was given a special dispensation to go on nature walks wearing tweeds of a colour 'which the birds wouldn't mind'.[79] Hennell went on to paint and write about the country life he knew and loved as a boy.

The budding botanist, Jocelyn Brooke, did not look forward to going to boarding school, a threat which hung over him for years. He had learnt the Latin terminology for plants by the age of four and he spent many hours hunting for wild flowers in the Kent countryside. When he was sent to St Michael's, Uckfield (called St Ethelbert's in his semi-autobiographical *Orchid Trilogy*), he 'botanized semi-secretly, with a sense of shame'. This was because the activity did not fit into the school's 'ideological framework'. Hating cricket and Scouting, he was relegated to the Fourth Game and nearly expelled from the Troop. But he found green-winged orchids growing on the playing field and spotted foxgloves (uncommon in the chalky lands of East Kent) while marching down a sandy lane on a Scouts' field day. Nevertheless, he resented not being at home for the crucial early summer months to continue his hunt for rare orchids. He was upset when some other children found a lizard orchid in the park near his house:

> Untold ages of school – an eternity of cricket, of Mr Wilcox, of equations – lay between me and the time when I should be able, myself, to walk across the Park in June and July.[80]

Jocelyn stuck it out at St Michael's, despite his dread of 'THE STICK', but was to abscond twice from King's School, Canterbury.

Another self-taught naturalist was Gavin Maxwell. At his isolated Scottish home, he and his two brothers and sister had 'a sort of primary school for the study of life'. An aunt presided over it and all the children contributed to its aquaria, vivaria and cages. They also studied wildlife in the surrounding countryside. Gavin wrote and illustrated his own 'Book of Birds and Animals', which he dedicated to his mother (a First World War widow). When he and his older brother Aymer went to prep school in England they took with them 'some small memento of our high, wild upland; a sprig of white heather or of fragrant bog myrtle, even a little piece of peat'. They were symbols of hope. But nature study now had to be reserved for the holidays except when opportunities were provided by Mr Sillar, the 'devoted naturalist' who taught Art and Geography at St Cyprian's and 'loved us all with an all-embracing affection'. Even Orwell had found comfort in this master (Mr Brown in his essay), who used occasionally to take him by train for an afternoon's butterfly hunting followed by tea in the parlour of a pub. But Flip had poured scorn on these expeditions, which formed Orwell's only good memories of the school. Sillar now fostered Gavin Maxwell's talent for painting flora and fauna and, when the boy left St Cyprian's 'in a quaking jelly of misery and self-pity', urged him never to give up his interest in natural history. Back at Elrig, Gavin was touched to receive from Sillar a parcel containing his whole collection of bird skins. They kept up a desultory correspondence, but the devoted schoolmaster did not 'live to see any form of the success that he so doggedly predicted'.[81]

Peter Scott received much more support at West Downs for his early efforts as a naturalist. Sending his mother instructions to look after his menagerie at home, including the 'little snake in the back dining room under the glass funnel', he spent all his spare time at school studying nature in one form or another. His beautifully illustrated unpublished letters describe hissing adders, birds' nests full of eggs, and the lizards, slow-worms and frogspawn he collected. He specialized in caterpillars but, unlike Peter Squire at Seafield, he did not have to send away for glass-topped tins in which they could turn into puss moths. The helpful Helbert gave him the use of a greenhouse for this activity, which he shared with the other members of his Caterpillar Club. Peter also got together a group of boys intent on finding birds' eggs and watching for the babies to hatch out. 'They are all very keen and very quiet,' he told his mother, 'bieing on their honour not to touch or tell of nests.'[82] Clearly his schoolfellow Duncy Sandys did not belong to this club: he and two friends 'got five Jay's eggs' but packed them so badly that on the way back to school 'they fell off our bikes and got smashed'.[83] No doubt Peter Scott's almost obsessive pursuit of nature seemed odd to other pupils but, even under Kenneth Tindall, the spirited boy 'went his own way'. One undated letter ends: 'Oh how good it is to be alive!'[84]

There were other forms of juvenile joy to be found amid the trials of prep school. Alan Turing hated being parted from his parents in 1922 when they went back to India, leaving him at Hazelhurst School in Sussex. His mother had a 'painful memory of his rushing down the school drive with his arms flung wide in pursuit of our vanishing taxi'.[85] But soon Alan's letters were preoccupied with his inventions: a typewriter, a fountain pen and a bicycle with paddles. It was lucky, he thought, that he did not have 'to show up any letters to Mr Darlington' (by a special agreement with his mother), for they were written in green ink which he had made himself. By 1925 (when his parents were closer at hand after his father's retirement from the Indian Civil Service), he was teaching himself organic chemistry and conducting experiments without help or hindrance from the school authorities: 'I wonder whether I could get an earthenware retort any-where for some high-heat actions.'[86]

Other independent-minded pupils rehearsed, often unwittingly, for their future careers. Argentinian-born Tom Harrisson felt like a foreigner and pariah at his 'loveless' Winchester prep school, where he kept index cards on every boy, anticipating the pioneering social survey Mass Observation he set up in 1937.[87] After being exiled from India to St Andrew's, East Grinstead, Alan Ross found solace in the 'revival of fortune for Sussex cricket'; he left the school as cricket captain and went on to write lyrical verse and prose about the graceful game.[88] Johnny Bell, future owner of a Newmarket stud, would escape from the pressures of Falconbury by making up commentaries on imaginary horse races. Terence Rattigan (who insisted on being called Terry and using Christian names with other boys), began his first play, *The Parchment*, while at Sandroyd. As often as possible he would sneak out to matinees and when offered the choice in 1921 between abandoning his part in the school play and a beating he chose the lat-ter. He admitted also to 'experimenting with one or two boys'. His headmaster innocently concluded that Terence had 'taken a leading part here in things grave and gay'.[89]

A little later, Humphrey Lyttelton played a leading part in school entertain-ments at Sunningdale. In his last concert there he led a jazz band, consisting of three kazoos, a master on the swanee whistle and himself on the drums. A tune called 'Whispering' was a great success with the audience. The 'reams and reams of music' which Benjamin Britten composed in odd moments at South Lodge, Lowestoft, did not reach the public until 1953, for he had flung them into a cup-board. At the same time he had distinguished himself as head prefect and Victor Ludorum. Arthur Marshall did not cover himself with such glory at Stirling Court, but he did reveal a rare talent during his last term. While taking part in a school debate, he was 'surprised and delighted' to find that he could make people laugh. 'I was anxious for more,' he wrote, 'and since that time I have made laughter the prime consideration in life.'[90] Another boy who embarked on the pleasures of life was Ian Fleming. Before leaving Durnford for Eton in 1921, he had acquired his 'abiding love of the sea and its creatures' at the Dancing Ledge, the nude-bathing pool 'blasted out of the rocks at the edge of the sea' by the headmaster Tom Pellatt. Unconnected with this, he had also developed a crush on Pellatt's 'strapping daughter'.[91]

Waugh's *Decline and Fall* has little to say about such boyish activities, which would have escaped the attention of his fictional pedagogues, preoccupied as they were with their own pleasures and problems. Of course, many pupils did benefit from the encouragement of more dedicated teachers. Frank Giles, a sickly child at The Grange, was given some worn records of Mendelssohn's violin concerto by one of the masters. These not only relieved the boredom of days spent in the sanatorium but taught the future editor of *The Sunday Times* to appreciate music, a 'great and lifelong boon'. Peter Squire derived similar benefit from his music-loving History master, who inspired another enduring passion by giving him a book in which he had marked the pages of a P. G. Wodehouse school story.[92] Richard Cobb developed his 'enormous curiosity about the past' thanks to his favourite master at The Beacon, Mr Atkinson – or M. Ratkinson as he was called. And Cobb's devotion to France stemmed from the French primer he used with Mr Wright, known as the Green Pig. The painter Keith Vaughan did not admit to any such legacy from Christ's Hospital, which he hated after being sent there at the age of nine. Fifty years later, he recalled only 'the smell of the long deal benches in Prep A against which I pressed my forehead in agony and longing for oblivion. . . . A smell of oil, deal, sweat and my own breath and salty tears.' Yet his work was influenced not only by Frank Brangwyn's murals in the chapel but also by the Art teacher, Arthur Rigby, who introduced him to Italian Renaissance painting and taught him 'the rudiments of self-discipline'.[93]

Other pupils had the excitement of being taught by aspiring young writers. Nigel Nicolson had happy memories of C. Day Lewis talking about books at Summer Fields. A pupil at The Downs compared W. H. Auden's classes to 'a glorious firework display': 'Completely unconventional, striding about in a large black Flemish hat, waving an umbrella, he entranced us with his eccentricity, tireless energy and sense of fun.' The boys addressed Auden as Uncle Wiz.[94] Doubtless, too, some boys at Arnold House and Aston Clinton benefited from Waugh's genius before the first appointment ended in a suicide bid and the second in his dismissal for drunkenness.

Talented teaching and early promise did not always bear fruit. One of the ablest schoolboys of the 1920s was the older son of the Liberal politician, Reginald McKenna. As the *History of Summer Fields* proudly records, Michael McKenna was captain of the cricket eleven and head prefect, as well as a member of the choir and a writer of poetry commended by W. B. Yeats. Finally, he won the top Eton scholarship of 1923, tying with a fellow pupil. At this point, Michael told his mother, he felt 'very genial and exceedingly happy'. Letters from his former teachers to 'Dearest Mikey' at Eton reveal how cherished this brilliant pupil had been at Summer Fields. They assure him that he is tremendously missed 'both in school and out', and that they look forward to his visits and trust that 'our little talks and confidences . . . are only suspended', before they sign off with 'heaps and heaps of love'.[95] But, after shining at Eton and at Cambridge, Michael suffered a nervous breakdown. His letters and reported conversations of 1929–30 suggest a troubled young man going 'deeper and deeper into my being', crying out for God's help and sensing that he was not 'meant to be in this world very long'. After his early death in 1931, his doctor judged that exhaustion and toxaemia following an operation were important contributory causes but that 'the spiritual factor was the strongest of all'. Among the many letters of condolence extolling the 'beautiful, good and gifted' Michael was one which blamed his demise on 'the Eton system' and 'the tremendous responsibility that is put upon outstanding boys'. A Summer Fields master compared him to the doomed youth of the Great War, to the 'Julian Grenfells and Rupert Brookes of this world [whom] the Gods cannot fail to love'.[96]

Had he lived, Michael would undoubtedly have fought in the Second World War, as did his brother David, some of his teachers, Evelyn Waugh (and Guy Crouchback, the hero of his later *Sword of Honour* trilogy) as well as most of the prep school boys mentioned in this chapter. Looking at a school photograph of 1934, George Perkin observed that a few years after it was taken 'most of us were in the forces'. For those who, like George, had been away from home since the age of seven, service life was in many ways an extension of boarding school; the sensitive child susceptible to dormitory ragging became a natural victim below decks in the Royal Navy.[97] But it was unusual for a former prep school boy or master to move on to prison as does Waugh's hero, Paul Pennyfeather.

He consoles himself with the thought that 'anyone who has been to an English public school will always feel comparatively at home in prison'.[98]

It is true that aspects of many inter-war boarding schools resembled prison: the scrutiny of private letters, limits on family visits, harassment by other inmates, unappetizing food, punitive bread-and-water regimes, square-bashing and harsh physical chastisement. Prep school boys often compared their grand mansions to prison-houses and their masters to 'a species of gaolers'.[99] Alistair Horne used astonishingly emotive language, going so far as to describe Ludgrove as 'a Belsen of the spirit'.[100] Former detainees of concentration camps or HM Prisons might well find these metaphors inappropriate. But Pennyfeather's view is shared by at least one convict who was also a prep/public school product.

Lord Montagu of Beaulieu was a pre-war pupil at St Peter's Court, where he *thinks* he was happy, before going on to Eton and serving in the Grenadier Guards. In 1954 he was sentenced to twelve months' detention for homosexual offences. He felt very bitter about his trial and conviction, which occurred three years before the Wolfenden Committee recommended the legalization of homosexuality between consenting adults, partly as a result of his case. But he did not find Wakefield gaol as unpleasant as he had expected and attributed this largely to his schooling.

> I was educated as a child to being away from home, cut off from family and close friends; I was used to an all-male society disciplined by routine and the clock; I was already hardened by indifferent food and a degree of physical discomfort.[101]

Like school, prison had its lighter moments. One was a concert party in which Lord Montagu, partnered by the Duke of Sutherland's former butler who had stolen the family silver from Sutton Place, sang Noel Coward's 'The Stately Homes of England'. Containing lines that must have reminded Montagu of his days at St Peter's Court, it is a comic elegy on the collapse of the landed aristocracy, whose education lacked coordination although its sons knew 'how Caesar conquered Gaul/And how to whack a cricket ball'. It was a tableau worthy of Waugh himself.

6

'A Higher Sense of Sacrifice'
The Second World War

When the Second World War began in 1939, Raleigh Trevelyan was only two years out of Horris Hill, 'a Spartan place . . . where objectionable little boys used to be swung by arms and legs by other objectionable little boys into holly bushes'. But the conflict was so protracted that he was called up before it had finished. In 1944, as a twenty-year-old subaltern, he fought in the Battle of Anzio, one of the grimmest of the war. He was wounded and taken to a dressing station where, just as he was succumbing to the effects of morphia, he recognized a signals officer as Mr Richards, his favourite Horris Hill master. 'Hello Trevelyan,' he said, 'any better at your Logs since I last saw you?'[1]

Trevelyan was not the only former prep school boy to feel at ease in the services. William Buchan, inured as he was to discomfort and communal living at the Dragon, did not find it hard to adjust to the RAF in 1940: 'I was simply back at boarding school.'[2] It was the same for Peter Collister, who had arrived at his Bexhill prep school from India in 1929 with profuse curls and an angelic countenance; he was the victim of merciless teasing until he turned on one tormentor and stuck a pen nib into his forehead – for which he was beaten in front of the whole school. When Collister joined up after leaving Cheltenham College in 1939, he did not find it hard to merge into military life.[3] For Alan Ross, matters were more complicated. When he entered the navy in 1942 after St Andrew's and Haileybury, his lack of family ties made him feel 'expendable'.[4] All these men served bravely. Trevelyan returned to the fray only to be wounded again; Buchan led air squadrons in Palestine, Ceylon and India; Collister fought the Japanese in Burma and Ross manned highly vulnerable convoys to Russia.

Of course, there were many other heroes among the old boys of these schools. Johnny Bell told a wartime story which epitomized, for him, the prep school ethos. Lieutenant Peter Roberts, a 1920s Falconburian, was awarded the Victoria Cross for volunteering to dislodge a ticking German bomb from the casing of his submarine. Much was made of this at Falconbury, whose old boys reacted by asking 'Wouldn't everyone have done that?'[5] But not all prep school products had this sense of patriotic duty. A West Downs boy, John Amery, even went on to betray his country by making propaganda broadcasts from Germany and attempting to recruit a fascist volunteer force in Britain. In evidence submitted to the Home Office, his former headmaster, Kenneth Tindall, said that he had 'no code of morals at all'. Amery was hanged for treason in 1945.[6]

Other boys emerged from prep school as conscientious objectors. Peter Pears, a well-adjusted pupil of The Grange keen on cricket and the Classics, had gained there a lifelong aversion to violence. The experience of being made to box and of beating younger boys with thick wedges of wood led him to vow at the age of ten: 'I'm never going to fight . . . [or] to take part in any war.'[7] Sure enough, he gained exemption from war service in 1940 on the grounds of his pacifist convictions, as did his partner Benjamin Britten. The two musicians did, though, contribute to post-war reconstruction and reconciliation; for the re-dedication of the bombed Coventry Cathedral Britten composed his *War Requiem*, in which Pears sang tenor and the German Dietrich Fischer-Diskau baritone. Other non-combatants among the pupils encountered in earlier chapters participated bravely as code breakers, medical auxiliaries or war artists. Thomas Hennell, for example, depicted hazardous battle fronts in Europe and the Far East before disappearing without trace in 1945 while visiting internment camps in Java.

This long war demanded courage from all classes of British people, even if they had not been educated by the public school code which was said to demand 'a higher sense of sacrifice and leadership than is expected from the under-privileged'.[8] The RAF, which had been the almost exclusive preserve of public school boys, now had to recruit more widely. As well as giving fitters and riggers from the Apprentice Training School the opportunity to become pilots, the Air Ministry created the Royal Air Force Volunteer Reserve in order to attract grammar and even elementary school recruits.[9] It was both incorrect and unwise for the president of the Headmasters' Association to claim that the Battle of Britain was 'fought largely by our old boys, for few apart from them had the education and training necessary to become air crews'.[10] In October 1940, Lord Beaverbrook (at that time Minister of Aircraft Production) told Churchill that only 30 per cent of RAF pilots came from public schools, prompting the prime minister to wax eloquent 'on the disappearance of the aristocracy from the stage and their replacement by these excellent sons of the lower middle classes'.[11]

Churchill elaborated on this theme in a speech at his own old school, Harrow, which had been hit by German bombs. Referring to Hitler's boast that men who had been through the Adolf Hitler schools would soon beat Britain's Etonians, he told the boys:

> Hitler has forgotten Harrow, and he has also overlooked the vast majority of the youth of this country who have never had the advantage of attending such schools, but who are standing staunchly together in the nation's cause and whose skill and prowess is the envy of the world.[12]

The Battle of Britain was won not so much on the playing fields of Eton as on those of state schools.

Beneath the war being fought in the air, on the green cricket and football pitches or the asphalt playgrounds of schools in south-east England, children witnessed scenes which they would never forget. Edward Montagu 'fell in love with fighter aircraft' and hero-worshipped daredevil pilots even before 1939, for St Peter's Court was very near Manston airfield in Kent. He longed to see Spitfires in battle but, once war came, the school was evacuated from this vulnerable spot to Devon, where he had to content himself with model aeroplanes.[13] The comic novelist Tom Sharpe had more excitement at Hazelwood, Oxted, which did not move despite its proximity to Biggin Hill. He often saw Spitfires going over and remembers a master throwing a bag of flour at one which flew too low. The Latin master, who had joined the RAF, delighted boys and alarmed parents by swooping down close to the cricket field when a match was in progress. Tom also delighted in collecting cartridge cases from the playing field. Otherwise school carried on as usual, with rugger games, tree climbing and regular beatings from the headmaster, Mr Goodbody Parry, for boys who received too many NS (*non satis*) marks for their work. Sharpe recalls with much glee the time when the wooden rapier Parry habitually used to beat him broke and gashed his (Sharpe's) head. After he had been patched up by Matron and put to bed, the headmaster actually came to apologize. Mr Sharpe removed Tom in 1940 not because of that incident but because the family moved to the safer Midlands.[14] This was a wise precaution since Parry insisted, once the Battle of Britain began, on going ahead with Sports Day 'as a gesture of support for the pilots overhead, despite parents running for shelter under a rain of shrapnel'.[15]

Even away from the immediate flight path of the Luftwaffe, known as 'Bomb Alley', there was plenty of excitement. From the Somerset country mansion to which his prep school had been evacuated, Roger Hancock (brother of the comedian Tony) saw the crash landing of a German Heinkel aircraft. He recounts that he and a friend secretly retrieved the swastika from its tail, which they hid in the dusty, out-of-bounds cellars they had explored a few months earlier. Roger thinks it is probably still there.[16] Some of the oldest prep schools in the country also saw action. The headmaster of Temple Grove had decided to stay put in Sussex despite parents' anxieties, and he had also argued his way out of being requisitioned as a hospital over 'quite a good glass of port with an official in Whitehall'. Thus boys on a picnic party, wondering why 'so many aircraft were passing overhead in the clear blue sky', witnessed the start of the Battle of Britain. Over the next few months the greatest danger – and the most exciting spectacle – was the 'drunken zigzag course' of a stricken plane. No doubt pupils followed the exploits of Temple Grove's heroic old boy, Douglas Bader, who took part in the air battle despite having lost both his legs in a pre-war flying accident.[17]

Meanwhile at Twyford near Winchester, Douglas Hurd and his companions 'followed the progress of the war with great care', plotting it with flags on their own operations map. And very indignant they were when, in September 1940, they had to go down to the air-raid shelter 'while the masters were allowed to follow in the sky the latest instalment of the Battle of Britain'. Enthusiasm palled in the ensuing months, which saw 'air raid after air raid', with hours spent in the stuffy shelter 'made even less endurable by the record of George Formby played over and over by one of the masters on his portable gramophone'. After a series of nights like this, pupils were understandably 'rather tired'. But the next day they would get on with their lessons and matches. They also engaged in school-boy feuds, dividing into parties in pursuit of what Douglas (a future Home and Foreign Secretary) described as 'the politics of the school'. Adults were more concerned about the bombers. Mrs Hurd, who had another son at Twyford, wrote to the school about the danger of splintering glass. The headmaster's kindly wife reassured her that they kept the shutters closed so that the 'amount of glass left unprotected is practically negligible'.[18]

Both schools survived these wartime ordeals as well as lesser hazards, such as an infestation of nits due, the headmaster of Temple Grove reckoned, 'to the influx of evacuees'.[19] He probably had in mind the guests who arrived at his

DOCTOR BLIMBER'S YOUNG GENTLEMEN AS THEY APPEARED WHEN ENJOYING THEMSELVES

Dickens's illustrator 'Phiz' contrasts the procession of Doctor Blimber's young gentlemen, who are allowed nothing 'so vulgar as play', with the rough-and-tumble of less privileged youngsters.

THE BRITISH CHARACTER
ABILITY TO BE RUTHLESS

Cartoonists view the journey to school before and after the Second World War: a small boy between his parents and a group of pupils bound for st custards (including nigel molesworth sitting on his tuck box).

Uckfield premises from an East End school rather than the pupils of Brightlands Preparatory School, Dulwich, who moved into ivy-clad Tavistock Hall at neighbouring Heathfield. Among the Brightlands pupils were Jim and Mark Hammer, whose unpublished letters to their parents (preserved in the Imperial War Museum) vividly conjure up the war experience of prep school children. They were in less danger than they would have been living as day boys in Dulwich, where their grandparents were killed by a bomb in October 1940. 'James felt the blow severely and showed much distress,' wrote his headmaster, 'but he was very courageous.' Still, as Jim remarked, their Sussex site was 'in the direct line of flight from the coast' and the boys had plenty of enemy action to report. They collected 'Amo' after 'footer' games interrupted by 'Syreens' and observed the barrage balloons over neighbouring Mayfield. Only a few days after his grandparents' death, Jim sent a long description of his 'most interesting, exciting and altogether best day'. He had seen 'a Spitfire zoom by very low and a Hurricane circle round about 900 to 1000 feet up', and he heard explosions as bombs fell in Heathfield Park. Half an hour later all the boys were summoned to the hall because some Messerschmitts had been spotted: 'We heard a terrific lot of zooming, climbing, banking and diving about. At one time there was an absolutely TREMENDOUS zoom and I thought that a plane was coming through the roof any minute.'[20] Other letters that autumn told of dogfights between planes 'criss-crossing with smoke trails following', a Polish pilot whose parachute failed to open falling to his death in the playground of Mayfield school and 'the glow of a jolly big fire' as bombs fell over London. In his spare time Jim informed himself about aeroplanes from the *Illustrated London News*, read of further wartime adventures in such books as *Biggles Defies the Swastika* and *William and the Evacuees*, and made models of fighter planes, including 'a Messerschmitt 109 out of rosewood'.[21]

The boys' leisure was also taken up with a great deal of knitting for the war effort. By November 1940, Jim had completed sixteen squares of a blanket, and a year later Mark reported that he had not had much time for reading 'as I have concentrated on my knitting'. They did not complain about this tame occupation but they probably preferred more energetic forms of helping out such as cutting down trees, digging trenches, growing vegetables and shooting rabbits. As time went on they had, like everyone else in the country, to 'Make Do and Mend': they wore second-hand shirts 'a bit on the small side', put up with blazers thinner and coarser than usual, had difficulty in scratching together a football kit and saved the peel of their rare orange ration for making marmalade. 'Anyway it's war-time!' Jim reminded himself.[22]

Despite all the excitement and activity, the Hammer brothers longed for home with its 'warm fires and wireless when you want!' They hated the thought of spending the holidays at school and hoped there was room for them in the Dulwich air-raid shelter. 'MAY WE COME HOME???' begged Jim in December 1940. In July 1941 he was longing for 'freedom from *don't* do this, *don't* do that, *don't* come here, *don't* go there!!'[23] After Jim left Tavistock Hall (the renamed Brightlands) in 1942 to take up a public school scholarship, Mark missed him very much and was grateful for a half-term family reunion: 'Now I look back on it with pleasure and think of that nice evening walk we had after supper. It was so nice seeing Jim again.' When German flying bombs and rockets struck in 1944, he sounded brave but no longer exhilarated. 'Everyone was shivering in their beds' during a 'deathly half-hour' on the night of 20 January as planes crashed and sticks of bombs fell, making 'the windows rattle and almost fall in'. Mark's letters over the following months described other such nights in which he got little sleep. By June many boys had gone home, but Mark told his parents not to worry about him; he said he was safer at school with slit trenches to use in the daytime and gas masks at the ready. But he worried constantly about his parents: 'Every evening I think of you, and wonder how you are getting on with all these "pilotless planes" crashing in London.'[24]

Needless to say, the war brought similar experiences to state school children, who demonstrated comparable pluck, patriotism and family loyalty. At a village school in Hertfordshire one of the biggest boys, 'an ardent and knowledgeable plane spotter', would run out when an alert sounded and stand on top of the shelter: 'If he thought it looked as if one of theirs might be coming down nearby he would shout 'Miss – Quick!', whereupon the whole school would stream out and huddle in the shelter.'[25] In September 1940, boys at a council school in Cirencester were reported to be 'industriously knitting during their playtime' and one seven-year-old had 'already completed two full-length scarves, a balaclava helmet and a hot-water bottle cover'.[26] All over the country, children in schools, clubs and holiday camps were lending a hand, digging for victory and eating their greens. As the headmaster of a Portsmouth school noted after it had been moved to Winchester, many children were as fearful as the Hammer boys about the safety of their parents in bombed cities. 'We had a couple of the big fire blitzes in Portsmouth and some youngsters, when the news came of the attacks, got on their bicycles to go home. . . . Well, who can blame them?'[27]

Such comings and goings were not unusual, for evacuation was never compulsory. When the Blitz petered out thousands of homesick children drifted back to the cities while their schools remained billeted in the country; indeed the old school buildings had often been destroyed or requisitioned for military purposes. 'The nation's education system had reached a consummation of chaos,' concludes the historian Angus Calder. He contrasts the many ordinary children receiving part-time schooling or none at all with 'the young relatives of Cabinet ministers [who] continued to enjoy an uninterrupted education' at private schools.[28]

A boy who experienced both educational systems during the war was Bryan Magee. His elementary school was evacuated from Hoxton in East London to Market Harborough, where it occupied a Baptist church hall. When he was eventually billeted with a family which made him welcome, Bryan, who had never got on with his mother, felt happier than he had ever been in his life. He enjoyed the community of purpose created by the war with 'each one doing his bit'. But school was a problem for this clever child; by 1940 he had already been through the syllabus of the top class three times. The headmaster tried to provide separate teaching in subjects like algebra, but it became apparent that he was none too clear about them himself. Nevertheless, in 1941 Bryan did so well in the scholarship examination that he was offered an assisted place at Christ's Hospital. This public school still 'remained true to the spirit of its original purpose' by educating a proportion of boys from poor homes, taking them in at the age of eleven to fit in with the state system. Thus Bryan trod the same path as Charles Lamb, Leigh Hunt and Coleridge, though it took him to the school's new premises in West Sussex (with its own railway station) rather than to the Tudor buildings in Newgate. 'Blimey Magee', as he was nicknamed because of his cockney accent, did not enjoy everything about Christ's Hospital, a conformist institution which derided Colin Davis for wanting to be a musician and nearly expelled Magee for atheism. But he thinks himself lucky to have experienced the type of education he had previously read about in school stories, which gave him 'a solid academic foundation' for the rest of his life.[29]

Another advantage which prosperous parents could give to their offspring was to choose a school with a safe location. Gayhurst, a day/boarding prep school situated in Gerrards Cross, north-west of London, had found that its numbers fluctuated in the uncertain months of 1940 and 'a good many more left than came'. Furthermore, in November 1940 it suffered damage, though no serious injury, when a bomb fell near the Junior House. The school stayed put under the leadership of Stormont Gibbs MC, a First World War survivor with pacifist convictions, and parents came to appreciate that its position was nearly as safe 'as anywhere else in the centre or south of England'. By September 1944 the school was full and 'had to refuse a considerable number of applications'. The renewed air attacks of 1944 brought some 'anxiety and irritation' but pupils rose to the occasion. When there was an alert, a boy would go to the highest point in the school to look out while another stood by the bell. 'He was to ring it on a signal from the first boy if he saw a bomb coming in the direction of the school.'[30] The bell never had to be rung and the school continued to play cricket matches, organize Scout camps and perform plays al fresco. Thus Gayhurst provided a stimulating and happy environment for Rodney Barker, now an immigration lawyer in America. From 1940 to 1947 he was a day pupil at the school, living with his divorced father, who did not wish to send his only child away. Rodney remembers Gibbs as 'another father figure' who only gave 'mild beatings' and Gerrards Cross as a neighbourhood around which he could bicycle without restraint during his boyhood.[31]

Other parents chose places of still greater safety. Schools such as Maidwell Hall in rural Northamptonshire were inundated with applications. Among its 'trained little winners' was Jeremy Wolfenden, who arrived at the age of nine in 1943, got into the top form within a year and gained the highest scholarship to Eton in 1947. Examiners were impressed both with his parsing of the word potato as if it were Latin and with his essay on dreams.[32] In North Yorkshire, too, 'you would not have known that there was a war on,' remembers James Day. He spent his 'idyllic schooldays' at Terrington Hall under a 'forward-thinking' headmaster known as Clemmie. In the evenings, pupils were given free access to Clemmie's study where they could read his books, learn to play bridge or add to their stamp albums with gifts from his own 'fantastic collection of British Commonwealth sets'. During their free time they built dens on the rough ground, went tobogganing in the frequent deep snowfalls and, on fine summer days, piled into Clemmie's Armstrong Siddeley tourer for expeditions to Castle Howard 'where we would all swim naked in the lake'. The boys were well fed, thanks to home-reared pigs and a kitchen garden. The only adverse effect of the war was that James's mother could make the train journey from Stockton to York only once a term – but lunch at the Railway Hotel was a treat in spite of rationing.[33] Terrington was evidently far enough away from York not to have been affected by the heavy air bombardment it suffered in April 1942. This was one of Hitler's 'Baedeker Raids' on Britain's historic cities which had already destroyed Exeter's choir school, killing the headmaster's daughter. Further raids on Bath, York and Norwich razed many ancient buildings and caused thousands of casualties.

It was not easy, therefore, to predict which parts of the country would escape enemy action. In 1941 Christopher Wood's London-based parents sent him to board at Edward VI Grammar School, Norwich. At first, the greatest peril he faced was a gang of bullies who waited until lights-out to start tormenting the new boys. Christopher was not alone. Another victim, Philbrick Minor, was his companion in suffering – until the leader of the bullies took Christopher aside and explained how he could become one of their gang. Following the advice he had been given, Christopher crushed a sock full of gooseberries into Philbrick Minor's bed, leaving the boy 'alone in his misery'. Christopher himself was left with a sense of shame at his betrayal which stays with him to this day. By comparison, the war was a source of entertainment, as glamorous American airmen from the surrounding airfields fought local squaddies outside the Samson and Hercules Dance Hall across the road from the school. These punch-ups puzzled the eight-year-old Christopher since the brawlers were supposed to be on the same side. It was only later that the author of *Confessions of a Window Cleaner* realized that Norwich girls, who favoured the elegantly dressed and nylon-bearing Yanks, were the cause of these nightly battles. In 1942, however, Norwich became a Baedeker target. The cathedral escaped more or less intact but a bomb fell on the adjacent medieval school, as Christopher has good cause to remember – he was beaten by the headmaster after a senior boy ordered him into the rubble to retrieve a tennis ball.

It was safer back in London, where Christopher resumed his preparatory education at King's College Junior School, Wimbledon. But now he was at risk from certain 'drunken, mentally disturbed, sexual predators' among the staff, whose peccadilloes were blamed on their being shell-shocked survivors of the First World War. (Or perhaps, as John le Carré surmises about Magnus Pym's prep school masters in *A Perfect Spy*, 'the fever of war encouraged brutality', which was intensified by the guilt feelings of non-combatants.) Christopher reported some of his masters' more outrageous behaviour to his parents but they, having scrimped and saved to give their only child the finest education within their means, preferred not to believe him. Despite all this Christopher found solace in his day-boy status and eventually became head boy and captain of rugby in the senior school.[34]

A city lucky enough to escape German bombs was Oxford. It was thought to be on Hitler's Baedeker list but, wrote Summer Fields master Geoffrey Bolton, 'our turn never came'.[35] Thus the Dragon School did not implement its planned evacuation to a large hotel in Cornwall. Charles Williams, who was a pupil there throughout the war, remembers no ill effects of any kind. He never went hungry, he took part in no war effort, he met no evacuees, he wore the Dragon's simple uniform of shorts, shirt and jersey and he was well taught by masters who 'were out of the services for one reason or another'. Moreover, he was fully occupied with getting through large amounts of prep, captaining the cricket, football and hockey teams, acting Shylock in *The Merchant of Venice* and singing in Gilbert and Sullivan operas. In fact, Charles was 'a star' in a large school full of keen, clever dons' children, tough 'little Dragons'. Despite his triumphs, though, he had his reservations about the school. His 'bolshie' rejection of its inhumane 'rugby ethos' and his dislike of the headmaster, 'Joc' Lynam, meant that he stood no chance of being appointed school captain.[36] By contrast, his contemporary and fellow historian, Antonia Fraser (née Pakenham), recalls being 'intensely happy' at the Dragon. One of forty girls in a school of 400, she played on the wing in the rugby team and felt that she was 'really a boy' – a conviction which did not make life easy for her when she moved on to a convent.[37]

Not all schools in favoured areas prospered. Julian Critchley concluded that his headmaster, R. P. Marshall, was losing money despite Brockhurst's 'remoteness from the Luftwaffe' in Shropshire. He disliked the 'ferocious' Marshall and the Edwardian building which 'smelt of sweat, stew, embrocation, fear and excrement'. So he did not mourn when it was sold in 1942 and moved to Staffordshire to share premises with another prep school, Broughton Hall. The merger had its disadvantages: the two sets of pupils infected each other with their epidemics and 'Matron was forever thrusting thermometers into our mouths'. But in general the new regime, under the 'affable, approachable and friendly' John Park and 'a bevy of ageing assistant masters brought back to life by the war', suited Julian better. For him the war now meant making model warships and doing his bit for Mrs Churchill by lifting potatoes. However, a passion for sweets led him into a bout of crime. He and the boys from the senior Brockhurst dormitory regularly broke into the cupboard where Matron stored all the boys' supplies that were to be doled out in weekly rations. They took care to steal only from the Broughton boys and 'expunged any feelings of guilt by pretending to ourselves that we were British prisoners of war, imprisoned in Colditz'.[38]

One of Critchley's victims was probably his future Conservative colleague in the House of Commons, Michael Heseltine, whose three years at Broughton Hall were 'the happiest of my schooldays'. There he engaged in such blameless pastimes as gardening and setting up the Tit Club with fellow birdwatchers, in which he was known as the Great Tit. A less benign activity was the boys' persecution of the French teacher as a German spy – she was rumoured to be communicating her messages in Morse code signals disguised as owl calls. 'Night after night we solemnly recorded the hooting of numerous owls in order to interpret the messages we believed she was sending to neighbouring spies.'[39] Conflicts more serious than sweet raids were to follow the merging of the two schools. According to Critchley, there was a battle in which the Brocks overcame a barricade mounted against them when they tried to return to the Broughton premises in 1943. Heseltine has no recollection of this confrontation but he does remember being called upon to testify in court on behalf of his headmaster, who was claiming damages for trespass and assault against John Park. Michael's 'piping tones' apparently won the day and Brockhurst moved to another 'palatial home'.[40] This particular 'Battle of the Old School Tie' hit the headlines in the *Daily Mail* and inspired the film *The Happiest Days of Your Life*, starring Margaret Rutherford and Alistair Sim as the headmistress and headmaster of a girls' and a boys' school billeted together.

It was usually evacuation which brought about such unlikely liaisons. John Starling recalled how his Portsmouth grammar school was 'squashed in with Peter Symonds', a public school in Winchester. One set of pupils attended in the mornings and the other in the afternoons for six days a week, with 'an awful lot of prep'. There was no contact between the boys and the Portsmouth lads envied the Winchester pupils their 'lovely swimming pool in the grounds, which was strictly *verboten* so far as we were concerned'. Things became easier when extra accommodation was made available for the Portsmouth pupils at Winton House prep school, which moved to Rugby to double up with Dunchurch Hall. But they were still not able to swim since the Winton House pool was boarded over to make a large classroom. Despite all this boxing and coxing, added to the anxiety which John felt about his parents back in Portsmouth, he got nine School Certificate passes with some credits in 1942.[41]

Another common wartime arrangement was for young pupils to move in with older ones. This happened when George Melly went from Parkfield, his day prep school in vulnerable Liverpool, to board at Oakridge, a public school on the Welsh borders. He had not much liked the regime at Parkfield, where the burly headmaster, Mr Twynne, known as Twimbo, used to pull boys to their feet 'by grasping either the short hairs over the ears or the fatty part of the cheek between thumb and forefinger and then shaking you like a rat'. But he found Oakridge, which replaced Twimbo's slipper with the more painful cane, even less congenial. Apart from that, the main change George experienced was that 'with all of us sleeping in the same dormitory' mutual masturbation became more widespread. To his surprise he was glad to return to Twyne's sole jurisdiction when Parkfield found its own boarding premises, an Edwardian house in Southport. Anticipating his later career in jazz, he brought in records such as *Yes, We Have No Bananas*, which Twimbo pronounced 'distinctly vulgar'. George also insisted on going home to Liverpool at weekends despite the headmaster's warnings that he was 'entering the lion's jaws'. There were indeed such heavy raids on Liverpool in early September 1940 that Mr Melly decided to move the family in with Twynne at Southport for the rest of the school holidays. The arrangement was not as gruesome as George had feared, because he had now left Parkfield and his old headmaster was 'like a sorcerer who had lost his power'. In fact, the enforced proximity revealed the secret behind Twynne's unpredictable temper: he was 'a serious boozer'.[42]

Summer Fields, too, experienced difficulties when it played host to three evacuated schools. First to reach Oxford were twenty-one 'nervous arrivals' from Farnborough, who had to adjust to a more regimented system and a 'far more stringent scholastic programme'. Julian Slade was disconcerted when the 'fearsome' Geoffrey Bolton tore a copy of *Biggles Flies North* out of his hands, pronouncing it to be 'rubbish'. Yet Slade later blessed 'GB' for introducing him to the works of Gilbert and Sullivan, which did much to inspire the musical plays (such as *Salad Days*) he went on to write.[43] Next came the pupils of Summer Fields' less formal 'daughter school' at St Leonards-on-Sea, getting out of the path of the threatened invasion. Unhappily, the two headmasters did not see eye to eye: John Evans of Oxford disapproved when Ken Barber's wife attended church without a hat, even though the Archbishop of Canterbury decreed that this was acceptable. Relations were easier with the third set of evacuees, from St Cyprian's, although one of the newcomers, Peter Nathan, was not popular when he was selected as cricket captain in preference to a Summer Fields player. Since neither Farnborough nor St Cyprian's returned to its old premises at the end of the war, Summer Fields gained a permanent benefit from additional pupils. The school's historian thinks it is 'no exaggeration' to claim that it was saved by the Second World War.[44]

The ideal outcome for private schools, which had to make their own evacuation arrangements, was to find a country mansion or hotel spacious enough to house all their charges – but preferably no others. Many were successful, though by no means all found accommodation resembling Blenheim Palace.[45] To be sure, Malvern College did find temporary quarters at Blenheim in 1939 but it soon had to make way for the Ministry of Air Production. Nearly as grand was the second evacuation home of West Downs, Blair Atholl Castle in Scotland, where they were 'rigorously segregated' from the Glasgow slum children occupying the basement. Pupils were impressed by their new quarters but some found the long corridors lined with innumerable antlers spooky. What they really liked was the ducal estate, with plenty of room for Scouting games like 'Smugglers and Excisemen'. The woods were 'fragrant with wild garlic' and full of red deer, which sometimes appeared as venison for Sunday lunch. One ex-pupil said that Blair Atholl was a 'glimpse of heaven on earth'.[46]

Another entranced school child was Eva Figes. She attended Ardenside Preparatory and Kindergarten School for Officers' Children, which was now in peaceful Cirencester, having been evacuated from Leigh-on-Sea. After her unpleasant experiences as a middle-class Jewish refugee from Germany at a 'wild council school' in London, she now found herself in a 'little Eden'. Here she read books at will, learned to play the piano and went for 'long afternoon walks down country lanes'. Her brother wilted in the austere conditions imposed by the spinster sisters who ran Ardenside but for Eva they opened 'doors behind which lay untold riches; songs, stories, books, legends, walking, memories caught in a sepia photograph, hedgerows filled with history, the flotsam of a world as miraculous as dandelion clocks blown into the wind.'[47]

Eleven-year-old Anthony Brown recounted more prosaic experiences even though he was billeted (with the rest of Seafield Park School from Lee-on-the-Solent) at the Duke of Devonshire's shooting and fishing lodge on the River Tamar. Now a luxury hotel and a Grade One listed building, Endsleigh occupies one of the most beautiful sites in Devon. But Anthony was no more interested in such aesthetic matters than was his fictional namesake, Richmal Crompton's William Brown; when William arranges for the children of Marleigh to be evacuated to Bolsover Lodge, his main concern is that there is 'quite a good garden for Lions and Tigers'.[48] Similarly, Anthony's unpublished diary, a rare survival from 1940 now in the Imperial War Museum, is emphatically preoccupied with his own affairs. About having to go back to school he groans, 'Oh, Lord!' He is pleased to have been moved up – 'Oh boy!' He is delighted to get three sausages for breakfast – 'Good Egg!' He dreads being sent to the headmaster to be whacked – 'Help!' He is disappointed on Good Friday when there are 'NO HOT CROSS BUNS', but cheers when Mr Dyer takes him out to tea on Easter Sunday – 'Super!' And he often has 'jolly good fun' or a 'super rag'.

All the same, Anthony's interest in the war is apparent in the diary. He makes a scrapbook of war cartoons and follows the news closely on the radio and in newspapers, getting worried after the fall of France: 'Great consternation, French Army ceases hostilities. Invaded any minute! Help!' He is delighted when his father and stepfather send him souvenirs from the front – a German bullet and Italian badges. During the summer holidays he and a friend write a play in which they act as Hitler and Göring, having their photograph taken in improvised German uniforms. When Plymouth is bombed early in the autumn term, Anthony lists the German planes he has spotted. On 5 October he listens to a broadcast by Lord Haw-Haw. And at the top of his Christmas present list is *William and the Evacuees*. The diary does not include much about Anthony's school work, except to list his exam results and to complain about getting 'blown up in all directions for Maths as well as Latin'. But it is clear that his schooling proceeded as normal, apart from a 'new idea' introduced in November probably as a daylight-saving measure: 'We get up half an hour later and have 5 minutes off each lesson.'[49]

More revolutionary practices were introduced at Brambletye, which had moved from East Grinstead to another West Country beauty spot, Lee Abbey

Hotel on the north Devon coast. Pupils' memories of the war years include not only spotting planes in the sky and imagining spies out at sea but also gaining a certain amount of pupil power. This came about after the Australian second master took over when John Blencowe, the founding headmaster and a wounded veteran of the First World War, succumbed to the pressures of the Second and became seriously ill in 1943. Jim Wilson, who had been invalided out of the Australian Navy, now organized the school 'on naval and democratic lines', one old boy remembers, aware that this might seem to be 'a contradiction in terms'. Wilson renamed the colour-coded houses Drake, Nelson, Wellington and Marlborough and ruled through the senior boys (or officers) who were given naval ranks ranging from Captain to Petty Officer and the power to run activities outside the classroom through their own parliament. As the boys themselves proudly explained in a book they produced in 1944, they could make regulations, run their own societies, referee their own matches and dispense discipline through a Defaulters Parade: 'The few people who try to slack usually find themselves on Defaulters pretty quick and lively.' Most of the memories quoted by the founder's son in his history of Brambletye speak fondly of such juvenile rituals as daily parades, falling in for hand inspection and marching into meals. But one 'slacker' ventures a comment on the punishment 'fatigues' which had to be worked off during the half-day holiday: 'All this made life more miserable if you were the type who didn't readily toe the line.' Another pupil was convinced that 'the discipline was far stricter than if a master had been involved'.[50]

The boys of Dulwich College Preparatory School (DCPS) had a more interrupted wartime education. Before the war even started, their formidable headmaster, J. H. Leakey, had built a camp of huts on his father-in-law's land at Cranbrook in Kent. When forced to abandon this as invasion threatened, he made an unsuccessful bid for Lee Abbey against Brambletye, whose headmaster he describes bitterly as 'very wealthy'. Eventually in June 1940, he took most of the boys (without consulting their parents) to the Royal Oak Hotel, Betws-y-Coed, in the 'Adventureland' of Snowdonia. When the army attempted to take over the coaching stables they were using as classrooms, even Leakey's protests might have been in vain had not the requisitioning officer recognized the cap of his own old prep school. Leakey's well-known book, *School Errant*, tells the story of the dedication, hard labour and good contacts that went into his triumphant venture.

The 'view from the valley and the scree slopes', as opposed to the summit, is rather different – as appears in DCPS pupils' recollections and correspond-ence.[51] Most of the boys appreciated the beauty of the place. 'It is lovely up here at Wales,' wrote one eight-year-old, 'there are a lot of hills and mountains.'[52] They also enjoyed the outdoor pursuits, enough to comprise an Outward Bound programme. They joined enthusiastically in all manner of war work, ranging from forestry to playing chess with wounded servicemen. Above all, they liked the fact that in these circumstances they were allowed 'more freedom and had to rely more upon their own initiative'.[53] As William and the Outlaws found, the cares of war meant that 'grown-up vigilance was modified, rules were suspended, discipline relaxed'.[54] Consequently, incidents took place of which the Dulwich staff were unaware: 'buying cigarettes for "Uncle's birthday" at the shop and taking the purchased items up the mountain and smoking them' or 'building a secret hut and burying a biscuit tin to conceal contraband tuck'. The boys, most of whom did not board when in London, also felt homesick and anxious about their families. Those whose homes were destroyed or damaged had no choice but to spend their holidays at the Royal Oak, where a 'wonderful programme of outings' helped to ease the pain of exile. Although most felt that the experience had changed their lives for the better, a few had unhappy memories of both the 'terrible first winter' encamped in Kent and their 'total isolation' in Wales. William Gruby viewed it as 'the nightmare result of the best of intentions' which he survived by developing a 'carapace of character'.[55] Those pupils left behind in Dulwich kept 'the flag flying in the old school' after it reopened in January 1940, carried on through the Blitz despite heavy damage to the school, but had to resort to correspondence lessons during the flying bomb raids of 1944.[56]

Such experiences indicate that prep school pupils did not always enjoy the undisturbed education in comfortable mansions which some historians describe. But it is true that prep and public schools generally 'weathered evacuation with students and staff intact' while educational standards fell in the country as a whole.[57] Even within the private sector, boys' schools apparently fared better than girls'. The historian Gillian Avery blames this on the male-dominated society of the time, claiming that 'high-ranking government Etonians, Wykehamists, Harrovians and Carthusians . . . saw to it that their old schools were never req-uisitioned'. She even maintains that officials got 'savage satisfaction out of an opportunity to crack the whip' by taking over girls' schools such as Wycombe Abbey and Cheltenham Ladies' College at very short notice.[58]

The old school tie, as well as the old school cap, certainly proved a wartime asset. But is it right to claim that private schools showed 'selfish indifference to both the national need and common sense' by insisting that these garments must still be worn? Norman Longmate cites his own school, Christ's Hospital, as evidence that old-fashioned formality continued. Throughout the war, boys wore the full Tudor ensemble so that they looked as if they were 'expecting the Spanish Armada rather than the German Army'.[59] Furthermore, schools' insistence on elaborate uniforms was an extra worry for parents. Sydney Butler, for example, did not know how she could find enough coupons to kit out her nieces, Jane and Susan Portal, for St Gabriel's Wantage, as well as her two oldest sons for Maidwell Hall. Her task became even more difficult when one son moved on to Eton, which suspended only the top hat from its uniform requirements. But the picture is mixed. Schools such as Gayhurst accepted that pupils would become scruffier as a result of the national shortage of combs and the difficulty of buying new clothes. The headmaster, who was himself so shabby that he was sometimes mistaken for the groundsman, even conceded in 1941 that 'some may consider this an advantage'.[60] Similarly, Leakey said that DCPS had not applied strict uniform rules during its Welsh evacuation. Yet on this matter, as on other aspects of school life, the juvenile view does not quite square with the pedagogic perspective. A former pupil remembers that the boys used to climb Mount Snowden 'in full school uniform' complete with blazer and cap.[61]

A particularly poignant memory of school uniform comes from a child who was on board the *City of Benares*, a ship full of evacuees torpedoed on the night of 17 September 1940. When the alarm bells sounded, Derek Bech got dressed: 'I put on my school trousers and blazer and raincoat and even my school cap and my gym shoes.'[62] He and his two sisters were saved but seventy-three children died, bringing to an end the Children's Overseas Reception Board, a short-lived government scheme for sending young people to safety overseas. The Bech youngsters had not been part of CORB but were on their way to Canada with their mother. They were among about 4,000 children of affluent parents, who travelled privately to the shelter of Canada, America, South Africa, Australia and New Zealand.

Winston Churchill disapproved of this exodus and swore that no relative of his would run away. Nevertheless, his Minister of Information, Duff Cooper, sent his son, John Julius, to the preparatory school of Upper Canada College in

Toronto. And this was despite his own experience at Wixenford School, which had convinced him that it was 'a cruel thing to take a child ... away from his home and the loving care of his mother'. John Julius was apparently happy and well taught, acquiring the necessary grounding to get into Eton on his return.[63] Twelve-year-old Edward Montagu (already a peer of the realm) was also sent to Canada in 1940. Unlike John Julius, he found it 'extraordinarily traumatic' to leave his school, friends, mother and dogs, though he hoped at least to see some action on the sea voyage.[64] Both these boys were able to return early, says historian and fellow-evacuee, Jessica Mann, as a result of 'the usual strings being pulled by influential families'.

Children who made longer journeys nearly always had to stick it out until the end of the war. By this time they had often become, like Ann Thwaite (née Harrop), rather 'grown-up and independent', unwilling to return to the state of 'being a child'.[65] In 1941 Ann and her brother David were taken to stay with relations in New Zealand. It was a perilous journey during which their ship, the *Ceramic*, collided with another vessel – the following year it was torpedoed with the loss of everyone on board. The evacuation gave David the opportunity to compare two very different prep schools. In 1939 this 'difficult' child had been sent to Burgess Hill progressive school, because a psychiatrist had decided that he needed 'an encouraging atmosphere, free from the necessity of marks'. David liked the teachers who were addressed by their Christian names and he does not remember being punished for anything. His reports gave the prescribed encouragement, pronouncing him 'keenly interested in miscellaneous information'. He feels, however, that he made more progress once he arrived at Southwell, a traditional 'English' prep school in New Zealand. Whether this was due to the school, to his being older or to being away from his mother, David cannot now judge. He got on well with the English-born headmaster, Henry Godfrey Sergel – who, he was to discover much later, had been christened Heinrich Gottfriech by his German parents. Over the next four years David 'came right', as he puts it: he enjoyed the academic work, won his rugby colours, got caned for talking too much, sang in Gilbert and Sullivan operas and, because of his English accent, acted as compère in a production of *1066 and All That* and as Sports Day announcer. Sergel, who was intensely loyal to 'the old country', kept the boys fully informed about the progress of the war and the heroic deeds of old boys, including his own son. By the time he returned home in 1945, David had had a thoroughly English prep school experience on the other side of the world; but New Zealand must have left its mark, for David went back there as a dairy farmer after he had completed his education.[66]

Meanwhile, some English schools prepared to go off to the colonies en masse, an idea considered but rejected by the Dragon. The prep school attended by eleven-year-old David Wedgwood Benn planned to take its pupils to Canada. When David heard of this he wrote to his father, begging not to be included in the party because he would be even more homesick than he already was and because he did not want to leave Britain in time of war: 'It would be kinder to let me be killed with you than to allow me to drift to strangers and finish my childhood in a contrary fashion.' This 'splendid letter' won the approval of the prime minister when it was printed in *The Times* in July 1940. Nevertheless some prep schools went ahead and advertised for financial backing to take their pupils abroad 'for the duration'.[67]

Abinger Hill Boys' School was among those which crossed the Atlantic. It found a haven at Ashbury School in Ottawa and in the holidays the boys went 'to whoever would take them'. When it became too much of a 'drag on Ashbury', Abinger Hill had to appeal to the British government for funds. Such problems were common all over Canada, according to Leonora Williams, vice-principal of Byron House School. Miss Williams had already evacuated this progressive mixed and multi-faith prep school from Highgate to Cambridge before she decided to take a group of pupils to Canada in June 1940. There they stayed until 1943, experiencing difficulties similar to those of Abinger Hill. Their energetic leader found two schools to take the children, a house for them to live in and Jewish benefactors to help them out financially. As luck would have it, her unpublished memoir recalls, 'the children weren't really homesick'.[68]

The pupils' own reminiscences are not quite so sanguine. Ann Perry (née Fawell) looks back on the experience as 'a huge struggle to cope' and thinks it explains why she still finds it 'hard to leave home'. She adds at the end of her contribution to a collective memoir in the Imperial War Museum: 'This isn't what I expected to write really; it just came out like this.' Mary Henderson (née Ferguson) says that she has spent many years trying to soften the stiff upper lip she acquired during her exile. Andy Richards, one of the school's 15 per cent of Jewish pupils, found Ottawa 'horribly anti-Semitic'. He was so 'psychologically mixed up' that he stole a watch belonging to the rabbi's wife. To be sure, the archive contains many fond memories of Canadian life: sleigh rides, swims in the Ottawa River, journeys to school on roller-skates, maple leaves and Mounties. Some ex-pupils cannot recall being homesick after the first few weeks and did not relish coming home – in certain cases to parents who did not recognize them in the gloom of a blacked-out London station. Geoffrey Carlton missed 'the chatter and bustle and comradeship of our little tribe' and resented 'that feeling of being possessed that parents, however well-meaning their motives, now engendered'. To this day he yearns for snow in winter.[69]

The happiest travellers were those who were whisked away from English prep schools to join their parents in different parts of the Empire. 'After Dunkirk,' wrote Tony Orchard, 'my parents in India decided they could, after all, cope with their offspring.'[70] Sometimes these children made the sea journey in the charge of special matrons; one ten-year-old rarely saw these ladies during the voyage, but he and his companions did learn from the sailors how to smoke Woodbines.[71] The reunion with parents was often short-lived, as many youngsters were sent off to established boarding schools in the colonies or to new ones set up for the duration. Michael Foss and his brother spent some time at the Highlands School, Coonoor, 'a small enclave of white boyish faces that studiously followed the pattern and ethos of the British prep school'. Foss learnt 'much about England' but his mind would wander to the 'wild tales of Vijayanagar' told by the one Indian pupil. Despite the school's efforts, Foss was 'entirely bathed with India'.[72] Michael Emtage describes a similar 'good English prep school' in the Nilgiri Hills, where the only Indian feature was its menu of hot Madras curries and chappatis. Otherwise, the diet of Latin, nature study, elocution, cricket, route marching and bullying was not very different from what he would have been offered in England – but Michael was glad that he could still hear 'the night cry of the jackal'.[73]

The most famous example of a wartime English prep school in an exotic setting is Sheikh Bagh, established by Eric Tyndale-Biscoe in Kashmir. Tyndale-Biscoe, whose father was a missionary in Srinagar, had been 'sent Home' to boarding school in time-honoured English fashion. He left 'fully resolved that nothing would induce me ever to set foot inside a school again', but he saw the war as an opportunity to give English boys the chance of a different sort of childhood. He was determined to avoid traditional prep school practices: individual competition in sports, over-concentration on cricket, subservience to the Common Entrance exam, reliance on beating and endurance of grim English Sundays.

Influenced by the Outward Bound ideas of Kurt Hahn, Tyndale-Biscoe encouraged the spirit of adventure and independence and the ideal of 'service for others before self'.[74] Boys who went to Sheikh Bagh have vivid memories of climbing Mount Mahadeo, bathing naked in icy streams, swimming across the Dahl Lake and camping in houseboats, all against the 'magical background' of Kashmir. As Jonathan Lawley concludes, the ethos of the school 'was deeply influential on the lives of all who went there'.[75]

Not all small boys could cope with Sheikh Bagh's arduous physical regime, with its nine-month terms, or with the expectation that they should live up to the school motto: 'In All Things be Men'. Michael Thomas did not like having so little contact with his parents and he thinks that the academic teaching was 'deeply suspect', though he passed his Common Entrance, causing the school to have a half-day holiday.[76] Other Indian war schools were less spartan but equally remote. At the Hallett in Naini Tal, Hilary Sweet-Escott (née Johnston) suffered the 'absolute heartbreak of homesickness' during its lengthy terms. One of her fellow pupils was Patrick Gibson, who had already had to flee from the Highlands School, Sumatra, as the Japanese invaded and believed until 1943 that the rest of his family had been killed in Bangkok. As Hilary observes, 'there were some very valiant little children' mixed up in the war in the East.[77]

Children in Britain suffered less than their contemporaries in the invaded countries of Asia or Europe. Yet David Pritchard, evacuated from the Blitz on Plymouth to a nursery hostel in Falmouth, can rightly conclude: 'We were part of a whole generation who experienced things that children of our age should never have had to go through.'[78] Prep school pupils were certainly not exempt from blood, toil, tears and sweat. But headmasters like Leakey could still boast of 'a most gratifying list of scholarships' to public schools, while many intelligent children Bryan Magee had known in London's East End 'grew up illiterate'.[79] The war made such inequality of opportunity more obvious and more unacceptable. The evacuated city children who arrived in villages like Evelyn Waugh's fictional Malfrey showed the local gentry, whose offspring were away at boarding school, 'how another part of the world lived'.[80] The normal educational experience for a working-class child was to go to an elementary school up to fourteen, leaving for the world of work at an age when prep school pupils had just moved on to public school. By the early 1940s, many hoped that a more democratic educational system would emerge from the people's war.

'How to be Topp'
The Post-War World

In 1941 a group of prep school headmasters known as the 'Devon exiles' met for luncheon in Barnstaple. Among them was Arthur Harrison, who had opened a small school in a 'pleasant Georgian house on the Kent and Sussex borders' and seen its numbers decline during the 'troubled thirties'. He and his fellow heads were in pessimistic mood: 'There were few of us at that time who did not believe that the Preparatory Schools were finished.'[1] Such worries mounted in 1942 with the appointment of a government committee under Lord Fleming to consider the place of public schools in the education system. Apprehension increased further in 1944 when the Fleming Report was published and it turned to despair in 1945 when a Labour government was elected. Edward Blishen, drawing on his experience as a young teacher at The Hall in Hampstead, reports that prep school masters held socialists responsible even for the icy post-war weather: 'Mr Attlee and his ministers were deemed to have Nature herself in their inept, seditious hands.'[2]

It seemed very likely that prep schools would be affected by Fleming's main proposal that public schools should make a quarter of their places available to children from state primary schools irrespective of parents' income. If public schools were to put their age of entry down to eleven to fit in with the state system (as did Dulwich College), prep schools like DCPS would lose many of their older pupils. Or if, as the Fleming Report suggested, prep schools took in eleven-year-old 'bursars' (children on free places) for two years, they would have to be 'recognized as efficient after inspection' and not be 'conducted for private profit'.[3] Gathered at the Randolph Hotel in Oxford, some headmasters declared themselves ready to cooperate by letting their schools become charitable trusts. Others, such as Oliver Wyatt of Maidwell Hall, voiced strong opposition to 'any form of state restriction or interference whatsoever'.[4]

In the event, prep schools were not put to the test since Fleming's proposed changes won little support elsewhere. Churchill had lost the enthusiasm for equal opportunities which he had extolled at Harrow in 1940, and Clement Attlee, the new Labour prime minister, made a speech at Haileybury (his own public school) expressing his conviction that 'the great traditions would carry on and might even be extended'. Once the Conservatives came back to power in 1951, the danger was past. The Fleming Report became, in the words of David Kynaston, 'the great educational might-have-been in post-war years'; the private and state systems continued to inhabit 'two utterly separate worlds'.[5] Establishments such as Attlee's former prep school, Northaw Place, were safe for the time being, though there were signs of class hostility towards these privileged academies. In the early 1950s, Jeremy Lewis felt that 'revolution was in the air' when two town 'oiks' shot the head boy of Seaford in the eye with an air gun: 'With his scrubbed pink-and-white features and neatly combed hair and rosebud lips, the head boy must have presented an irresistible target.'[6] The incident lends credence to the plot of Tim Heald's novel *Class Distinctions*, in which 'village yobs' destroy huts built by the boys of West Hill School in their 'Dingle' and cut the ropes of the marquee erected for their smart Speech Day.

Such episodes apart, independent schools flourished in post-war years, meeting 'an unexpected but overwhelming public demand'.[7] The boost was due partly to the fact that grammar school places were now dependent not on parents' ability to pay but on success in the new eleven-plus exam. With prep school numbers rising by 5,000 between 1947 and 1952 it was all too easy to set up in the business. Andrew Loog Oldham had to leave Cokethorpe School in 1952 when the new headmaster, a Jimmy Edwards figure who sported a handlebar moustache, double-breasted blazer and Guards tie, was arrested as a confidence trickster. He and his gang had opened and closed seven private schools, getting away with about £80,000 each time. Andrew was sent to a 'grimy and depressing' state school where he mourned the loss of his beloved Cokethorpe in its 'magnificent mansion with stables and many acres of lush green fields'.[8] For prep schools with less commodious premises, greater numbers often led to the overcrowded and unhealthy conditions which haunt the memories of former pupils. The whitewashed huts in which lessons were taught at Greenways suggested a penal camp; the stench of chamber pots at West Downs rivalled that of Winchester Gaol next door; girls at Ripley Hall queued for the single lavatory which served seven junior dormitories; impetigo, veruccas and chilblains were rife at Summer Fields.

The age of austerity witnessed other afflictions, such as the 'bugs that ran through prep schools like miniature versions of the plague'.[9] Richard Phillips remembers that he was 'invariably laid up for about a week per term' in the infirmary at Wellbury. At least that school had its own generator, which enabled it to keep the place warm and lit during the harsh winter of 1947.[10] During that bitterly cold Easter term, 'all but about ten boys were down with measles, flu or both' at Summer Fields.[11] Most worrying for boarding schools must have been the outbreaks of infantile paralysis (polio) which struck the country most summers during the late forties and early fifties, leaving thousands dead or crippled. Julian Critchley contracted polio when he was eighteen and was fortunate to be robbed only of the ability to run. This terrifying illness is rarely mentioned in the history of schools, even though their frequently inadequate sanitary arrangements and unhygienic swimming pools (like the black one at Temple Grove shared with the bodies of rabbits stricken with myxomatosis) were potential sources of infection. At Formosa, a mixed Quaker prep school near Hatfield, a boy died of polio in 1947. The school was closed and pupils like Ann Rosenthal (née Shire) spent 'a miserable time' in quarantine, avoiding all enclosed public spaces.[12] It is not clear, in view of what seems to have been almost a conspiracy of silence about polio in schools, how worried children were by the disease.

An unexpected consequence of the boom in prep schools was that there were too few public school places for the boys they produced. What would happen to those who did not get in? Boys were warned that if they failed Common Entrance (or in some cases even if they misbehaved) they would be sent to the local secondary modern school and 'end up running a garage or a pub'.[13] To avert this dreadful fate for their pupils and to keep up their own tally of scholarships, headmasters cracked the whip in the senior forms, even if so much cramming might jeopardize the avowed aim of producing 'a well-mannered person with cultivated interests and a sense of responsibility'.[14] During the summer terms, schools hummed with the sound of extra lessons 'conducted by men who knew by heart twenty or thirty years of Common Entrance papers in their own subject'.[15]

Many pupils have remembered the experience all their lives. In the scholarship stream at the Dragon, says Philip Steadman, 'we spent most of each morning on Latin and Greek.'[16] Michael Holroyd recollects the strenuous pace set by Denis Owen, the acting headmaster at Scaitcliffe which sent most of its boys to neighbouring Eton. The days were 'crowded with Latin gender rhymes, fielding practice, multiplication tables, gym, English grammar and spelling, cross-country runs, the recital of dates in history and appalling plunges into the open-air swimming pool'.[17] Norman Hale, headmaster of Milbourne Lodge in Esher, achieved legendary results with his equally rigorous regime. As he entered the sixth form classroom he would already be on question number three or four of his daily Latin test, several having been shouted out as he bounded up the stairs, the answers being scribbled down by the boys at a similar gallop.[18] All this helped to produce some fine scholars. It might even have taught the likes of nigel molesworth 'How to be Topp in Latin' at st custard's – though Ronald Searle's drawings to illustrate 'The Private Life of the Gerund' would not have gone down well in the Common Entrance.[19]

So vital was success in this examination that schools sometimes resorted to dubious measures to get their pupils through. Jeremy Lewis took his papers early at Seaford because his parents were emigrating to Canada. Before he started, the master's wife who was to invigilate him insisted on showing him a detailed item in the *Daily Telegraph* about the Queen's world tour of 1952. When Jeremy opened the geography paper, lo and behold, one of the questions required him to mark the royal route on a blank map of the world. Henley Smith has a stranger tale to tell. An undiagnosed dyslexic (and a fine sportsman) at Cheltenham College Junior School, he was hopeless at French, had always found Latin 'a nightmare' and could only learn anything parrot-fashion. He was usually bottom of the class and was not certain to pass his Common Entrance to Cheltenham College. As it happens, a piece of land adjacent to the college came up for sale at this time and Henley's wealthy father donated over £20,000 to make its purchase possible. There may have been an understanding that his son would be charged no fees. To Henley's relief he got into Cheltenham. He did not know about the gift until shortly before he left, when the headmaster, David Ashcroft, told him over a beer in his study that he had been so astounded to receive the huge cheque that he slept with it under his pillow. Much later still, Ashcroft, a man of formidable intellect with a double first from Cambridge, confessed to Henley that he had surreptitiously raised his Common Entrance mark from 54% to the 55% required to secure his place.[20]

Other pupils had less cause to be thankful. To this day Michael Croft* holds his masters at Brambletye 'personally responsible' for not requiring him to learn the twelve lines of poetry he needed to answer a crucial question on the English paper. And at Temple Grove the academic standard had declined so much, according to Simon Taggart*, that scholarships were won in spite of, rather than because of, the school's teaching. He himself was doing so badly in Maths and Latin (and was considered so 'bolshie') that he was asked to leave; he took his Common Entrance papers and gained a public school place from a crammer, where he found the teaching much better.[21] It was not unusual for boys who were unlikely to pass to 'go out of the window', as Blishen's colleagues put it, so that they would not tarnish the school's record. The dyslexic Richard Branson left Scaitcliffe in 1961 before he was thirteen and got a place at Stowe from another school, where he narrowly avoided expulsion for his nocturnal visits to the headmaster's daughter. At Scaitcliffe he had been bottom in every subject despite, he claims, 'being beaten once or twice a week for doing poor classwork or confusing the date of the Battle of Hastings'. His headmaster, Richard Vickers, later said that these weekly canings were a 'myth'. A contemporary also finds it unlikely that even a 'dunce' like Branson would be caned with such frequency, but suggests that his tally could be accurate if it included other masters' 'everyday sadism': whacks from the ruler in the classroom or the gym-shoe in the cloakroom.[22]

Richard Vickers was one of the twin sons of Ronald Vickers, who bought Scaitcliffe in 1896 and ran it until his death in 1942. There was then an interregnum under Denis Owen during the active war service of Richard Vickers, who took up headmasterly duties after his demobilization in 1946. Meanwhile, Ronald Vickers's widow and spinster daughters still played an active role. Thus, concludes Michael Holroyd, the school which he attended in the closing years and aftermath of the Second World War had not changed a great deal since his father's time there in the equivalent stages of the First. Basil Holroyd did not tell his son until much later that he had been miserable at Scaitcliffe, where he lived in terror of bullies and of getting 'six sharp cuts with the cane' from Ronald Vickers. He had 'wanted to believe that things were getting better and all was for the best', even after being advised by Denis Owen that Michael was not 'fit for the rough-and-tumble of a boarding school'. This warning came after a 'sensational episode' when the eight-year-old boy 'let out a vast cry' which echoed all over the school, while being beaten for wetting his bed. Michael stayed on to run, jump, bat, bowl and kick for his father until 1948, joining in while striving for 'invisibility'. Neither his nor Basil's time at Scaitcliffe much resembled the affectionate 'picture of an extended family' presented in the school history written by Richard Vickers. Nor does Michael's contribution to the chapter of 'Old Boys' Reminiscences' tell the story of his loud lament.[23]

The Vickers dynastic headship, which eventually spanned nearly a century, symbolizes the traditionalist nature of the prep school world. In the first post-war issue of *West Downs Magazine*, old boys described their school as 'immune from change' in personalities, in furnishings or in essence: 'The spirit of West Downs remains all that we remember it.'[24] Tim Heald considers that nothing much had changed at Connaught House (his Somerset prep school, on which he based *Class Distinctions*) since its foundation in 1870; he found in it 'a sense of security and permanence'. But the political journalist Robin Oakley remembers that he 'fitted awkwardly' into Aldro, Godalming, in 'the days of compulsory boxing, corporal punishment and domineering matrons', when the boys swam in a muddy lake and played rugby on pitches 'shared with defecating geese'.[25] In both boys' and girls' schools, 'the 1950s showed unexpected continuity with the 1930s'.[26] Even the same visiting speakers seemed to be going the rounds of south coast schools. The deep-sea diver who clanked on to the stage in a complete rig at Seaford in Jeremy Lewis's time sounds remarkably like the Captain Smith who thrilled the boys of Brambletye in 1929 and those of Falconbury in 1932 and again in 1948. Jeremy found out later that the Seaford visitor was really a retired bank clerk in a hired costume – but perhaps Captain Smith was the genuine article. Another sartorial oddity was the headmaster at Farleigh House; Captain Trappes-Lomax always dressed in the boys' full school uniform, including grey corduroy shorts, though he rather spoilt the effect by smoking Turkish cigarettes through an elegant holder.

It is not clear whether His Majesty's Inspectors ever witnessed this unusual attire. Many schools refused to admit 'the ministry', as Norman Hale termed such officials. Others did not care if their teaching methods were pronounced old-fashioned. The 1947 report on DCPS, for example, was generally complimentary but found fault with the Drill and PT taught by the glass-eyed eccentric Captain Fleming, who was told to 'model his lessons on the recommendations of the 1933 syllabus'. The Captain ignored this advice and stayed on for another ten years at the school, where he also taught Latin 'by somewhat draconian methods'.[27] Boys seem to have enjoyed his lessons as well as his stories of life on the north-west frontier. For the future foreign correspondent John Simpson, they were an early introduction to a 'world of excitement' with its 'strange places' and 'questionable people'.[28]

The 'paters' (fathers) caricatured by Willans and Searle continued to assure the 'old gurl' that schools had changed: 'Boys are no longer cruel to each other and the masters are frends.'[29] In truth, most sons entered regimes remarkably similar to those their fathers had known. Prince Charles, as a 'painfully shy' little boy at Cheam, was haunted by the shadow of his father, whose sporting prowess and popularity he could not match. Despite the schoolboy plumpness for which he was taunted with the nickname 'Fatty', Charles was eventually made captain of the first soccer eleven – which went on to lose every match it played that season. The prince apparently used to apologize chivalrously to anyone he felled on the field – a practice he had not learnt from the Duke of Edinburgh.[30]

Another boy to follow a family tradition was Anthony Heath. He told me that Highfield had hardly altered since his father, Graham, had been there before the First World War. Headmaster Mills, a close friend of the Heath family, had now been made a canon of Portsmouth Cathedral in recognition, he liked to say, 'of my work among boys'. Many of them (including young Graham) were 'tiresome boys' who ragged in the showers and had to be beaten, which made him late for the early celebration of Holy Communion. A contemporary of Anthony's remembers that Mills once had to take his slipper to a great many bare bottoms because no one had owned up to a bout of thefts. Such stern methods (as well as the thorough teaching of his masters) ensured that Highfield still occupied a place among the top twenty or so prep schools. It prided itself on the major scholarships and the distinguished careers achieved by its old boys – who could always bring to mind Mr McIintosh's helpful diagrams of Marlborough's four great victories and the four major battles of the Thirty Years War. Some post-war pupils found the canon a fatherly figure and were moved by his annual readings of *Journey's End*, made all the more heartfelt by the death of the heir to Highfield in the Second World War. In 1953 Mills died and his younger son took over. By all accounts, Peter Mills was 'not the man his father was'. He ran an even tighter ship than the old canon, perhaps being too anxious to assert an authority he had not expected to inherit.[31]

War cast a long shadow over many prep schools, which now added the names of more dead masters and old boys to their chapel memorials. It was impossible, felt Simon Taggart, to escape from the 'atmosphere of sacrifice and guilt' at Temple Grove. In this school, still owned and run by Meston Batchelor, it was the First World War which (as often happened) made more impression on modern memory.[32] Pupils blamed it for Batchelor's pronounced limp; they drew endless pictures of dreadnoughts; and they thumbed through the library's multi-volume *Times Illustrated History of the First World War*.[33] Boyish reading at Summer Fields seems to have been more up to date. Anthony Cheetham's generation in the early 1950s was 'deeply infected by the rash of paperback war escape stories', from which arose a craze for digging tunnels, protracted planning 'for a full-blooded jail-break' and the creation of mantraps for unsuspecting masters.[34]

Not even the escape stories met with masters' approval – Geoffrey Bolton, for instance, continued to favour boys who played cricket and read P. G. Wodehouse. During and after the war Bolton shared the arduous headship of Summer Fields with John Evans, 'a squirearchical figurehead' who suffered breakdowns in 1943 and 1953. Since he was unmarried (like most of the staff) there were no heirs to take over when his health finally collapsed in 1956. Thus Bolton became sole headmaster when he was 66, not an age at which a deeply conservative man was likely to implement change. The removal of some ancient six-seater desks during an overhaul of the school caused him to weep. The most daring innovations during his four-year headship were a less frequent celebration of Sung Eucharist (known as 'Long Chapel') and an annual dance with the girls of Greycotes. No doubt both were popular with the boys, but some might also have benefited from more physical comfort and 'feminine influence'. Nicholas Aldridge remembers that 'the place could still be a bear-garden for the weak, the shy or the unusual boy.' While the school flourished academically and culturally, pupils had to put up with inadequate food, smelly changing rooms, boring, chilly, blank weekends and prefects who 'would frequently knee one's back and pull one's hair with great force'.[35] Nobody asked children for their opinions in those days – but now these post-war pupils can talk freely (if sometimes anonymously) about their boarding school experience, often recalling it with great clarity. 'It is still with me,' said Michael Croft, 'as though it were yesterday.'

Some remember with affection a benign world akin to Linbury Court, the term-time residence of Jennings and Darbishire, whose exploits were followed by thousands of young radio fans and readers in the 1950s. To be sure, the bespectacled son of the Reverend Percival Darbishire cannot at first understand why his father has sent him to a place 'governed by clanging bells and threats of being bashed up'. But, after an early bid for freedom intercepted by the wise Mr Carter, the two boys find their feet. Jennings wins renown for a spectacular header in the closing stages of a crucial football match, while Darbishire avoids being taken for 'a terrible sissy' by writing up the game for the school magazine. In a later volume the friends succeed in setting up a Natural History Club despite opposition from the tidy-minded headmaster, Mr Pemberton Oakes, and the irascible Mr Wilkins, who 'don't see things in the same way as sensible people like you and me'.[36] They even escape the detention (Linbury's worst punishment) due to them for illicitly taking a boat onto the river, because they have rescued an elderly naturalist from drowning. In real life good deeds did not always win absolution. When Martin Gilbert (later the official biographer of Churchill) was at Highgate Junior School, he reported some pupils of a neighbouring school to the RSPCA for drowning a cat in Hampstead Ponds. An RSPCA representative subsequently came to Highgate with a special certificate to recognize Martin's vigilance and public spirit. Once the visitor had left, Martin received six-of-the-best on the grounds that 'we don't believe in tale-bearing in this school'.[37]

Other reminiscences, however, are as joyous as one of Jennings's adventures. David 'Fitzy' FitzGerald loved everything about his Methodist prep school, Prior's Court, under its headmaster Mr Maltby, 'who was brilliant with boys'. Later a City lawyer, Fitzy delighted in the steam-train journey to school, when the boys would put their heads out of the window and get covered in soot; in the beautiful Queen Anne mansion with its extensive grounds; in the entomology club which studied butterflies and moths; and in the Austin Seven car which pupils could dismantle, rebuild and drive around the site.[38] Fitzy also relished the academic work. This reached a very high standard, according to Ken Saunders, a pupil at Prior's Court just after the war. Ken considers that in subjects like French, Latin and Maths, Mr Maltby and the other talented masters brought thirteen-year-old boys up to present GCSE standards. He owes to them not only a successful career as a professor of medicine but also his enduring love of the Classics. Yet, like Fitzy, he had plenty of time for 'bug-hunting', team sports, wide reading and being 'in the middle of everything'. In his memory 'no one ever got beaten'. For Ken, Prior's Court acted as his home while his parents worked as missionaries in the Gold Coast (Ghana). He cannot imagine a school where he would have been happier.[39]

The most common key to prep school contentment was sporting prowess. 'Sport ruled it,' said Peter Pugh, a pupil at Oriel House in the early 1950s. He himself 'lived for games and was in the first team for everything', becoming captain of cricket and head boy in his last year. This prowess made him popular – though he did not win the prize introduced by the new headmaster, Mr Mainwaring-Burton, awarded on the strength of a school vote to 'the nicest boy'. Peter thinks that success may have made him rather big-headed. Certainly he had no fear of the headmaster, even though he acquired long-lasting scars from his cane for talking in the dormitory. Nor, as a bright boy, did he have to quake in his shoes before end-of-term 'collections', when all the pupils were told how they had done. He enjoyed nearly all aspects of school life, though he did not succumb to the craze for collecting snakes. He loved Scout camps, and when at one of them he came down with chickenpox, his English teacher, Miss Baker, looked after him in her own house. Peter, who is now a publisher, feels that he owes his expertise in English grammar to the buxom Miss Baker's lessons. He is also proud to have sneaked a kiss with the pretty young matron, aptly named Miss Redhead – an achievement often matched in reminiscences of this time when the age of puberty was falling. Peter remembers Oriel House with genuine affection, despite blaming its dreadful beds for a bad back, its poor lighting for his short sight, its terrible food for his hatred of milk pudding and pilchards, and its rapid turnover of inexpert masters for his failure to gain a scholarship to Oundle.[40]

Henley Smith was another 'school hero', winning great popularity at Cheltenham Junior School for his achievements in 'every sport going', his ready wit and his good-natured leniency as head boy. Of course, as a well-endowed and expensive school, Cheltenham could offer boys great advantages: it had about ten playing fields, two fives courts and the best team teas in the area. But Henley attributes the 'well-balanced' character of the school to its headmaster, Hugh Clutton-Brock. This huge, fair-minded man won boys' respect and infected them with his own enthusiasms. He took the pupils on nature rambles and to Peter Scott's bird sanctuary at Slimbridge; he provided a vivarium for their pet tortoises and snakes; he scared them stiff by reading stories like *The Monkey's Paw* on Sunday evenings; or he took his own 18-stone frame onto the lake when it froze before pronouncing it safe. For Henley, an ebullient only child whose mother did not like other boys coming to her 'clean house', the greatest advantage of boarding school was the camaraderie. There was always a lot of fun among the boys, although there might be a price to be paid. 'Dormy fights' carried the risk of a caning from the headmaster if things got out of hand; dares resulted in boys being made to parade around naked, which some perhaps minded more than they showed; and the trouble with mutual masturbation was that it could become 'more fun than anything else'. But, for all this, Henley blesses his five prep school years (1955–60) for the 'huge self-confidence' they gave him.[41]

At some schools it was possible for a boy to have a good time despite being hopeless at games. This was certainly the case for Philip Steadman, who went to the Dragon in 1950. What he liked was the relaxed 'family-like' atmosphere: winter uniform took the form of boiler suits; school was abandoned when the water meadows froze (as they often did in post-war winters) so that everyone could go skating; there was plenty of time for messing about in boats during the summer; and there was no prefect system. Joc Lynam was still in charge, but by now he was a 'rather remote' figure, according to Philip, who hardly saw him. What Philip valued was the 'light touch' of Lynam's discipline and the fact that he 'appointed good masters'. It is true that some used a certain amount of 'knockabout violence' in the classroom, throwing board rubbers, pulling hair or (on one occasion) breaking a pipe over a boy's head. But many were real enthusiasts whose lessons Philip found stimulating. Science, which was taught by a distinguished biologist, 'made a strong impression' on him and he went on to specialize in it at Winchester, to which he won a scholarship in 1954. By that time school had become Philip's real life, for he never saw his parents during the term; he even extended his school activities into the summer holidays by keeping a detailed diary for which he twice won a prize. The diaries reveal an early interest in architecture (which was to become his profession) as well as familiar pursuits of fifties children such as train-spotting, Meccano-modelling and bicycling. More unusually for that time, he went on annual foreign holidays and watched a lot of television.[42]

Clearly, Lynam did not conduct inquisitions like those of Norman Hale at Milbourne Lodge, who would quiz the boys about whether they had televisions and hold them up to ridicule. This did not worry Piers and Rupert Brendon, whose parents did not possess a set. But the brothers did incur Hale's noisy wrath when it turned out that they (like their father) supported Labour at the 1951 election – the only boys at the school to do so. In other respects, however, they got on well with this 'capricious, egotistical, whimsical, charismatic man' for 'his enthusiasm was infectious, his dedication total'. His eccentricities were especially endearing: he crammed his Ford V8 Pilot with boys and drove like Mr Toad, seldom remembering to fill up with petrol and telephoning the Station Garage to rescue him when he ran out; the mechanics took to hiding tins of petrol in his boot, but he found them, used them and continued to get stranded all over Surrey. Hale was sparing with the slipper or plimsoll, carried round by his dog Wagger. And he treated his pupils as individuals.[43] He allowed Piers and Rupert, who found the school food disgusting, to have lunch at the Cosy Café in Claygate with a generous half a crown supplied by their formidable mother. Sustained by egg and chips (at one shilling and sixpence) and two bars of chocolate (at sixpence each), they would return for an afternoon of compulsory games and more lessons, followed by plenty of prep, which was done at home. Unlike boarders, they managed to learn their Latin verbs and Sunday collects without supervision – the prospect of Hale's terrifying inquisitions was enough to keep them at it.

Food also cheered up the Londoner Anthony Rudolf during his three years as a day boy at Arnold House – where his surname inevitably got him likened to the red-nosed reindeer. He, too, hated school dinners and would tip his suet pudding on to the floor when he thought no one was looking. But the big red bus on which he made his homeward journey at the end of the day seemed homely, because his 'tastebuds were imagining tea and toast and jam, or sponge cake, on arrival home about fifteen minutes later'. After tea Anthony doubtless got on with his prep. Certainly he did enough academic work at Arnold House to keep him going for his first year at City of London School which, luckily, took 'far more Jewish boys than Westminster', whose quota was full for that year.[44] Day boys such as Anthony Rudolf and the Brendon brothers did not inhabit a self-contained world, cut off from home and did not have, like Jennings and Darbishire, to change at the end of each term from being 'a unit in a boarding school to a member of a family'. They did not have the experience of Richard Phillips whose 'parents seemed like strangers' on their visits to Wellbury where he was quite happy with his 'stern surrogate parents', the Kenworthy Brownes. They were 'very good at looking after us', and the whiskery Mrs KB even kissed the younger boys good night.[45]

For her first two years at Formosa Ann Shire found no difficulty in adjusting between school and home. She flourished under the enlightened regime of Lucia Beamish, though not all pupils were so enamoured. One boy ran away using money borrowed from other children, including five shillings from Ann. Meanwhile, she relished the freedom from uniform, from undue supervision and from the dread of punishment. No one got furious, for example, when the pupils played with pogo-sticks on the tile-floored loggia of the Georgian house, drew on its marble mantelpieces or got stuck up trees in the garden. But they were expected to work hard at lessons, which were structured and included carpentry, pottery and science. The situation was changed for Ann halfway through her time at Formosa by the death of her father after a botched operation, which took place while she was recovering from a bout of measles spent in a darkened dormitory. Mrs Beamish broke the news with more sensitivity than was usual in prep schools at that time but, even so, Ann rushed to the lavatories to cry rather than breaking down in front of the headmistress. She was left with a sense of guilt at not having seen much of her father in the weeks before he died. During miserable holidays with her grief-stricken mother she now pined for school so much that she did not say anything when she found nits in her hair, in case this meant a delayed return. At Formosa she continued to thrive, acting Miranda in a performance of *The Tempest* in the outdoor theatre and gaining a scholarship to Bedales after two days of rigorous tests.[46]

It was not always easy for children to lead two separate lives and the rupture could have physical consequences. Throughout his career at Seaford, Jeremy Lewis would sob convulsively before and after parting from his parents when they came on a weekend visit. He cannot explain why this happened, since he enjoyed the 'boisterous spirit' of the school, a 'genial, kindly place' whose two headmasters overlooked his own lack of team spirit and even invited him to watch the boat race in their sitting room on the strength of his father's rowing fame. Monday morning would find Jeremy 'trundling happily forward once again'.[47] The case of Ferdinand Mount is similar. The asthmatic boy was uncharacteristically healthy during the terms at Sunningdale, but for the first few days of every holiday he became 'breathless and helpless'. In his autobiography, Mount concludes that his 'bronchial tubes were registering a transfer of loyalty' for his 'real life was now lived on the school stage, while home life had retreated to the wings'. On the whole he liked Sunningdale, where the urbane Mr Fox (the headmaster appointed during Humphrey Lyttelton's time) 'knew how to mimic home comforts'. The place resembled a country house, in which 'every Hon. and Viscount was accorded his full title'. To Ferdinand, the son of a steeplechase jockey, it also seemed like 'an upmarket version of Beachcomber's Narkover Academy', in which most of the staff and boys were infected with racing mania. But it had a 'dark underside' in the form of Mr Burrows, who 'never slept' but kept his cane at the ready to administer savage midnight thrashings to miscreants in the dormitories.

In remembering the thump of his cane, Mount lapses into the historic present: 'It is all so terrifying that we do not think of telling our parents.' For good or ill, the life of the school possessed the young boy. His little garden plot at Sunningdale assumed more importance than the borders at home in which he had been a willing helper: 'Like some prisoner long penned in the gulag, my patch inside the wire had become my real garden.'

A reference to Stalin's dictatorship crops up surprisingly often in oral and written memories of boarding schools in this era – during which the boys at Wellbury said the rosary for the conversion of Russia every evening before supper. Ferdinand Mount remembered that his first school, Greenways, had an air not only of Llanabba Castle 'but also of a gulag in some distant region of the USSR just this side of Siberia'.[48] And Michael Croft's first, spontaneous remark about Brambletye was to liken it to the Soviet Union under Stalin, because it involved 'total immersion in a system so that you didn't know what was going on in the outside world'. Sent there at the age of eight, without having the 'first idea' why, he would have run away had home not been a daunting twenty miles off – and, in any case, it was his parents who had sent him there. But the post-war headmaster, H. V. Jones, clearly understood something of a new boy's feelings. In chapel on the first Sunday, he reassured boys who might be thinking that their parents had wanted to get rid of them. 'No,' he explained, 'the reason they've sent you here is so that you can learn to stand on your own feet.' Michael found this advice helpful and did his best to follow it. After a week of crying every night, he could not cry any more and learnt self-control. As he said to another homesick boy, 'You have to think of something good about the place.' He found his own ways of coping. He was pleased when he was placed higher up in form order than the sportsmen who viewed him as a dud: 'It was the one chance I had of excelling.' He loved the free afternoons when gangs of pupils were allowed to roam the woods – a pastime prized by generations of Brambletye boys. He took consolation in the twice-daily chapel services, especially when they sang his favourite hymn, 'The day Thou gavest, Lord, is ended'. He joined the other boys in cheering an announcement that Matron was to marry the History master.

In time, Michael became accustomed to the militaristic routines of Brambletye, which had survived the return to East Grinstead but without the famous par-liament to give a veneer of democracy. He 'didn't mind playing at soldiers' and learnt to do as he was told by the officers to avoid being sent to the Study for a painful 'whack, whack, whack, whack'. But he could never resign himself to the 'gulag fare': 'You hit bottom with sheep's neck.' He deplored the 'collectivist spirit' which placed team games higher than 'selfish' intellectual effort. And it took him years to get used to the separation from his family. Symptomatic of his emotional deprivation were nightmarish fears about the eleven-plus exam, which his father arranged for him to take so that 'if anything happened to him' Michael could go to a grammar school. This was not properly explained to the boy, who was convinced that if he failed he would be taken away to 'some place where there were no holidays'. In fact, no worse fate befell him than gaining a place at a public school and going on to work in Africa, for the various rigours of which Brambletye may have prepared him.[49]

It is, of course, less common for old boys to liken their prep school to the gulag archipelago than to st custard's. Tim Rice, editor of the 1985 edition of *The Compleet Molesworth*, says that the academy it features bore a precise resemblance to his own prep school. nigel himself describes it as 'a bit of a shambles' with 'nothing but kanes, lat. french, geog. hist. algy, geom, headmasters, skool dogs, skool sossages . . . and MASTERS everywhere'. As Anthony Heath says of Highfield, it was 'all right' once you had settled down and anyway, for children of a certain class, there was no escaping it: 'It was the done thing to be plonked on the school train at Waterloo and left to get on with it.' David Blandford felt much the same about Brambletye. His first journey from Victoria, dressed in the school's conspicuous bright-pink uniform, was not auspicious; he nearly got left behind when everyone changed at Three Bridges, because he thought he had to stay with his shiny new trunk and consequently arrived at school with the last batch of boys. There he was confronted with the terrifying fangs of a tiger-skin rug in the hall. But he had always known that 'this was what happened and you had to accept it'. Neither Anthony nor David had the advantage of sporting skill but they held their own. Anthony got through with the help of singing in chapel, games of Tri-Tactics and his weekly delivery of *The Eagle*. David, in the meantime, became a leading light in the puppet club, attempted to smoke grass and ferns in the privacy of woodland dens and had fantasies about escaping down the stream known as 'the Amazon'. Like nigel molesworth, these boys learnt to survive each term, with 'super rags wheezes japes and pranks' along the way and to cheer when the end was in sight. They were glad to get home – followed by reports bearing such helpful comments as Mr McIntosh's on Anthony's Geography: 'His maps would be worth a lot if Picasso had done them.'[50]

Robin Baird-Smith (the publisher of this book) has impressively precise memories of both the pains and the pleasures of West Downs between 1954 and 1959. The train journey of the Scottish contingent (known as 'Scottish mush'), which had been acquired during the school's wartime evacuation, took him exactly 385 miles away from his home in Glasgow. His mother gave him a ten-shilling note as his term's pocket money. Every day of term, Matron, in her starched white headdress, gave out a thermometer and a dose of Radio Malt to each of the 150 boys. A master who habitually interfered with the pupils in his classroom, before being sacked, was six feet three inches tall.

For many of the school's hardships Robin managed to find some compensating factor. Its great distance from home meant that he never saw his parents during the term – but his mother promptly sent food parcels when he wrote saying that he was 'very hungry'. He was terrified when first beaten by the new headmaster, Jerry Cornes – but he got used to it and it prepared him for Winchester where 'you were thrashed all the time'. He was not keen on sport, the speciality of Cornes (an accomplished cricketer and former Olympic athlete despite his chain-smoking habit) – but he loved the school's traditional activities of Scouting, drama and music. West Downs itself lacked 'warmth of any kind' – but Robin had his own group of friends who are 'still very fond of each other'. The repressive Mr Potts might land on him 'like a ton of bricks' if he made a mistake in Greek – but the avuncular David Howell-Griffiths, an inspired teacher of English, Latin and History, was always very good to him. His encouragement helped him to gain the intellectual self-confidence he had lacked because of having always been compared to a brilliant older brother. Robin's verdict, delivered with some hesitation, is that West Downs gave him a good enough education, for which he paid a high emotional price.[51]

Highgate Junior School passed varying verdicts on Martin Gilbert during his time as a weekly boarder there between 1945 and 1949. Reports, which Sir Martin still possesses, found his cheerful countenance 'infuriating', his maturity 'disconcerting', his attitude towards work 'lazy', his behaviour 'unobtrusively satisfactory', his Latin 'far too erratic', his boxing 'not too successful', his work as house librarian 'most efficient' and his map work 'excellent'. He was 'too easily amused' in recorder lessons and his lack of useful interests (which means sport) 'left him too free to misbehave'. The historian's own verdicts on Highgate are equally diverse. Although the school had its 'share of tyrants and eccentrics', he considers himself very lucky in his teachers. Among those who had an important influence on his life were Mr Sorenson, who encouraged him to write comments on the books he had read, and the Turkish Gym teacher, Prince Fehti-Samy (known as Sweaty Sammy), who was patient with the 'awkward and gangly' boy and talked to him about the old days in Constantinople. The prince had, for instance, seen the German warships *Goeben* and *Breslau* pass through the Dardanelles, marking Turkey's alliance with Germany in the First World War. Martin owes most to Geoffrey Bell, the headmaster of the Senior as well as the Junior School, who had won a Victoria Cross in the First World War and whom the boys believed to be a pacifist. He found the time to teach History, Geography and Writing and to organize trips to the London docks, the gasworks, the House of Commons and the law courts. He encouraged Martin in particular to explore and map the bombed area around St Paul's, an imaginative project which helped to inspire his future work on the Second World War. Later, when Martin was in the Senior School, Bell had to leave because the governors considered him insufficiently strict. This was not a judgement which could have been made of the master-in-charge of the Junior School, Mr Miller, the 'affable beater' who punished Martin for sneaking to the RSPCA. Nor was there any leniency about the formidable First World War veteran, Mr Markham, with his habit of taking the wind out of errant boys by hitting them hard on the back of the neck. For all the masters who gave encouragement, there were others who made Martin feel ashamed when he could not do well at subjects like sport or Latin or singing. This was the aspect of the school which he found most difficult.

In general, however, Martin was not 'an unhappy schoolboy'. Like molesworth, he knew how to survive. When he wanted to read after lights-out he would go to the toilets. To avoid being taunted as a 'swot', he would make himself useful by helping others out with their essays. Rather than complaining about forties food, he cultivated a taste for corned beef and powdered eggs. And he learnt how to protect himself, a knack which proved useful one evening in 1947. After the boys had finished listening to *Dick Barton Special Agent* on the wireless, the BBC News announced that the bodies of two British sergeants, hanged and booby-trapped by Jewish terrorists, had been found in Palestine. Before he knew what was happening, Martin, the only Jewish boy in the room, found himself being attacked by twenty of his fellow pupils. He simply curled up so that they could not hurt him and thought no more about the event. It is only in retrospect that he is shocked by the hostility which, he has since discovered, affected at least one other boy in the school on the same day and reverberated throughout the country. Most of the time Martin was not persecuted, unlike Jewish refugees from Europe whose foreign accents made them subject to bullying. There was a fellow feeling among most of the boys, who had all been through the war; many had suffered the loss of a father or a home and Martin himself had been separated from his parents as a three-year-old evacuee to Canada. He still saw little of them, because their flat in St John's Wood was too small to accommodate him as well as a sister born while he was away. Thus he spent weekends with a favourite aunt (the one who had taken him to Canada), making the long journey to her home in Hammersmith by bus and trolley bus. And during the week he liked the routine of boarding and some members of staff became a kind of surrogate family.[52]

However, a substantial minority of post-war prep school boys recall being really miserable for one reason or another. As if living in ancient Sparta, one remarked, they had no alternative at the time but to bury their feelings – which can be brought to the surface by later events. The first piece of music chosen by David Suchet for his *Desert Island Discs* was the song 'You'll Never Walk Alone' from *Carousel* (1945). This reminded him of his schoolfellows at Birchington House, who sang it as they followed the headmaster into the 'freezing-cold sea' in a compulsory daily ritual. David hated this school, at which he was given six-of-the-best for having a Mars Bar in his locker.[53] A college dinner can sometimes bring back unwelcome memories of institutional life. One such occasion prompted Cambridge scientist, Peter Murray Rust, to pour out the story of his unhappy time at Moffats in Shropshire from 1948 to 1953. The school's regime sounds quite normal for its day, with its cricket, cold showers and cross-country runs. Like other schoolboys, he learnt his Latin from the textbook whose title was altered to 'Kennedy's Eating Primer' and amused himself at church services by calculating the date of Easter. Peter was 'not much bullied'. He found the food edible, apart from baked dates in custard. He liked the Maths master and shone at that subject. And he was beaten only twice with the headmaster's cricket bat. But he did resent the way in which boys were exploited on the 250-acre farm occupied by the school. He remembers having to mow the lawns with a dangerous machine, to pick up and sack potatoes during the working school day and to carry large bowls of hot food, which once caused him third-degree burns. He was even made to copy out a manual of French verbs written by an old boy, like some 'medieval scribe'. Peter's real problem, though, was sheer loneliness. He never managed to make friends because he was young for his class and clever in a way that alienated other boys. Nor did he have any friends when he returned to his home in the remote Somerset countryside. He hated the separation from his parents whom he never saw during the term and he dreaded the return to school – though he did enjoy his solitary train journeys during which he played I-Spy and spotted engines. Peter describes himself as 'socially crippled' as a result of these desolate prep school years.[54]

It was not usually possible for a child in this situation to complain to his parents. John Peel (né Ravenscroft), who was initially bullied at Woodlands School, Deganwy, did manage to smuggle 'a tightly rolled cry for help into a sealed envelope'. In reply, his father advised him to punch his persecutor 'firmly on the nose', a tactic which proved effective.[55] At Temple Grove, by contrast, Simon Taggart got into trouble when he was found writing in his Sunday letter, 'Mr Batchelor is a beast'. Indeed, he never succeeded in conveying to his parents his hatred of the 'appalling martinet' whom they found so charming. With no telephone contact, no home visits during term and 'no route out' from the remote location, Simon felt so isolated from family life that 'it was like being at sea'. His heart would sink every time he approached the school up its long gravel drive lined with damp rhododendrons.[56]

Tim Jeal was no more successful in sending messages out of Boarzell in East Sussex. In his first Sunday letter to his mother he wrote that he 'felt homesick at night, and also longed to be with her during the day'. Later on that day he was summoned by the headmaster's wife, who tore up the letter, suggesting that 'it would be kinder and braver' to say that he had got over any homesickness he may have felt. Tim never did tell his parents how much he disliked the school, nor did he mention to them 'the mauve and purple bruises that dappled my buttocks in term time and earned me admiring comments in the showers'. After all, he thought, if he did tell them and they failed to remove him, how would he know that they still loved him? Towards the end of his time, however, he and another boy devised a novel method of getting their own back 'for so many beatings and restrictions on our liberty'. They wrote an obscene anonymous letter, addressed to the sister of a fellow pupil at her respectable neighbouring boarding school, designed to cause maximum embarrassment to their headmaster.[57]

Meanwhile, at Highfield, Paul Knight had fantasies about leading a revolution against the authorities – an anticipation, perhaps, of the insurrection in Lindsay Anderson's film *If*. Paul had never recovered from the shock of being sent to the school very soon after the death of his beloved grandmother. There had been no censorship to stop him sending an urgent plea to his parents to 'get me out of here', but they failed to oblige. He can remember very little of his first two terms during which he did not function very well, except that a kind woman teacher used to read to him in the evenings. Looking back, he cannot really explain what made him so wretched. He found Canon Mills 'genuinely kindly' if over-committed to achievement; he hit it off with some of the masters although he had strong reservations about Peter Mills; he did not come in for much bullying until his last year when a group got at him for being too competitive. Paul had, it is true, got into the first football team, sung solos with the school choir and won several prizes for academic achievement, eventually gaining a place at Winchester. All this, and *The Eagle*, helped him to survive. His greatest comfort was going to bed at night with the blankets tucked in like a cocoon and rocking himself to sleep. Just before leaving the school he felt 'a kind of euphoria', but at Winchester the misery of his early Highfield days returned with shattering effect. Boarding school did not suit him even as an adolescent. But eventually something good came out of the 'pain of childhood'. Paul followed a career in child care, becoming a Director of Social Services and helping to steer through parliament the 1989 Act which enshrined certain rights for future generations of children.[58]

The comedian Peter Cook also helped to shape the future. Straight after the war, he went as a small asthmatic boy to St Bede's, Eastbourne, where he was an easy prey for bullies. His 'brave enthusiasm' on the football field and 'academic brilliance' stood him in good stead. But Peter never stopped pining for his family who lived abroad – his father was in the Colonial Service. His sister Sarah remembers that he was desperately unhappy at school, although he 'never moaned' to his parents. Both at St Bede's and afterwards at Radley he kept his emotions 'firmly battened down', while using his wit to deflect the bullies and win popularity. Not long after leaving school, while still at Cambridge, Cook hatched the pioneering review *Beyond the Fringe*, which used a 'tone of manly understatement' to mock sacred British institutions such as public and preparatory schools.[59] Later he created the patrician character Sir Arthur Streeb-Greebling, who has wasted his life trying to teach ravens to fly underwater. When asked by Ludovic Kennedy in one of a series of comic interviews why he had his son, Roger, educated privately by goats despite his own 'childhood experiences with goats', Sir Arthur replies: 'Well it was either that or King's School, Canterbury. I'm not entirely heartless, you know.' Roger's education is completed when he and the goats 'go down to a very good prep school near Lymington in Hampshire'.[60] Such sketches were calculated to make it hard for stuffy headmasters, overbearing fathers, complacent chaplains or visiting dignitaries and deep-sea diving experts ever to be taken seriously again.

8

'Boiled Mince and Incense'
The Swinging Sixties

When eight-year-old Stephen Fry arrived at Stouts Hill School in 1965, he became acquainted with the school pets. Among them were 'a profusion of ponies and horses', including an elderly grey called Cloud 'with a great Thelwell-style underhang of a belly'; a squadron of dogs including 'something fluffy and loud called Caesar'; and an aviary of exotic birds including a mynah bird who became Stephen's particular friend. The presence of these creatures symbolized the 'kindly familial warmth' for which Stephen's parents had selected the school through the renowned agency of Gabbitas & Thring. Perhaps when they made their preliminary visit to the school Mr and Mrs Fry did not hear the bird's prodigious imitation of 'the dull bang of the cane being thwacked on to tight trouser seats in the headmaster's study'. Or perhaps they did and found this a perfectly normal practice, as did their young son for whom 'the whack' was as much part of 'the Game' as compulsory cricket and the 'nightly spoonful of Radio Malt'.[1] Yet in the world outside the confines of prep school, Dr Spock, who had replaced Truby King as child expert of the day, advised parents against the physical punishment of children. Moreover, teachers belonging to the Society of Teachers Opposed to Physical Punishment (STOPP) campaigned against its use in schools.

This chapter examines whether anything was swinging in prep schools of the 1960s apart from the teacher's cane so gleefully wielded by 'Professor' Jimmy Edwards in the long-running television and radio series, *Whacko!* It uses the evidence of memoirs, letters and interviews, although such testimony is a little harder to find than for earlier periods since former pupils now tend to imagine living parents and teachers looking over their shoulder or listening to conversations. However, Royston Lambert's major inquiry into boarding education was based on diaries kept by pupils. These certainly reveal more about children's experience than do the questionnaires filled in by headmasters for Philip Masters to use in his *Preparatory Schools Today*, a survey which was evidently intent on showing that all was for the best in the best of all possible worlds.

The sixties decade is usually associated with challenges to hallowed traditions and taboos. The 'wind of change' blew through colonial Africa; homosexuality was legalized, capital punishment was abolished and flogging was removed from the penal code; *Lady Chatterley's Lover* was published despite its alleged obscenity; girls' skirts became shockingly short and boys' hair grew daringly long; the pop scene made public school accents and respectable demeanour unfashionable among young people. 'The times', Bob Dylan sang, 'they are a-changin'.' Philip Larkin famously identified the turning point as 1963, just after 'the end of the *Chatterley* ban' and just before the Beatles' first LP.[2] But did anything happen to disturb the cherished customs and established routines of preparatory schools?

There is little reason to think that the world of Jennings and molesworth altered much in the sixties or even in the seventies, during which time boys still devoured books about Linbury Court and st custard's. Martin Rowson's abiding memory of his High Church prep school in Harrow is the time-honoured smell of 'boiled mince and incense' rather than any newfangled whiff of bean sprouts or marijuana. In Mrs Threadham's class, six-year-old Martin was stripped of his first name, as was customary in private schools, barracks and prisons. He witnessed her tying a classmate to his chair until he got his spellings right and forcing another to eat 'everything on his plate, predigested and otherwise'. Dr Spock had clearly not superseded Truby King in these classrooms, where 'time seemed to have stood still'.[3]

Two pupils from this era draw similar conclusions about St Aubyns under W. H. Gervis. This school demonstrated its reverence for the past with frequent memorial services and flag ceremonies, and with houses named after historic fighting bands. New apparel for choirboys took priority over heating the dormitories and the brass band prevailed over any other kind of culture, just as titled parents took precedence over others, who had to give up their seats to them in chapel. Tom Ponsonby summed up the school's ethos at that time as 'strong bodies and military discipline', while Vivian Bickford-Smith likened the place to a male club in which favoured members enjoyed privileges such as being taken to Glyndebourne by the headmaster. Mr Gervis's canes (all twenty-six of them, varying in ferocity) loom large in both men's memories. Vivian was their victim three times while his more exuberant friends were beaten nearly every day for offences such as talking after lights-out. Tom was never caned but he once dared to go into the headmaster's study to view the cupboard where he kept the dreaded weapons.[4]

Some headmasters, it is true, put away their canes and slippers in this period and Norman Hale's dog, Wagger, no longer carried round a plimsoll at Milbourne Lodge. Newly appointed headmasters sometimes made a fresh start in this respect. One of the first decisions taken by John Briggs at King's College Choir School in 1959 was to abolish this 'repressive and brutalising' form of punishment.[5] Hugh Woodcock, who took over the headship of Dulwich from John Leakey in 1962, upset the old guard by abandoning the use of the 'Tolly' – though boys found that he was quite 'scary' enough without it, 'not a man you wished to cross'.[6] David Walker does not remember any boy being beaten at Forres once Mr Strange, a benign family man, took over from the flagellant Mr Mackray, otherwise known as 'The Fish'.[7] At Scaitcliffe it was the birth of his own sons which caused Richard Vickers to see 'things in a very different light' and give up corporal punishment. It is not clear from his own account when this self-denying ordinance was implemented, but it was too late for Richard Branson and also for Rupert Morris, a pupil at Scaitcliffe from 1960 to 1964. Rupert remembers being caned four times for various escapades, which included lowering the flag from the roof and laying a 'trip-wire' (in reality a dressing-gown cord) which, unfortunately, felled the young Mrs Vickers. Under the new regime he would have had to write a letter of apology instead of submitting to the cane.[8]

Most prep school headmasters, like Jerry Cornes of West Downs, did not feel that they had to 'apologise for the continuance of this ancient remedy'.[9] It was used to a greater or lesser extent. One of Arthur Marshall's correspondents (at prep school from 1964 to 1969) remembers that his headmaster beat all ninety-eight pupils in his school for defying a prefect ban on talking during elevenses. On the other hand, Hamish Pringle cannot recall anyone being beaten during his time at The New Beacon, although he is sure that the deterrent was still in place.[10] At West Downs, John Passmore got four strokes of Cornes's own cane for refusing to translate the sentence 'Puer Amat Mensam' on the grounds that it was unlikely that a boy would love a table. Meanwhile, his classmates gleefully chanted: 'Bendo, Wackare, Ouchi, Sorebum.'[11] Such whacks could indeed cause injury to the recipient. At Orley Farm, recalls Anthony Horowitz, 'the headmaster flogged boys till they bled'. Tony Mitton, who once got six underserved strokes at St Felix for throwing darts onto the gym floor in a game organized by a master, could tell that Matron was shocked to see the multi-coloured marks on his bottom at bath-time a few days later. At Falconbury, attended in his turn by Johnny Bell's son, Robin, 'beatings would cease two weeks before the end of term, because the headmaster did not want to send boys home with bruising that would be evident to parents'. Robin also thinks that Mr Devitt got satisfaction from beating because it 'worked out his anger'.[12]

Other boys were sometimes under the same impression. Dan Fairest remembers his 'Dickensian' Classics master at Stancliffe Hall running at full pelt down the hall to whack his victim with a gym shoe. Dan could sense the difference between him and the kindly headmaster, Ken Wareham, who would carefully explain why he had to administer the butterpat – the smooth or the crinkly side depending on the severity of the offence.[13] Referring to Maidwell Hall's Oliver Wyatt, Andrew Motion claims: 'Beak enjoyed beating.' Clearly speaking from experience, he enumerates the many crimes which gave rise to the penalty:

> He beat us if we did badly at work, if we were cheeky, if we walked with our hands in our pockets, if we left the middle button on our jackets undone, if we walked on the grass by the statue standing on one leg, if we slammed doors, if we barged ahead of masters, if we swore, if we made a mess in our lockers, if we didn't have our towels, if we had fights, if we damaged the flowers, if we hid our food.

Even Tom Fort, a schoolfellow who criticized Andrew Motion's disobliging memoir, conceded that Maidwell's 'regime of constant corporal punishment' was so severe that it would, if emulated today, 'land the perpetrator in prison'.[14]

Occasionally, the blows had a sinister feel to them. Richard Aldwinckle recalls that a master who 'went too far' with his vicious use of the slipper at Christ Church Choir School, Oxford, moved on to another local school.[15] The neighbouring Dragon is the setting for a story told by Paul Watkins, an American pupil there in the early 1970s. A master he calls 'Pa Winter' played a frightening game of chase with Paul and a friend. Both had been left behind during an exeat weekend, when the school resembled 'a ghost town'. The man deliberately pursued the boys on to the muddy playing field which had been put out of bounds, beat them for committing this offence and then hugged Paul when he burst into tears: 'He pressed my face into his sweaty shirt and then he shook my hand and gave me a chocolate bar.' Some time later, the friends heard that Pa Winter had been fired and mentioned the chasing incident to the headmaster. They could not understand why the head was furious with them for not having told someone at the time.[16] As is now clearly recognized, certain adults can derive a sadistic thrill from the exercise of dominance, from flagellation itself or from witnessing its effects. Michael Barber, who was at Hildersham during the 1950s, recalled a 'rum old pervert' of a Latin master who would pay a boy sixpence after a swishing to see his 'cherry bottom'. No doubt, as a modern authority concludes, there were often 'sexual factors at work in the beating system'.[17]

An even more hidden aspect of prep schools is the paedophilia for which they could provide ideal conditions – isolation from the world, masters' position of power and boys' craving for affection. Moreover, when it was difficult to recruit staff, heads did not always 'inquire deeply into an applicant's background'.[18] It is not unusual for former pupils to hint at an unhealthy atmosphere or a 'dark side' to school life. Witnesses from earlier periods have described masters making favourites of the more attractive pupils, taking a voyeuristic interest in the boys' showering and nude bathing, or being sacked 'for that sort of thing'. Several men have told me of masters who would take boys onto their laps during lessons and fondle them under their shorts. But there have been only a few direct allegations of past abuse in written or oral memoirs. One of the most controversial is Richard Meinertzhagen's *Diary of a Black Sheep* (1964), which tells of Walter Radcliffe's homosexual advances and sadistic beatings at Fonthill in the 1890s (*see* Chapter 3). In casting doubt on the authenticity of this account, the historian Brian Garfield makes the point that it was published in the 1960s when 'child-abuse had become a hot topic'. Curiously, Garfield attributes this to the popularity of Dr Spock's *Commonsense Book of Baby and Child Care* which 'encouraged torrents of pop psychology and sexual pathology books'.[19] In fact, Spock's manual gives practical and humane advice on subjects like infant feeding, potty training and the management of young children. All this was invaluable to mothers, but it can hardly be said to have stimulated an unhealthy interest in paedophilia. On the contrary, it seems evident that Meinertzhagen wanted to tell his story before he died and felt freer to write of such matters in the more open atmosphere of that time. Other memoirs published in the same year as *Diary of a Black Sheep*, such as Randolph Churchill's *Twenty-One Years* and Evelyn Waugh's *A Little Learning*, were similarly frank about sex.

As it happens, Anthony Storr's *Sexual Deviation* was also published in 1964.

Far from being a work of 'pop psychology', it is an entirely sensible description of various conditions, including paedophilia. Storr explains that this may take the form of verbal approaches, genital exhibition, fondling and (rarely) intercourse. He isolates the factors which make youngsters vulnerable: 'Children are both less demanding and more ready to give affection than adults ... [and] are easily pleased with small gifts of sweets or money.' Although 'many children survive such incidents' unscathed, Storr concludes that society should protect them from such advances which carry 'the risk of emotional damage'.[20] There was now more protection than there had ever been; after 1957 all private schools were subject to inspection and to closure 'if the proprietor, staff, buildings, accommodation or instruction are found to be unsuitable'.[21] But inspectors in the 1960s were rarely on the lookout for child abuse, which was not such a 'hot topic' as Garfield supposes. Nor did Royston Lambert's survey find much evidence of 'sexual deviation on the part of the staff', concluding that 'such activity does not remain undiscovered long'.[22]

This seems now to have been a rash assumption. It has taken forty years, for example, for boys abused by several masters at Caldicott School at different times between 1957 and 1974 to tell their stories, which featured in the BBC television programme *Chosen* (2008). Mark Payge, whose abuser was reported by Matron, denied that anything had happened to him when he went to wake the master each morning – for he felt that he himself was incriminated. Only after his parents were dead did he admit that he had been 'ridden like a blow-up doll' by a man who attempted suicide when the truth came out but has never been charged. Tom Perry did not tell anyone about the French kisses and masturbation bestowed on him regularly by Peter Wright, who taught French, rugby and cricket at the same school, because he had been so well groomed that he felt complicit. He, too, could only get the words out after the death of his mother. In 2003 Wright was charged on sixteen counts of child abuse but the case was stayed because it all happened so long ago. In the early 1970s Alastair Rolfe did admit under questioning by Matron that he had been a sexual victim of Martin Carson, a popular Caldicott master, but he did not tell the whole story of his sodomy. Peter Wright (by then the headmaster) convinced Mr and Mrs Rolfe that the episodes had been a 'blip' and that 'the best thing for Alastair was to get straight back on the rugby field'. Carson was dismissed, went to teach at another school and was only convicted of indecent assault thirty years later, when he received a two-year sentence.[23]

These distressing stories corroborate each other and make it possible to imagine the special circumstances in which abuse could happen. It required a complicit or remote headmaster or one to whom 'pederasty was quite unthinkable', a matron who was unobservant or turned a blind eye, and perhaps a group of like-minded masters.[24] In the course of my discussions and interviews (during which I never raised the question of paedophilia), I heard of several similar cases relating to prep schools of the sixties. Peter Franks* told me that his well-known school contained some 'painfully enthusiastic pederasts'. Their preying on defenceless boys was ignored by its elderly headmaster and by a 'wilfully ignorant school nurse'. 'Until the pederasts came' he was happy at this school which gave plenty of opportunities for 'inspiration and creativity'. But he blames it for the 'early demise' of his innocence.[25]

Another story related to Allen House, a 'brutish and unpleasant' school in Surrey. Luke Spiers* told me that the headmaster used to touch boys inappropriately as he pushed them like seals into the bathwater. He was also 'too physically friendly' with boys in public, but Luke does not know whether he pursued this further in private. Luke is clear about his own encounter with another master who engaged him in 'non-invasive' sex. Even though he was a weekly boarder, Luke never discussed this with his father, who had attended the same school under the same headmaster. Thus he has always been worried that his father might have known what was going on, which is what bothers him most about the experience. Eventually, Luke understands, a group of parents did object to the 'culture of the school' and encouraged the head to take a world tour and consider his position. On his return, the property was sold for a large sum of money and Allen House merged with a neighbouring school under a different name.[26]

There can be no doubt that some prep boarding schools have harboured active paedophiles, although it would be wrong to assume that this was common or that large numbers were affected. Over the last twenty years or so, with more rigorous inspection, greater use of trained teachers, freer communication between parents and children and wider publicity, it has become harder (though certainly not impossible) for such criminal behaviour to go unnoticed.

While Harold Wilson conjured with the white heat of the technological revolution in his famous speech, the main form of communication between pupils and parents in the 1960s remained the supervised Sunday letter. School prospectuses

announced telephone numbers (such as Brill 237), pupils' homes were likely to
be among the 50 per cent which possessed a telephone and most prep school
children would have known how to use it – after all, Jennings has no difficulty
in ringing for the fire brigade from Mr Carter's office in the first book of the
Linbury Court series. But pupils were rarely given the opportunity to speak to
their parents from school (though seniors who were allowed out sometimes used
a municipal telephone box). The reason for this was explained to Andrew Motion
by Miss Hardwick who taught the junior boys at Maidwell Hall:

> We must try to forget our mums and dads because thinking about them would make us
> miserable. That was why we weren't allowed to make telephone calls home. And that's
> why Sunday letters had to be checked, in case we said something upsetting.

Andrew was amazed when he progressed to Radley public school in 1965 to find
that there was a pupils' pay phone – and 'a queue that went on for ever'.[27]

Letters were better than nothing, as Pat Savage, the new headmaster of
Summer Fields, realized; he assured the parents of new boys that boys' Sunday
letters were 'never censored' and urged them to write regularly to their sons
since 'going to a new school is such an upheaval for small boys'.[28] But, as I was
told by David Barton*, a former pupil of St Dunstan's, Burnham-on-Sea, such
a correspondence was not always 'very relevant to our lives.' He remembers his
father (a naval captain) sending news from his ship in the Far East, while he
wrote about St Dunstan's winning matches against St Peter's: 'Not a lot of it
connected.'[29] The letters, which some families have kept, can sometimes recap-
ture emotions felt at the time. Henry Lytton Cobbold had forgotten that at
Wellesley House he continued to write fantastic stories about a so-called 'Donk
gang', which he had begun at home and now sent back to his parents. His later
letters illustrate the skill he developed at boarding school of getting around the
rules rather than breaking them. Often written with multi-coloured felt-tipped
pens in various forms of script, they were hardly the orthodox Sunday missives favoured by the masters; one is headed 'Colditz alias Wellesley House'.[30]
Some of Vivian Bickford-Smith's letters reflect the glow cast by his glamorous
twenty-year-old sister, Gillian. He asked her to send pictures of herself for his
friends and looked forward to her coming to the carol service 'because all the
boys want to see you'.[31] Richard Aldwinckle found that reading the school letters

he had written to his parents (who were serving with the Allied Forces in Paris) released feelings he had 'put on hold in the memory bank'. They conjure up, for example, his recurrent homesickness at school in Oxford: 'Every time I hear a train whistling by, or a plane over-head I get a lump in my throught.' And a letter written on a cold February afternoon evokes the bleakness of a boarding school Sunday:

> Nobody took me out last Sunday and it seems as if nobody's going to take me out today. It's been dull all week, just done the same as usual. If my hands weren't so cold I'd try and write some more. They're all cracked. I've got a *S-T-I-N-K-I-N-G* !!!!!! cold.[32]

Rupert Morris, too, only recaptured the misery he had blocked out when, many years later, he read the letters he had sent home as a small asthmatic boy from Scaitcliffe. They brought back his feeling of being, in January 1960, 'abandoned like an orphan at this strange big house'. At first he was terrified of the 'bashing up' he thought he would get from other boys if he ever sneaked to Matron or a master: 'They say that strong people . . . whip you with barbed wire and kick you in the stomach with their football boots on and tie you to the table and throw balls at you.' He does not seem to have suffered such terrible reprisals but he was frequently very unhappy. Despite assuming that 'most people like bording school better than day school', he found himself crying 'whenever I am alone' and begged his parents 'to come every Sunday'. By the summer, he reported that he was less homesick but his letters still betray signs of anxiety. He was having 'asthma attacks galore'. He implored his mother to 'please for goodness sake send some short socks' because otherwise he would get a minus mark. He sent frequent assurances to his sister Laura that he would never forget her. And he found it difficult to go for three weeks 'without the slightest glimpse' of his family. Of course, in the end, Rupert became one of the boys, flicking pellets out of rubber bands, burning things with the help of a magnifying glass, throwing conkers at cars from hideouts in the garden, circulating his funny school story called 'Cooper's Adventures' and arranging to take friends home for delicious birthday lunches of roast duck and chocolate cake. But he continued to have periods of hating the 'whole wretched school', longing for the time when the 'old family' would be back home, 'eating potato crisps and talking together over odd things in the drawing room'.[33]

Rupert does not remember being able to seek reassurance on the telephone, but his headmaster, Richard Vickers, claimed that he would let a homesick boy have a word with his mother once the initial 'emotional traumas were partially over'. As with the matter of beating, Vickers found that his attitude to new boys' sorrows changed once he had his own sons.[34] No doubt it was such fatherly feeling which prompted him to let boarders see their parents more often. Rupert went home about once every three weeks, as seems to have been customary by this time – except for the 30 per cent or so of boarders whose parents lived abroad. Rupert still cannot understand why he had to be sent away from a home which was nearby in London and from a mother who (like most contemporaries of her class) had a housemaid and did not go out to work. Henry Lytton Cobbold's letters suggest that he had regular weekends back at Knebworth House despite the three-hour journey from Broadstairs; he often thanks his parents for 'letting me go home' or asks what is on at the local cinema so that he can indulge his early obsession with films. He longed for home throughout his time at Wellesley House and could never grasp why he had to go away to his father's old school.[35] The usual justification given by headmasters at the time was that prep school boarding served 'to go between the home and the harder life of the public school'.[36]

So although mothers were beginning to demand a more homely school environment, most pupils still slept on iron bedsteads in cold, bare dormitories and gathered around the few radiators to be found downstairs. Richard Aldwinckle was scarcely exaggerating when he complained to his parents in October 1963: 'I hope you realize this school *has no heating*. Not in the dorms or the classrooms.'[37] The martial regimes which still prevailed were as spartan as the physical conditions. Girls' prep schools were no exception. New Court, Cheltenham, for example, was run along naval lines by Miss (known as 'Admiral') Peplow, who was rumoured to be an admiral's daughter. Other teachers were called Captains, prefects were Lieutenants and classes were given the names of destroyers such as HMS *Courageous, Renown* or *Vanguard*. Rituals dramatized the seafaring theme. The diminutive Admiral Peplow would be piped into Assembly on the First Lieutenant's whistle; this daily ceremony took place in a hall adorned with lifebelts, photographs of battleships and a ship's bell; and every Friday each class would follow a procedure known as 'Ships', in which log books of the week's events were read out by a Lieutenant. Even the teachers found all this odd and none of it meant much to the pupils in their surprisingly girlish pink uniforms. Ten-year-old Elizabeth McKellar was preoccupied at first with her own misery in a bleak place 'full of emptiness' and with her difficulty in making friends after arriving from South America with a Spanish accent. She found solace in reading and later she came to enjoy nature study, Latin and netball. But she never got used to the cold, impersonal atmosphere of the school, which seems to have been designed to fulfil Miss Peplow's nautical fantasies.[38]

In boys' schools the break from home was still emphasized by the widespread use of surnames, as a seven-year-old boy explained in his diary for Lambert's survey. 'They kept asking me my name and when I said John they all laughed and said not that one stupid, the real one, and then I said Ashton and they nicknamed me 'Ashcan'.'[39] Paul Watkins had the same experience at the Dragon where 'there was no point in having a first name because nobody used it.' Nicknames were handed out in the dormitory on the first night and some surnames 'could ruin your life' – Codrington became Cuddlybum and Bessom became Bosom while Paul got off lightly with Watty Dog.[40] Henry Lytton Cobbold's double-barrelled initials meant that he was known as Elsie. Rupert Morris was called Wheezebag because of his asthma or Morris Minor to distinguish him from an older namesake – though he was pleased to note that his form master knew his Christian name. Even brothers would use surnames and see little of each other. Things had not changed since the mid-fifties when David Blandford had to tell his bewildered younger brother that they could not call each other by their first names – and David has always felt guilty that he did not look after Chris when they were at school together. 'I'm not your bro any more,' said Kit to Andrew Motion at the beginning of a term, 'see you in twelve weeks.'[41] But some headmasters did encourage a more domestic atmosphere. Dan Fairest remembers the teddy bears' party organized for new boys by Ken Wareham, who would dress up in an Egyptian costume to judge the teddies. Dan found the presence of his older brother at Stancliffe Hall a great comfort, as did Rupert Everett on his first day at Farleigh House, when his brother held his hand as they bade farewell to their parents.

After that, writes Everett, 'we were left to make our own way ... in the tradition of our Empire-ruling forebears'. The next morning he took part with everyone else in 'the three-course meal' of prayer, followed by defecation and (if summoned by the headmaster) punishment.[42] Such memories, as well as Lambert's research, suggest that boys' 'most intimate behaviour' was 'scrutinized by others' in ways which could often be cruel.[43] A child who wet the bed, called the lavatory by the wrong name, blubbed when he was hurt or upset, dirtied his pants, was embarrassed about undressing in front of other boys or had 'foreign characteristics, such as curly hair or a greasy complexion', could be ragged without mercy.[44] Dan Fairest, who was himself very happy at Stancliffe Hall, criticizes domestic arrangements which humiliated some other children. Whatever happened, boys could change their underwear only twice a week; those in the 'wet-bed dorm' had to get up earlier than everyone else and wash their sheets in the bath in full view; and pupils had to share the bath water with about four others.[45]

Weeks of this grim communal life could get a child down in an era when homes had become more comfortable and openly affectionate – and when the Beatles' refrain insisted that 'All you need is love'. Memories as well as letters belie the assertion of Philip Masters (formerly headmaster of The Beacon) that by the 1960s 'the old bogy of homesickness' was a 'thing of the past'.[46] Even, or perhaps especially, if there were difficulties at home it was hard to be sent away. Tony Mitton and his older brother were packed off to boarding schools because the doctors insisted that their manic-depressive mother could not cope with them; they understood this but nevertheless missed her hugs and cuddles.[47] Duncan Wiltshire always hated being 'dragged away from home' and from his loving mother to The Abbey (the preparatory part of Woodbridge School), which was still 'a harsh environment' in the 1970s. The regime was directed by two dour Scots, the ferocious headmaster, Mr Dewar, and the equally tyrannical matron, always known as 'Haggis'. Dewar was apt to lose control of himself, as when he found Duncan in the cloakroom engaged on an errand for one of the masters. Rather than listening to the boy's explanation of why he was in the wrong place at the wrong time, he picked him up by his ears, shook him and flung him out. Duncan has never forgotten or forgiven this injustice. Haggis would also brook no disobedience. She stood over boys until they had eaten everything on their plates (including maggot-ridden apples), accused them of malingering if they reported sick and sent them to bed at an impossibly early time. Duncan remembers only one occasion on which she was defied. After the annual pageant in The Abbey's beautiful grounds, she rang the bedtime bell at seven o'clock while parents were still gathered on the lawn with their sons. Encouraged by the Rev Pizzey, the sympathetic young master who lived in the attic, and emboldened by the presence of their parents, the boys defied three clangings of the bell, each angrier than the last.

Duncan plucked up more courage when he and a friend decided to escape from this 'dictatorship'. Unwisely, they leaked their plans to the other boarders who all turned out to see them off. But the young runaways lost their nerve once they had climbed over the fence into forbidden territory and were back in school before the staff knew they had gone. It would not have done Duncan any good had this venture succeeded, as he found when he made a later bid for freedom on his own. After cycling twelve miles home on a flat tyre one Saturday afternoon he was taken back at his father's insistence, before his absence had been discovered. Like most other prep school children of his time, Duncan would have to solve his own problems – and he certainly found that The Abbey trained him for the more brutal environment of Woodbridge School.[48] Other boys had no means of escape. Tom Ponsonby could not contemplate fleeing from St Aubyns, Rottingdean, because his home was in Ireland. In his 'miserably unhappy' second term he contemplated suicide and he still has the 32-shilling Harrods penknife with which he came close to cutting his wrists.[49] One eleven-year-old in the Lambert survey summed up his feelings about school life in a prayer:

> Here I am, lone and friendless,
> I'm one of them
> Nobody in particular
> Just one of them,
> 'Smith' they call me;
> But I may not cry Lord,
> You know why.[50]

In the end, the toughening-up process often worked and boys 'made it through' in one way or another. When Paul Watkins split his lip while playing goalie and managed not to cry, he realized that he would not 'die of the homesickness, or the teasing, or the modelling-clay bugs in my desk. I would be all right, but I would have to make sure of it by myself.'[51] Tony Mitton used his skills as a story-teller to win credit with the other boys at St Felix, where he sensed that the headmaster saw him as 'a workhouse child' because he had some sort of state funding. Tony did even better as a mimic, imitating Kenny Ball's jazz trumpet favourites during 'loo-time'. Such talents proved useful to other boys. Tom Ponsonby made up for not being in the least sporty by telling stories after lights-out, while other boys kept *cave* for the sound of Gervy's squeaky shoes. In his novel *My Affair with Stalin*, Simon Sebag Montefiore has the same idea: his bespectacled hero, William Conroy, taunted as a cabbage because of his lack of prowess in sports, wins popularity at Coverdale by telling blood-curdling murder mysteries. Rather less plausibly, he leads a successful revolution against the elite sportsmen by modelling himself on Stalin. Boys with more serious handicaps than poor eyesight could also survive. Patrick Cockburn, a polio victim, did not repine when he exchanged a country-house existence where he was 'cosseted by parents and servants, for the dull routine of a schoolboy sleeping in a crowded dormitory' at St Stephen's prep school in Dublin. With a ten-year-old's desire 'to behave in the same way as the other boys', he threw away his crutches and 'left them lying on a lawn behind the main schoolhouse'. He could not, of course, play games but he nevertheless made plenty of friends. He found that St Stephen's was an improvement on the isolation ward and the orthopaedic hospital, where the doctors 'never seemed to realize what their younger patients were going through'.[52]

Other vulnerable pupils used their wits in similar ways. David Barton, a clever boy with coeliac disease who remained the smallest of a hundred boys at St Dunstan's until he was ten, coped by being a 'fly-on-the-wall', always very careful in what he said. Like the short-sighted Richard Aldwinckle, he found a sporting role by scoring in cricket. It was better than having to report, as did Henry Lytton Cobbold in a letter to his parents, 'I batted last, I was bowled first ball, I did not bowl because I can't, I missed a catch. That shows how bad I am at cricket!'[53] Henry made up for this shameful performance by holding the hurdles record for seven years, despite his flat feet. Rupert Morris, too weedy to excel in the games he adored, would act as touch judge in rugby matches and get the all-important 'grub' which followed. Rupert also received a certain amount of protective care from the headmaster's elderly mother, 'Ma Vickers', who fussed over him and provided him with a room on his own when his asthma was bad. Such attentions were a help. David Walker, whose parents lived abroad, had a little mothering from his headmaster's wife and from a young matron, who once escorted him and his brother all the way to Liberia. A 'shy and reserved' boy, David got through the terms by keeping busy and by being 'just sporty enough' to keep in with the crowd.[54]

It is clear that sport retained its traditional prestige in prep schools, doubtless enhanced by the fact that England won the football World Cup in this decade.

Hamish Pringle found that 'a lot depended on being sporty' at The New Beacon. He loved everything about the school and cherishes glowing memories, especially of playing in the nets late on summer evenings. He got into all the first teams, became head boy and, like Tom Brown, did not abuse his position by bullying those who were lower down in the heap.[55] Some of the prefects and house captains in Lambert's survey took their duties equally seriously. One boy saw fit to pray:

> Thank you, Lord, for giving me the leadership of Hawthorn House; thank you for my privileges and my prefect's tie; for the house cup which we so closely won and for the trust of the boys in my house, thank you, Lord, thank you.[56]

Only one sport became less popular, in line with current ideas. Year after year, *St Dunstan's Magazine* reported fewer volunteers for the boxing club and in 1963 expressed fears that its days were numbered for 'one reads of so much opposition to this sport in the press'. No boxing reports appeared in the 1965 and 1966 editions.[57] By this time, boxing had been discontinued in Summer Fields after 'memoirs of many who had suffered at school had been published, suggesting that, rather than making a man of one, being hit on the head and body might have a deleterious effect on both the mind and body'.[58] No doubt this trend was reflected in other prep schools – though in the boarding house of DCPS boxing was actually introduced in 1961 by a new housemaster, who administered the place as 'a sort of junior Army in Civvy Street'.[59]

That did not, of course, mean that boys stopped fighting in their free time, when they could enjoy 'the life we lived separately from the teachers'. War games dominate childhood memories of this time – as of many other times. In the extensive grounds owned by most prep schools, boys built forts, laid mantraps, constructed camps, dug tunnels, incarcerated prisoners and fought pitched battles. Paul Watkins recalled: 'We killed [Japanese and Germans] hand-to-hand by the river banks, the dead ones vanishing as they hit the ground and new ones jumping to life from the bushes.'[60] Sometimes teachers would intervene, as when they forbade water pistols at Summer Fields, confiscated rubber-band catapults at Scaitcliffe or broke up dangerous underground shelters in the 'giant sand-pit' at St Dunstan's. At West Downs, Jerry Cornes clamped down on roof climbing. He would not even visit Freddie Browning in hospital after he had seriously injured his leg while engaged in that forbidden activity: 'I was very much aware that the boys might think that Freddie was a wounded hero and this is one reason I have not visited him myself at any time.'[61] Masters at Forres had special reason to be cautious because of the danger of live underwater mines being washed up on Swanage beach; rumour had it that two pupils had been killed while throwing stones at one in the 1950s. And at Montefiore's fictional Coverdale (which may bear some resemblance to Ludgrove, the prep school attended by the author in the 1970s), the police are called in after knives appear in a terrifying battle between Stalin's troops and the 'White Guards'.

Some pupils found it difficult to join in rough games. The unhappy Andrew Motion spent 'muck-about' time in solitary activities, such as building Airfix models of 'aeroplanes like Spitfires, Mustangs, Messerschmitts, Dorniers, Lancasters, Wellingtons, Heinkels, Mosquitos, Hurricanes'. He liked to do this on a particular window ledge: 'If I sat there for long enough the radiator heat made the school disappear as it wobbled up through my brain and mixed with the glue-smell.' And he would think about his beloved mother who had bought the kits and posted them to him.[62] Others preferred to spend time in the library, often immersed in the popular *War Picture Library* series. Richard Aldwinckle became 'terribly interested' in Churchill's *The Second World War* and begged his father to bring him 'that little black book with German planes in' and some photographs of the war 'out of the photo tin'.[63] It was in the library that Robin Bell found 'a place of refuge' from the aspects of Falconbury he so hated: the constant scrutiny and supervision, the 'inexorable competition', the bullying and harassment and the headmaster's terrifying moods. He also discovered prisoner-of-war stories such as *Colditz* and *The Great Escape*, from which he learnt how to plot his own breakout from what he always calls 'the Institution'. After some months of secret planning, he got away, but was taken back to school by his parents. After walking out again, Robin was deemed 'an uncontrollable boy' and sent home for good.[64]

The Second World War also infiltrated pupils' lessons and supervised leisure time. In Mr Thursby-Pelham's History classes at St Aubyns the boys would wonder how many Germans this former Grenadier Guardsman had shot with the trigger finger now wielding the chalk. Visiting speakers liked to tell of war heroes and the weekly film show would often be something like *Cockleshell Heroes*, *The Dam Busters* or *The Guns of Navarone* – though Brambletye must have regretted its choice of *The Great Escape* when successive groups of boys emulated the prisoners by getting out of school and making triumphant journeys home. Of course, prep schools were not alone in being preoccupied by the war. In 1968 over 8 million television viewers watched *Dad's Army*, that 'mild-mannered comedy about the wartime Home Guard'. The series, says Dominic Sandbrook, captured the spirit of the age 'just as much as any of the Beatles' records or the trendy films of Swinging London'.[65] In fact, this warmly irreverent drama was not usually among the programmes which prep school pupils watched in their limited viewing time. More likely fare were state occasions such as Churchill's funeral or Trooping the Colour, international rugby matches, straightforward adventures like *Robin Hood* and *The Lone Ranger*, escapist dramas such as *Dr Who* or (that schoolmasters' favourite) *The World of Wooster*. The boys would relish these TV sessions as 'a bit of home' – and they were certainly more fun than the 'exceedingly boring lecture on birds' endured by Henry Lytton Cobbold in 1974. Rupert Morris went so far as to write: 'There is only one thing nice about this school and that is TV.'[66]

The closest contact that most boarding school pupils had with youth culture during term time came through music. Many took transistor radios or crystal sets to school, with or without leave. Increasingly, 'the nights were restive with the mosquito-buzz of furtive trannies'.[67] On them they might catch *Pick of the Pops*, with Alan Freeman playing hits like Helen Shapiro's 'Walking Back to Happiness', Billy Fury's 'Halfway to Paradise', Roy Orbison's 'Pretty Woman' or the Beatles' 'Please, Please Me'. Quite unusually, Nicholas Aldridge, as a young master at Summer Fields, managed a boys' pop group himself, with the active support of Pat Savage. Formed in 1963, 'The Scholars' went on to make a record in 1964, the school's centenary year. Meanwhile, the future pop star Mike Oldfield was a day boy at the 'prim and proper' St Edward's in Reading, whose headmaster reminds him of the cane-wielding teacher in Pink Floyd's album, *The Wall*. Mike sought 'an alternative life' by playing the Eko acoustic guitar he persuaded his dad to buy him and by listening to the new pirate stations, Radio Luxemburg and Radio Caroline.[68] Even the school chapel could be a source of popular music, at least if Rupert Everett was at the organ, on which he would play some quieter numbers while 'everyone shuffled up to receive the sacrament'. His favourite was 'Where is Love?' from Lionel Bart's *Oliver!*, an item which would not have been allowed by the chaplain at Summer Fields, who proudly boasted 'that he altered nothing in the Chapel during his seven years there'.

Rupert became extremely religious while he was at Farleigh House, a Roman Catholic establishment, and he would spend hours 'praying for a visitation from Our Lady'.[69] It was not unusual, Lambert found, for prep school children to 'respond warmly and positively', at their impressionable age, to the worship that was still compulsory during the 1960s. He quotes one eleven-year-old who wrote of being very moved by a sermon: 'Sister Mary's talk . . . taught me a great deal about my dealings with other people.'[70] But juvenile faith did not always last. Rupert Morris was inspired by some of the sermons in chapel and would go there on his own and pray to God – until he began to wonder whether there was anyone there. Anglo-Catholic notions 'infected' young Martin Rowson for a time after the death of his mother. He remembers buying some holy water when taken on a school visit to the Marian shrine at Walsingham and drinking it to see what happened:

> But nothing did, neither my mother coming back to life, nor me growing a thick prehensile tail or being able to fly or clamber up the wall like a gecko or my grandmother dropping dead or anything.

For him, the only long-lasting effect was that 'religion, by and large, always smells of mince'.[71]

Of course, Mike Oldfield, Rupert Everett and Martin Rowson may not have been typical little boys. A diary kept for Royston Lambert's inquiry recorded the more ordinary experiences of an older prep school pupil. Punctuated with exclamations like 'Phew!', 'Ugh!' and 'Crumpets!', it describes what Lambert calls 'a normal schoolday, packed full of work and play, all to a strict timetable'. In general, the example supports the sociologist's conclusion that most prep school pupils seemed 'happy, highly committed and fulfilled in the gregarious world of pre-adolescence'. But the boy's panic about getting back a 'crummy maths prep' and his relief that his practice scholarship papers are satisfactory suggest the anxiety many children felt about reaching academic standards that were frequently high enough to enable boys to coast through their first years at public school.[72]

In the senior forms at Maidwell, Andrew Motion certainly experienced pressure: 'It made me feel I was walking into a tunnel that was getting steadily narrower and darker and soon the ceiling would be pressing so hard on my head, I'd never be able to think straight.'[73] It was the same for Tony Mitton when his linguistic abilities got him promoted to a higher class, where he could not understand anything about the geometry and algebra he was expected to tackle: 'I remember the awful sick feeling in my stomach, the welling up of tears, the feeling of hopelessness and uselessness that resulted.'[74] 'Getting bad marks for bad work' ranked highest in Lambert's list of worries afflicting prep school children, above the fear of parents dying.[75] Perhaps this is not so extraordinary in the light of what happened to the 'unhappy and overweight' young Anthony Horowitz at Orley Farm. The headmaster made him stand up in assembly and announced to the whole school: 'This boy is so stupid he will not be coming to the Christmas games tomorrow.' To relieve his misery, Anthony began his writing career by making up 'tales of astounding revenge and retribution'.[76]

With a new 'bulge' going through the prep schools, competition for public school places was fierce and the Common Entrance exam became 'a stern test', according to the *St Dunstan's Magazine*. The editor and co-headmaster, Rupert Martin, warned boys that it was 'most perilous to delay their efforts until they actually reach the Fifth Form' and advised them to take the eleven-plus 'as a useful safeguard'.[77] Martin had helped to write *Foundations*, an IAPS report of 1959. It made the daring recommendations that less time should be devoted to Latin, that Science should be introduced, that 'cultural interests' should be promoted and that greater account should be taken of boys' differing needs. At the same time, it insisted in schoolmasterly fashion that 'a boy must work hard at a subject he does not like'. Neither this report nor a later one, *Prospect* in 1965, brought about a revolution in the prep school curriculum, harnessed as it was to public school demands.[78]

Yet some schools did try to enter the jet age. With the help of Shell and Esso, instruction kits on such topics as Pond Life and Astronomy and, if they were lucky, generous donations from wealthy fathers like the publisher, Robert Maxwell (whose four sons were at Summer Fields), most prep schools taught some Science. But few boys have any recollection of such lessons – even when, like Richard Aldwinckle, they still possess handwritten timetables showing that they took place twice a week. The only one of my interviewees to recall them clearly was motorsport expert Duncan Wiltshire, who reckons that he developed his bent for engineering at The Abbey. Some schools also pioneered language laboratories, taught conversational French, built pottery kilns, introduced the 'new maths' and experimented with creative English – often upsetting the old guard among parents and staff.

In addition, many prep schools offered wonderfully enriching extra-curricular opportunities. Echoing progressive educational ideas he had gained at Bryanston, John Briggs wrote in 1961 that every boy should find an interest 'in which he loses himself'; the King's College School magazine for that year carried lively reports from the Photography, Model Railway, Pet, Squash, Chess and Young Farmers' Clubs.[79] At DCPS, seven-year-old Ian Bostridge performed in one of his first concerts, singing an animal part in a performance of Britten's *Noye's Fludde.* Even something quite simple could nourish the imagination of a lonely little boy. Tom Ponsonby thinks that his devotion to French culture was partly inspired by the black-and-white tourist posters of cathedrals and châteaux with which the pipe-smoking old Mr Webber decorated his classroom. And when Tom sang with the school choir in St Margaret's, Rottingdean 'the seed of church music was planted'.[80]

What prompted many schools to keep up with the times was a fear voiced in the *St Dunstan's Magazine* of Summer 1964, soon after Harold Wilson had formed a Labour government:

> Private education may soon come under new political scrutiny ... We must continue to do everything we can to justify a way of life which has worked so long and so successfully.

This defensive position was understandable in the light of manifestoes such as Anthony Crosland's *The Future of Socialism*, which predicted 'the gradual closure ... of private preparatory schools, and the disappearance of one early and influential source of class insemination'.[81] Moreover, experts with no political axe to grind now questioned the value of these 'socially divisive' establishments and suggested that they should form close links with the state-maintained middle schools which served the same age group in some parts of the country.[82]

Pupils did not usually take much interest in these debates. If they read the newspapers in the school library they were more likely to follow wars, sporting fixtures or, in the case of Hugo Vickers at Scaitcliffe, the activities of the royal family. He has confessed to cutting out photographs of the Duke and Duchess of Windsor from the school's copy of *The Illustrated London News* and sticking them into scrapbooks that provided material for his later biographies.[83] Nevertheless, children absorbed the social and political attitudes of parents and teachers. In 1964 Richard Aldwinckle wrote home after a Current Affairs lesson: 'We talked about the election. Down with Labour.'[84] One twelve-year-old confirmed Crosland's view of prep schools with this diary entry:

> It is the sons of the important men really who come to a school like this and when your dumped into a third class school with all the village children it shows up a considerable amount because they all talk rotten, like 'urry up'. If you are talking sophisticatedly like we do here then I think they would poke fun at us.[85]

He was right about that. Dan Fairest remembers pitched battles with the VKs (Village Kids) who would invade his Derbyshire school 'looking for a fight'. Although sticks and stones were used, Dan describes the affrays as good-natured fun. But clearly this was not always the case. The two 'Bovvers' recruited by William Conroy in his role as Stalin were glad of the opportunity 'to punch up some snobs'. 'They were creatures from another world,' thought William, 'like Red Indians in a cowboy film. They wore earrings, army boots, T-shirts, blue jeans and denim jackets. Their denims were groovily faded.'[86] At a time when Mods and Rockers were clashing on the promenades of British seaside resorts, Denis Owen warned Mr Morris that Rupert's end-of-term escapades were 'the beginning of the road that leads to Clacton'.[87] Deploring the persistence of class antagonism, the Labour politician Shirley Williams wrote that 'the freedom to send one's children to an independent school is bought at too high a price for the rest of society.'[88]

In the event, fee-paying schools 'were let be', as the historian Peter Clarke says, although they perpetuated privilege more effectively than grammar schools, most of which were abolished to create the new comprehensive school system.[89] Even so, these were hard times for prep schools which were closing at the rate of about one hundred a year during the sixties. Cyril Annick in *The Honours Board* (who may well be based on the headmaster of Cumnor House, Hal Milner-Gullard, to whom Pamela Hansford Johnson dedicated the novel), found it difficult to 'believe in the permanency of the world that was his'.[90] In Seaford, writes Jeremy Lewis, 'blackboards and canes and rolls of honour were committed to the flames, and the games fields that had been so distinctive a feature of the town were covered with desirable residences suitable for retired tobacconists.'[91] This was caused not by any growth of Flower Power among the pupils or by schoolboy revolutions such as that portrayed in the film *If*, but by the combined pressures of compulsory inspection and higher rates of taxation. Many schools found it difficult to pay the Selective Employment Tax, which was imposed on service industries in 1966. Some passed on the 'iniquitous' SET to parents; Ashfold, for example, added £7 to its 'truly inclusive' fee of £165 a term.[92]

The situation did not get any easier under Edward Heath's government in the early 1970s, when the oil crisis and a series of strikes led to galloping inflation, power cuts and the three-day week. Pupils, like the homesick Tony Hanania (alias Toby Shadrach) from Beirut, heard their elders raging against 'the unions, the communists, against *fainéant workers*, against *poltroon management*, against the socialists who will abolish private schools if they are given half a chance'. Boys rejoiced when blackouts meant cancelled lessons and prep as well as exciting torch-games.[93] But even William Conroy was taken aback by his adored headmaster's outburst against his Stalinist escapades: 'This bloody country's in a terrible fix. The unions run the place and they're COMMIES. . . . There's not a parent who is not suffering: we've NEVER had fewer pupils here. Soon no one will be able to afford to come to Coverdale.'[94]

In fact, Montefiore's alma mater has survived – indeed, both Prince William and Prince Harry attended Ludgrove in the 1990s. And, as the next chapter will show, many of the other schools mentioned in this chapter have managed to adapt to changing times. One of the casualties was Stouts Hill, which closed down in 1979, ten years after the departure of Stephen Fry. This was nothing to do with the reputation of its former pupil who had repeatedly stolen money from the boys' changing rooms to buy the sweets with which he was obsessed, before leaving early 'without ever having been made a prefect, selected for a single athletic team, or achieving any distinction whatsoever save a record number of canings and a handful of academic prizes'. As Fry explains: 'The fees were high, the uniform remained fabulously classy and meanwhile the parents became less interested in ponies and Greek and more interested in Common Entrance results and money.'[95] The fat pony and the clever mynah bird, as well as the old Majors and Commanders, had to go.

9

'The Harry Potter Effect'
Modern Prep Schools

At a recent family lunch party I expressed the view, suggested by historians, that prep schools had become 'much more agreeable places' by the 1980s.[1] But guests of the thirty-something age group were sceptical. Drawing on their experiences at Sunningdale, Abberley Hall and Buckland House, three cousins talked of enduring terrible homesickness, of writing the weekly letter to parents without being able to talk by telephone, of being addressed by their surnames, of suffering under bullies and beastly matrons, of being forced to take punitive cross-country runs and of getting the cane or the size-14 slipper for talking after lights-out. In subsequent interviews, two of the young men confirmed these initial reactions, adding stories about particular characters: the 'blind' headmaster who missed his true target and caned boys on their legs and the unpleasant bully rumoured to have had an affair with a young female teacher. One declined to talk any further. These schools hardly seemed very progressive, even though the boys had studied modern subjects like Science and Computer Technology. In truth, the 1980s did not witness radical transformation of prep schools, although some headmasters ran them more benevolently than others – as had always been the case.

Some change had certainly begun, for schools were anxious to avoid the fate of Stouts Hill. It usually took the form of new amenities such as the indoor swimming pool at Summer Fields or the Music School at DCPS, both of which would have been the envy of any primary school in the kingdom. Edmund Marler remembers the installation of an improved system for draining the Temple Grove sports field where he had the 'great thrill' of playing in all the first teams. A purpose-built gym was also opened during his time at the school (1977–82). Nevertheless age-old pastimes continued and these were just as important to Edmund: singing in the chapel choir, taking part in Gilbert and Sullivan productions, hut building among the bamboos and the rhododendrons, tree climbing in the woods, dam making in the stream, canoeing on the lake, playing croquet on the lawn and looking after his pet gerbils in the basement. All this helped to ease three-month separations from his parents who were on British Council postings overseas. Compulsory letters were still the main form of communication, though for boys with parents nearer at hand a pay phone was now available. Temple Grove sounds less repressive than it had been in the days of Ottiwell Waterfield or Meston Batchelor and Edmund says that he was happy there, apart from home-sickness in his earlier terms. He does, however, describe both the headmasters of his time as 'distant authority figures' who spoke at assemblies and administered discipline. Punishments consisted of detentions, lines and a slipper used 'only for the worst misdemeanours'. Among those were the traditional dormitory larks after bedtime ('as early as 7pm!'), for which Edmund himself was duly beaten. No weekly boarders and no girls, apart from one daughter of each headmaster and of the head matron, had yet entered the precincts of this ancient school.[2]

At Aldro, a new headmaster, Ian Argyle, began to transform the rather grubby conditions which Robin Oakley had experienced in post-war years. But what mattered to Rupert Pick when he started there in 1981 was that it was 'a caring school'. He found it a relief to move from Milbourne Lodge, where the academic pressure seems to have given him constant migraines. And he was ready, at the age of ten, to embrace 'the spirit of boarding' with lots of surrogate brothers and plenty of sport. Argyle and his wife created a family atmosphere and pretty young matrons looked after boys who were homesick – as Rupert quite often was. Luckily, his parents lived only twenty minutes away so that they could come regularly to matches, and Rupert went home for a good Sunday lunch about every other week. In addition, his mother would sometimes meet him for a surreptitious chat by the playing fields. As a good games player Rupert was not likely to be bullied, but he does not think that even 'geeky boys' were victimized at Aldro. He is pretty sure that boys could ask to use telephones if they needed to and that Walkmans were allowed. Thus the regime Rupert remembers sounds benign, even though there had been no radical changes.[3]

'Benign' is not a word which could be used of DCPS in the 1980s. Mark Randall,* a pupil of that decade describes the headmaster as a 'crass authoritarian', the staffroom as 'full of furious men', and the general atmosphere as 'arctic'. Despite having abandoned corporal punishment in the 1960s, Hugh Woodcock's regime in its later years conveyed a 'threat of violence' through the verbal rage of teachers and occasional assaults – on one occasion a master literally kicked a boy out of his classroom. Nor was the aggression directed only at pupils of the school. When a black boy from a neighbouring comprehensive came into the drive to retrieve a football the headmaster shouted at him, in front of numerous witnesses: 'Bloody monkey'. Production line methods of instruction, plenty of rote learning and a concentration of resources on the favoured scholarship classes ensured impressive examination results. But, in Mark's case, there was a price to pay. Despite the fact that there were a few masters who made their subjects enjoyable, he was left with an abiding sense that all teachers were his enemies.[4] Mark might well not have felt this if he had been at the school after 1991 under Woodcock's successor, George Marsh, who 'came from a different generation'. Marsh brought with him a 'strategy for change'. As will appear later, he not only kept abreast of developments in prep schools as a whole but forged 'closer links with the educational world outside the independent sector'.[5]

Both Aldro and DCPS have remained all-boys schools. But even by the eighties, some prep schools had found it economically advantageous to admit girls. These numbered over 7,000 by 1981, threatening to realize nigel molesworth's nightmare of classrooms full of soppy 'GURLS looking intent, eager, keen ect' and no one to 'pla tag with me in the break'.[6] Actually, historians see this change as helping to make prep schools more relaxed, as well as less tough and noisy. Duncan Wiltshire would agree. When he went back to visit a friend's sister at The Abbey, which took in girls soon after he left, he was amazed by the transformation in the headmaster, Mr Dewar. He could not believe that this man with 'girls climbing all over him' was the same headmaster from whom he had cowered.[7] Norman Hale, another headmaster who was persuaded to admit girls in the late seventies, 'expected his new entrants to take part in all the boys' activities, including rugby'. But he did organize a special female competition 'for the best chocolate log made at Christmas time'.[8] At Abberley Hall, the advent of co-education brought a bonus to boys in the form of girlish sports such as horse riding, which they could enjoy too. The co-educational trend has accelerated over the last three decades so that, of the schools mentioned in this book, only sixteen still cater exclusively for boys.

Even some historic choir schools lost their 'monastic atmosphere'. One of the first to change was Chichester's Prebendal School, which has been attached to the cathedral since Tudor times. In 1972 its governors agreed that up to a third of the pupils could be girls, although the dean observed that this might be the thin end of the wedge: 'Girls will only enter the Cathedral choir over my dead body.' His fears have not materialized, but for Angharad Gruffydd Jones, a weekly boarder from 1984, the Prebendal School helped to inspire a singing career. She describes it as a wonderfully happy school, where she benefited from a high standard of musical as well as academic education. Other ancient choir schools have followed Chichester's example, finding that girls not only boost numbers but also bring enrichment with 'their industry and their talent'.[9]

Another departure from tradition was the movement away from boarding. Traditionalists may dismiss the doubts of psychologists about the wisdom of sending children away from home, but over the years parents' attitudes have been profoundly affected by the views of Dr Spock and like-minded writers. Dr John Bowlby, for example, concluded after years of studying children that 'a secure base and a strong family' sustain rather than sap self-reliance.[10] Sociologists such as Royston Lambert agree that a boarding school cannot provide 'the unconditional love that a child expects to receive in his family'.[11] To the surprise of devotees of boarding such as Philip Masters, most parents really do believe 'that the contribution they can themselves make to their boys' development balances the advantages of boarding school life'.[12] Indeed, some school prospectuses echo the new ideas. Claremont (which took over Falconbury in 1968) 'places a very high value on family life', offering neither boarding nor Saturday school. St John's College School, Cambridge emphasizes that its boarding house 'should act as an extension of the child's family', allowing 'leave outs' every weekend and parental visits during the week. By 1990 only a quarter of prep school pupils were full boarders; the rest either attended daily or went home at weekends.

Some compromises occurred. Pupils at Abberley Hall were supposed to stay in school all the time except when there was a special exeat. But Max Hasler, a pupil there in the 1990s, was not particularly happy at his father's old school. In his first two years, this quiet, studious boy was homesick, finding himself 'alone quite a lot' and the target of bullies. Aware of all this and living just over an hour's drive from the school, his parents took Max home most weekends despite the school's disapproval and in time he found his niche. Relegated to the 'X-league' as far as sport was concerned, Max was gratified to find when taking part in a variety performance in his second year that he could make people laugh. This gave him the confidence to become involved in more drama and other school activities. Most important, he made some friends and discovered that it was 'okay' to enjoy academic work and to spend time reading in the library, which was well stocked and furnished with comfy beanbags. Proximity had been Max's salvation and by the time he went on to Winchester he could cope with boarding.[13] During the last twenty years increasing numbers of parents have chosen schools relatively close to their homes, with the result that some of the more remote establishments have found it difficult to attract pupils. Thus Temple Grove, beautifully situated in Ashdown Forest, had to close a few years ago, despite having admitted girls and day pupils.

New laws, themselves based on more liberal ideas of child care, brought about other important changes to all prep schools. In 1985 corporal punishment became illegal in state schools and many independent schools abolished it of their own accord. In 1994 the *Independent on Sunday* could find only four schools in which children were still being hit, though the ban was not extended to all schools until 1998.[14] The cane (and the prospect of it) could no longer strike terror into the hearts of pupils at school – but British children may still be smacked at home. At first, some masters found it hard to abandon old habits and they continued to strike, shake or throw things at boys in the privacy of their classrooms. In time, they devised new punishments, such as the time-wasting exercise known as 'Sergeants' remembered by Max Hasler. Wrongdoers would have to change into their boiler suits or games kit, present themselves and then change back into school uniform. A similar penalty existed when Sam Mahony arrived at Cothill House in 1998; alternatively, miscreants had to 'face the wall' near the staffroom, where passing teachers would 'invariably tut at you'. Sam thinks this practice was phased out towards the end of his school career, but Ofsted inspectors found it in use in 2005 and recommended a more constructive alternative. Into that category would presumably come the essays about their wrongdoings that Sam and other sinners had to write in their later years.[15]

In 1989 the Children Act placed a legal duty on independent boarding schools to 'safeguard and promote' pupils' welfare. This is defined not only by their perceived 'physical, emotional and educational needs' but also by their own 'wishes and feelings', in accordance with the UN Convention on the Rights of the Child of the same year, which 'laid stress on a child's right to participate in decisions affecting her or him'.[16] So, when inspectors visit a boarding school nowadays, they interview children and give them confidential questionnaires to complete. Some establishments were initially suspicious of the new system, which was indeed often presented in modish bureaucratic jargon. Neil Smith, who ran

Brightlands, the boarding house at DCPS, felt that the Act was 'inclined to show boarding school life in a poor light' and that the Southwark inspectors treated the school as though it were a children's home. But in time most schools responded by providing more pastoral care, thus enabling pupils to talk privately about their problems – which may themselves have been created by boarding. Max Hasler noticed the difference. When he went to his first headmaster, Michael Haggard, about being bullied 'he didn't do anything'. His replacement, John Walker, tried much harder: 'He helped me to feel better.'[17] There were now also more opportunities for pupils to express their views. At DCPS, George Marsh and a female deputy head appointed in 1997 introduced a Nurturing Programme with a regular Circle Time, a discussion period in which boys had 'a voice'.[18]

Another radical development was Marsh's insistence that boys should be addressed by their first names in class, a decree which some staff found very hard to obey. This usage was slow to catch on in other boys' schools where names and nicknames have always been a matter of tradition. At Abberley Hall, where a few masters were customarily known by their first names, Max Hasler found much variation in the forms of address used during the 1990s.[19] At Cothill House, practice changed over time. When Sam Mahony joined the school 'surnames were invariably used' in the classroom, but by the time he left in 2004 first names were in general use, reflecting a closer rapport between teachers and pupils.[20] In co-educational schools, which often contained siblings, it was obviously inappropriate for boys to be addressed in a different way from girls. Gone were the days when a boy would be ridiculed if he ever mentioned his sister's first name. But children themselves often stuck to the old formalities. At Caldicott, the boarders addressed each other by their surnames while day boys used Christian names. In similar vein, the pupils of St Aubyns, a third of whom are female, recently voted to keep their soldierly house names: Musketeers, Crusaders, Templars and Vikings. Nor do they appear to object to the use of the old motto: 'In All Things be Men', which was hardly fitting for small boys, let alone little girls.

Technology, too, has affected most school regimes. In the age of laptops and mobile telephones there is no point in staff trying to censor pupils' letters – even if they can get them to put pen to paper. While many boarding schools are holding out against the mobile phone, they now usually make it possible for pupils to have ready contact with their families through unchecked email and letters as well as private telephone conversations. Ofsted reports set much store by such free communication. Yet, while schools have become more electronically connected to the outside world, their premises have become sealed off because of current fears for the health and safety of pupils. They are locked in with the latest security equipment, and outsiders find it increasingly difficult to gain access unless their criminal record has been checked. Gone is the freedom children once had to roam the countryside, take long bicycle trips and rescue strange gentlemen from drowning.

Even within schools' spacious grounds, restrictions have been applied, much to the frustration of pupils who see them as unnecessary curbs on their freedom. When John Walker, a 'modern, efficient administrator', took over Abberley Hall in 1996, he soon put a stop to the boys' age-old custom of building 'living-spaces' in the school's 99 acres. The older boys had even been given licence to use penknives and light fires. Max Hasler shared the 'bitter resentment' caused by Walker's ban, even though one of his friends had broken his wrists while engaged in unsupervised recreation. Similar regrets were felt at St Aubyns a few years ago, when children were forbidden to play on a piece of rough ground adjoining a public footpath. Back in the sixties, Tom Ponsonby had shown no interest in the smutty magazines which were sometimes thrown into this area, though other boys had devoured them with some glee. But the two pupils who showed me round this school in 2009 explained that after syringes and other nasty rubbish had been found, pupils were no longer allowed to build their dens and tree houses there. Sometimes these wild areas were destroyed altogether under a new regime. Thus the fictional Cyril Annick laments 'the destruction of those secret places so necessary to human life' when his successor at Downs Park hacks down the Thicket so that everything will be 'nice and open'.[21] In some schools unregulated activities have survived, risky though they can be. Summer Fields has kept up its popular annual traditions, the Hay Feast and the 'Bombers and Fighters' game, despite vagaries of the weather and occasional injuries. Two pupils of Old Buckenham Hall told me that they are allowed to play and make 'bases' in the 'big woods', as long as they are with a friend.[22] In 2004 the school's Ofsted inspectors noted that it could be dangerous for boarders to have the run of the estate but did not clamp down on this freedom. Nor did they disapprove of boys at Lockers Park making camps in the grounds and riding their bikes and skateboards.[23]

All these changes of the last thirty years have meant that the traditional prep school characteristics of rustication and separation have become less highly prized. But preparation remains a prime function. It is often said that pupils who are going on to board at public schools need some experience of being away from home, albeit in more comfortable surroundings than were ever offered in the past. Thus Old Buckenham Hall does not permit weekly boarding in pupils' last two years. Ten-year-old Rupert and Charlotte George are happy with this because full-time boarding 'prepares you for public school' – although they (and their parents) will miss their relaxed weekends at home. The twins already do practice Common Entrance papers, know which schools they want to sit for and what percentage they must gain.[24] The exam has changed in recent years, with more emphasis on English and Science and less on Latin, which is no longer a compulsory component. But Common Entrance is still 'a big thing', dominating the horizons of contemporary prep schools and looming large in the recollection of ex-pupils to whom academic work did not come easily or whose teachers prepared them for the wrong History syllabus.[25] Many parents provide extra coaching to ensure that their offspring gain entrance to the public school that they – or their teachers – have chosen. 'Aggressive streaming' is still the norm in prep schools today.[26]

The prep school system, by adapting to parental, juvenile and statutory demands, weathered the various storms of the late twentieth century, though some establishments only avoided closure by becoming part of a chain. Thus Milbourne Lodge was bought by Cognita, a consortium chaired by Chris Woodhead, former Chief Inspector of Schools and just the sort of functionary whom Norman Hale would have debarred in the old days. In the new millennium, prep and pre-prep numbers increased by 10 per cent and competition for places was fierce. The head teacher of a London school went so far as to advise mothers expecting to have babies by Caesarean section to opt for a date in the first week of the month, since 'date of birth is the deciding factor in getting a place'.[27] The greatest demand was for day places. But boarding held its own, often on a flexible basis to fit in with the busy schedules of two working parents. In 2007 a *Times* article described boarding schools as 'stand-in parents', helping out with 'sleepovers' when mounting pressures of work take parents away from home or prevent them from devoting time to their children in the evenings. With 'everything on offer – from tree-climbing to stabling your own pony, golf to sailing to film-making', schools offer plenty of diversion. A recent survey even showed a small increase in boarding, especially among boys. This was partly due to an influx of overseas pupils, but it is also attributable to 'the Harry Potter effect'.[28] Boarding has acquired a certain cachet among the young as a result of the popularity of boy heroes created by children's writers like Michael Morpurgo, Anthony Horowitz and J. K. Rowling, whose thrilling exploits take place within school walls.

All three of these writers add the tasty ingredient of magic to a traditional school-story brew, containing ingredients which have appealed to generations of children: house rivalries, exciting matches, esoteric slang and illicit adventures. While these old-fashioned preoccupations doubtless play more of a part in pupils' real lives than do witchcraft and wizardry, the novels hardly provide a reliable guide to what goes on in schools today. Nevertheless, the popularity of this fashionable fiction reveals something of the tastes, emotions, worries and fantasies of its readers – at prep school and elsewhere.

One of the favourites is Michael Morpurgo's *The War of Jenkins' Ear* (1993). 'Everyone was reading it' during Max Hasler's time at Abberley House and it is now used as a class book in some prep schools. Even when first published, however, the novel must have seemed something of a historical document, since it was based partly on Morpurgo's time at The Abbey, East Grinstead, in the 1950s. His hero, Toby Jenkins, 'was not Toby any more' at Redlands: 'He was Jenkins now, or 'Jinks'.' Letters to his parents have to pass inspection and he edits them 'so that they would think he was happy and always doing well'. His Sunday afternoons are spent 'messing around in the park – climbing trees, playing conkers, cow-pat fights, building camps'. If he arouses the anger of Mr Stagg, known as Rudolph, he has to bend over his leather chair in the study to be caned.

The supernatural element comes in the shape of Toby's friend Simon Christopher, a mysterious new boy who claims to be the Son of God. Christopher (who is called that throughout the book) seems to have the power to heal not only sheath-knife injuries but also a feud with 'a pack of roughs' over fishing rights – the war of the book's title.[29] But this intriguing plot is not the only means by which this book breaks new ground. Morpurgo deals with feelings deeper than the triumphs and frustrations of Jennings and Darbishire. Modern readers are invited to empathize with Toby, who (like his creator) is no good at any school activities except singing in the choir and rugby, who relishes an unexpected night at home when he attends his granny's funeral, who finds joy in his new friendship, who shyly develops a relationship with the cook's pretty daughter and who wets himself when beaten by Rudolph. The book, like Morpurgo's *The Butterfly Lion* and *Alone on a Wide, Wide Sea*, conveys more about the feelings of all children separated from their parents than about modern prep schools. But it provides an important clue to the emotional sophistication of young readers.

Like Morpurgo, Anthony Horowitz has used his own childhood as rich source material for his books. 'What happens,' he asks his readers in a preface, 'when, aged eight, you get sent to the grimmest, most gruesome boarding school in England? You end up writing *Groosham Grange*.' In fact, David Eliot is twelve when he is sent to this sinister establishment, 'a crazy mixture of battlements, barred windows, soaring towers, slanting grey slate roofs, grinning gargoyles and ugly brick chimneys'. It is situated on an almost inaccessible island off the coast of Norfolk. And, as David exclaims in his diary, it bears little resemblance to his former school (or to Orley Farm in the 1960s): '*Good* Latin teachers? A school with no punishments? Have I gone mad?' It is different also in the absence of bullies and the presence of girls. The only point of similarity is the food, so dire that David thinks he is 'going to starve to death'. Despite this typical schoolboy complaint, he is soon 'beginning to enjoy life on the island'. He does well in class, gets a place in the first football team and forms a close friendship with another new arrival called Jill – the name, incidentally, of Horowitz's wife. But David is frightened by a weird change taking place in himself and thinks that the school wants to turn him into 'some sort of zombie'. It turns out that Groosham Grange is a school for witches and that David has been selected for training in magical skills because he is the seventh son of a seventh son. In the end, he submits to Mr Kilgraw's 'rather agreeable' evil and begins his 'education in earnest', returning to Groosham Grange for further adventures in search of the Unholy Grail.[30]

Horowitz was also inspired by James Bond, who served as his escape route from a childhood rendered 'desperately unhappy' both by school and by his 'arid and distant' parents and 'completely horrible' grandmother. From the films he adored as a child Horowitz has evolved the boy detective Alex Rider, whom critics have rightly called 'James Bond in miniature'. Alex attends a West London comprehensive but is whisked away to engage in assignments for MI6. But even as they follow these imaginative adventures, readers are invited to share their author's more mundane preoccupations. The disturbed offspring of wealthy parents at the Swiss boarding school that Alex has to investigate in *Point Blanc* come from backgrounds similar to that of Horowitz. Alex soon finds, like David Eliot at Groosham Grange, that the school and the people in it are 'slipping under his skin, working their way into his mind'. The fantastic explanation, in this case, is that the pupils are all clones of the headmaster, Dr Grief, surgically transformed to resemble the original boys whom they have replaced. Bond-like, Alex manages to extricate himself from the situation, kill Dr Grief in all his guises and free the genuine pupils from their cells. This is all exciting stuff and it may be no accident that two of the pupils bear the names of Horowitz's sons. But the story is a heartfelt and highly charged parable. When Alex asks why parents have not noticed any changes in their offspring, Dr Grief replies:

> You are talking about busy, hard-working parents with little or no time for their children in the first place. And you forget that the very reason why these people sent their sons here was that they *wanted* them to change. . . . They would actually be disappointed if those children came back the same.

Grief likens these parents to all those who send sons to boarding school in the hope that they will become 'better, more clever, more confident'. Thus Horowitz raises grave doubts in his readers' minds about an educational system he rejected for his own sons, who attended day schools and had a 'normal childhood'.[31]

Unlike these writers, J. K. Rowling had no psychological ghosts to lay, for she attended ordinary state primary and secondary schools. She told the *Oprah Magazine* that Harry Potter had to be at a boarding school simply 'for reasons of plot': 'How would it be interesting if the characters couldn't get up at night and wander around?'[32] In Hogwarts she has created a self-contained environment set apart from tiresome Muggles and bound by long-established conventions. The uniform can be bought in London 'if yeh know where to go', Hagrid, the gamekeeper, assures Harry. The arrogant new boy, Draco Malfoy, boasts that all his family have been in Slytherin House – 'Imagine being in Hufflepuff.' When Harry on his Nimbus Two Thousand broomstick catches the Snitch in a crucial inter-house Quidditch match, he feels that he has 'really done something to be proud of'.

But Hogwarts appeals to its many fans all over the world because of its attractive modern features. The uniforms are glamorous. The benign headmaster administers none of the 'old punishments' such as hanging by the wrists from the ceiling for a few days. The girls are plucky, if somewhat too clever, and the food is scrumptious. Harry had never seen so many things he liked to eat as were spread on the table at the start-of-term banquet: 'roast beef, roast chicken, pork chops and lamb chops, sausages, bacon and steak, boiled potatoes, roast potatoes, chips, Yorkshire pudding, peas, carrots, gravy, ketchup and, for some strange reason, mint humbugs'. Of course, a fictional school is not required to offer too many unpopular vegetables or to work within tight budgets – any more than its pupils have to abide by tiresome health and safety regulations in their quest for the philosopher's stone.[33] Thus Rowling's fantasy world satisfies modern children's dreams of escape from an increasingly regulated existence. What eleven-year-old would not want to be sent from Privet Drive (or indeed from an ordinary prep school) to an establishment like Hogwarts?

If fiction fails to tell the whole story about conditions in reformed prep schools, there is plenty of alternative evidence, even though people under the age of thirty have rarely written their memoirs. When they can be tracked down at their public schools and universities or distracted briefly from busy working lives, they are just as willing to talk about their prep school days as older alumni. In addition, the visits of school inspectors can yield useful information. Boarding schools are subject to rigorous and regular scrutiny, particularly with regard to the social care they provide. As well as looking at the school's facilities and questioning pupils, inspectors insist on seeing a great many policy documents and records. All this can sometimes prove a stumbling block, as it did for Sunningdale, which has been owned and run by the Dawson family for at least four decades. When it was inspected in 2008, the school was unable to produce employment histories for all its staff, some of whom had been allowed to start work before the Criminal Records Bureau had subjected them to its statutory investigations. Nor had the Bureau made the necessary checks on the taxi drivers used to transport its pupils. So, although most of the boarders said that they felt safe and well tended, the inspectors judged that the school's social care was 'inadequate'. While the required paperwork may seem absurdly cumbersome and the inspectors little better than jobsworths, their scrutiny has helped to shed the light of day on institutions which once liked to set themselves apart from the world.

Hector Matthews experienced an innovative regime when he attended DCPS in the 1990s under George Marsh and the new head of boarding, 'Bunky' Symmes. In the school as a whole Hector did not see much of the anger described by Dulwich pupils of the eighties. Marsh was 'a reasonable guy', and there was only one master who 'didn't know when to stop'. All the teachers had by this time got used to calling boys by their first names. The worst punishment Hector remembers is the equivalent of the 'naughty step' favoured by many modern parents; it was a 'bit of a disgrace' to be seen sitting on the 'naughty chair' outside the headmaster's office. Sport was still hugely important. 'The social hierarchy was based on it', as it had been in Tom Brown's day, and Hector suspects that inept games-players may not have enjoyed the school as much as he did. While he does not consider that there was much bullying, he wonders now about the pain that certain nicknames may have caused; a boy who already had to shave was known as 'Puberty' and another who had been given an unfashionable haircut was called 'Pud'.

Hector speaks very highly of boarding life under Symmes, an American who, according to his predecessor Neil Smith, 'had his own ideas about how a boarding house should be run'. Family accommodation replaced the bachelor quarters Smith had inhabited and Symmes and his wife became known as house parents, 'reflecting the general emphasis towards pastoral care'. For Hector, whose father had left home, this was an important factor; the house had a 'warm and comfortable' atmosphere and there was always someone to talk to if he had problems. He also appreciated the way Symmes allowed boys to play in the grounds during the evenings, under supervision so inconspicuous that they were not really aware of it. Symmes even supported their more risky activities, reaching an agreement that they could use skateboards and rollerblades as long as they wore helmets.[34] Like the other thirty or so Dulwich boarders, Hector went home every weekend.

Children with much less parental contact could also fare well under new management, as did Jonathan (Johnny) Wall, whose parents put him into full-time boarding at Caldicott in 1996 while they worked in Zimbabwe. Although it was still a single-sex establishment with compulsory full boarding in the last two years, the school had obviously changed since the days of Peter Wright's long headship (1968–1993). One remaining legacy was that the rugby cult he had always promoted was still very strong. Johnny had to play this or another game at least four times a week, even though, as he cheerfully admitted, he was 'rubbish'. It is only on looking back that he sees this as 'a waste of so much time'. He preferred playing chess or hide-and-seek in Burnham Beeches – or, indeed, getting on with his work.

Johnny's strengths were academic and he loved being in the scholarship class, ending up in the top twenty on the Eton list for his year. But he remembers no pressure being put on him: 'Little boys like showing off.' Nor was there any disgrace attached to those in the bottom stream. He thinks he would have been aware of any bullying or other forms of abuse, for there were 'no secrets' among boarders. The worst punishment he remembers was being told off by a stern housemistress and having 'to stand outside the dorm'. Gaining points for the house gave most boys sufficient incentive to behave well. Johnny's strong memory is of being 'wonderfully happy' at Caldicott, where he was 'just too busy to be homesick'. It helped that he could communicate with his parents by email (only to repeat the same news in the compulsory Sunday letter) and that he saw them every four or five weeks when they visited at half-term or he and his brother flew to Zimbabwe for glorious holidays.[35]

Paradoxically, Johnny's schoolfellow, David Nicholson-Thomas, did find boarding stressful even though his parents lived next door to Caldicott. In line with the school's policy, David boarded for his last two years and he never lost the feeling of being 'quite separated' from his home 'just over the fence'. He admits that the experience helped to prepare him for Eton where, like Johnny, he became an Oppidan Scholar. He enjoyed chess, singing in the choir and scoring in cricket; he kept up easily with work in the scholarship stream; and it mattered little that he was not cut out to be a sportsman. But, unlike Johnny, he could not really say that he was happy at Caldicott and he does consider that there was bullying. He himself was a victim in the sense of being deliberately excluded, a persecution not perhaps very obvious to teachers or to other pupils.

Neither of these Caldicott boys much enjoyed mealtimes, for there was never a choice of menu and they had to finish up what was on their plates. Two years after Johnny and David left in 2002, Ofsted inspectors made the same criticism, as only vegetarians or boys with special dietary requirements were allowed to take the alternative dish on offer. That report also put David's difficulties in context by recording that only 41 per cent of the boys said that they had never, or hardly ever, been bullied. Another concern which the inspectors noted was the pupils' lack of privacy, especially in the communal showers, rather echoing Johnny's observation that there were no secrets among the boarders. On the other hand, the report praised the school's exceptional range of activities, from which both these former pupils benefited. By the time of the next report in 2008, most of the earlier defects had been remedied and the school was now praised for its strong anti-bullying policies.[36]

There is a similar consistency between Sam Mahony's memories of Cothill House, a boys' full boarding school in Oxfordshire, and the comments of inspectors a year after he left. Sam admits that he himself was 'a fussy eater' who survived on toast and the tuck shop, but he knew that the school food was good enough to have won awards. And he would probably not be surprised to hear that most boarders in 2005 expressed great satisfaction with the meals, especially with the home-made cakes and puddings. Sam told me that 'bullying was always punished with the greatest rigour if it was detected', as Ofsted confirmed. Yet he also said that when he first arrived there was 'a pitched battle every night' between his year and the year above, and that older pupils employed 'any means' to get the respect due to them from the younger boys. He does not count any of this as bullying but 'more as the natural way that things occurred' – just as they always have done in large boys' boarding schools. But perhaps this is what about half of the juniors meant when they informed the inspectors that they were bullied a bit. Teachers cannot be on the spot all the time.

There can be no doubt about the marvellous opportunities that Cothill provided 'to do other things outside of academia'. The nine-hole golf course was very popular and Ofsted noted a surprisingly egalitarian attitude towards sporting performance, with every boy having a turn at representing the school in a football team. Sam's fondest memories are of his very good guitar teacher, of three foreign trips with the choir and of a term spent in the school's French château. He concludes that Cothill, 'though not without its peculiarities, was a very enjoyable place', and he does not think that 'anybody who went there would say any different'. Presumably, the boy who told the inspectors that boarding at Cothill was like a 'massive sleepover but with rules' was of the same mind. Such a school is a world in itself and, although parents are encouraged to visit, boys do not necessarily want to break off from their absorbing activities. As Sam remarked, 'I think most boys had better things to do on their Sundays off than spend them with their parents.'[37]

Victoria Barron implied much the same about weekends at Beeston Hall, a mixed full boarding school on the Norfolk coast. They were 'the best bit of boarding', with so many activities that it was 'more like a holiday camp'. She did miss home when she first arrived at the age of eight, but 'there were so many people to cheer you up' and after a bit 'you were too busy' to be miserable. It also helped that Victoria's parents travelled from Suffolk every week to watch matches or concerts and that she spoke to them every few days on the payphone – no mobiles were allowed. She said that she was very happy at Beeston Hall and her mother confirmed that this was true of her other three children, including her oldest daughter who went there at a difficult time some years after the death of her father. Mrs Barron's opinion that 'the pastoral care was marvellous' is echoed not only by Victoria, who never lacked for 'lovely matrons' and 'parental staff', but also by Ofsted who reported during her time there (2002–06). The inspectors commended the school's sensitive policies on homesickness, enuresis and privacy. They approved of its hot chocolate sessions, in which children and staff could chat. And they liked such homely customs as allowing a birthday child to choose the menus for the day. As for Victoria, she valued being allowed, when she was older, to go to the beach and even into Sheringham with her friends, despite the potential risks noted by the inspectors. She considered a mixture of boys and girls (which Beeston Hall has had since the 1970s) very much healthier than sexual segregation. Perhaps this was what the Ofsted inspectors meant when they remarked on the spontaneous attitude of care and consideration in the school.[38]

Equal enthusiasm for co-education was expressed by Jamie Gardiner, who left St John's College School in 2008. He thought that the presence of girls made boys work harder and become more mature. The school's impressive record of scholarships to public schools bears out the former judgement and his own quietly confident demeanour is testimony to the latter. Jamie did not board but he told me that it became increasingly fashionable to do so, even among children living in Cambridge. He attributed this to its being fun and to the perceived need to prepare for public school. Boarding became slightly less attractive, he reports, after the retirement of a popular housemaster. Apart from this, the boarders' only complaint was about their suppers, said to be so dire that they lived off tuck. Jamie himself was 'brilliantly happy' at St John's, where he appreciated particularly the ambitious drama productions (as many as six or seven a year) put on by Mr Clarke, 'a great character'. Jamie was not aware of any bullying and thought there was never much need for discipline. These comments are astonishingly close to those of the Ofsted inspectors who visited the school in Jamie's last year. Like him they identified the food and some recent changes in the boarding routines as the causes of some resentment. In nearly every other respect they found the school to be outstanding, with warm relationships between staff and children, minimal use of formal discipline and a busy schedule for everyone, especially the choristers.[39]

Another school where boys and girls 'all mix together' is Old Buckenham Hall, according to the testimony of the George twins, who are still pupils there. As in other boarding schools, boys form a substantial majority, for they are more likely to be sent away from home and to start at an early age. Rupert George, for instance, was sent to board at OBH two years before his sister Charlotte. A few old distinctions and rivalries linger in a world which used to be a male preserve. At OBH it is still the custom for boys to address each other by their surnames while girls use first names. And in 2006 the boys complained to the inspectors that the girls were getting preferential treatment, with better showers and bedside lights. This unintentional discrimination is being corrected and it is clear that in general a family atmosphere prevails. The first thing many children do when lessons are over is to look after their pets in a shed known as The Ark; they can chat to their tutors about how the day has gone; and parents are welcome to come and watch matches on Wednesday afternoons. The twins do not wish to change anything except, as usual, the food. They do not even mind the punitive use of early-morning runs, since both of them happen to be keen runners.[40]

Few schools can have been transformed as radically in the last thirty years as Orley Farm. Inhabiting the very house from which Anthony Trollope used to run daily to join the more gentlemanly boarders at Harrow, it always had close links with its neighbouring public school. Yet, while Harrow has remained an all-boys full boarding school, Orley Farm abandoned all boarding in 1984 and admitted girls (up to the age of eleven) in 1994. The last three decades have also witnessed the building of the sports hall complex and a 'state-of-the-art' music school, proudly listed on the school's website. And the 'horrendously unpleasant' regime that Anthony Horowitz experienced in the early 1960s has been transformed into the enlightened and stimulating set-up described by Nell and Archie McCann, who both started in Orley Farm's pre-prep department at the age of four. They tell of stickers to reward good work and behaviour rather than a stick to punish misdemeanours and of special lessons with an 'extra-kind' teacher rather than ridicule for pupils finding it hard to keep up. Nell reports that she has never been teased for being small for her age. Archie speaks approvingly of the 'buddy bus stop': children stand there if they have been left out of playground activities so that 'someone will come over and talk or invite you to join in a game'. It seems that trust has replaced terror and communication is now more common then confrontation. But the McCann children have had a problem not shared by Trollope or by their schoolfellows who live in the prosperous precincts of Harrow: a long journey to and from school. Ten-year-old Nell was sad to leave after six years in order to attend a school nearer home, giving her more time for homework and music practice. Seven-year-old Archie cannot think of anywhere he would rather be than Orley Farm.[41]

School visits can reveal further contrasts between past and present, though, as the following accounts may suggest, the impressions gained are inevitably rather superficial. In May 2007 I attended the centenary celebrations of Highfield School with former pupil Anthony Heath. At lunch, I met some of his near contemporaries who had chosen to attend the occasion, even though their recollections of the school in the 1950s were not altogether happy. One was still indignant about being caned for 'stealing' his own McVitie & Price chocolate digestive biscuits and prohibited from keeping a teddy bear. But he consoled himself with the thought that the beating and bullying he had suffered at Highfield had 'made him tough'. Acting as a counterpoint to my companions' recollections, a speech by William Mills, grandson of the canon, emphasized the long service devoted to the school by its 'cultivated, kind, compassionate' headmasters. Another grandson, Jonathan Carey, said that his grandfather 'believed passionately in progressive education', a view as remote from Anthony Heath's memories as was Aubrey Upjohn's opinion, expressed in his slim volume on the preparatory school, from those of Bertie Wooster.[42] The centenary occasion also revealed the modern school in action. We saw traditional features like the cricket match in its spacious grounds, team photographs (some featuring Anthony's father) in the corridors and a plaque in the grey stone chapel commemorating the twenty-two Highfieldians killed in the First World War. But we also noted some novelties: girls' names on the scholarship board, bunk beds in cheerfully decorated dormitories and relaxed children of both sexes in an art class. And, of course, there was no cane in the headmaster's study, which was open for all to enter.

I also encountered a blend of past and present at a St Aubyns Open Day in January 2009. Knowing that I was a historian, my delightful guides, Ben and Mira, thoughtfully showed me parts of the school which evoked its earlier days: the shooting hut from which the short-sighted John Kipling fired at targets; the Boot Room with its antique benches and lockers; the mulberry garden containing a beautiful old tree; and the chapel displaying not just the names but the pictures of all the school's war casualties. The shabby house itself has, as Simon Hitchings found when he came to be interviewed for the job of headmaster in 2006, 'an old-fashioned feel' about it.[43] But my guides themselves, a boy and a girl, represented one break with tradition. Their appearance and conversation revealed further changes from the days of John Kipling, Wilfred Thesiger, Tom Ponsonby and Vivian Bickford-Smith. They wore comfortable tracksuits rather than blazers and ties. They are day pupils most of the time because both are scholarship candidates and feel they can work longer hours at home – though when they take up the 'flexi-boarding' option 'it's so good you feel you're at home'. Both are on the School Council which Simon Hitchings has introduced. The curriculum contains features they particularly enjoy, such as Global Eye (a blend of religion, geography and current affairs) and Arts Express Days, on which music, drama, art and literature revolve around a chosen theme. When pointing out notices telling pupils who to go to if they are worried or unhappy, my guides assured me that they were hardly needed because 'this is a really nice place'. Ben and Mira will be sad to leave St Aubyns but when they do it will be for public schools close to their homes, respectively Brighton College and Roedean, they hope. I believed the headmaster when he assured me that these two pupils had not been coached – but they could hardly have given a better advertisement for their school with what they proudly called a 'modern/traditional mix'.

Tradition is more immediately apparent at Summer Fields, which has remained a single-sex full boarding school with no pre-prep department and only a handful of day boys. Discussions with the headmaster and pupils (who made me welcome on an ordinary working day in February 2009) revealed, however, that the school has moved with the times. And the Ofsted Report of 2007 confirms this impression. The 'boys are not terrified', Robin Badham-Thornhill assured me – and, indeed, they did not seem to be as they greeted him cheerfully in the carpeted corridors. They have private contact by email, payphone and letter with their parents, who nowadays tend to live reasonably close to the school (though 10 per cent of them work abroad). Boys are 'nurtured' more than in the past and can take any worries to their tutors or lodge parents (boarding house supervisors). 'When I'm homesick staff make me feel better,' one pupil explained to the Ofsted inspectors. According to the headmaster, bullying is rare at Summer Fields, a verdict borne out by the inspection.

Ralph from London and Tayo from Nigeria showed me round the school with obvious pride in what it had to offer. Both boys are in the Remove, the class below the top form in the school, and have their sights set on Eton and Harrow respectively. Among the impressive features they showed me were the theatre, which puts on one or two productions every term; the music room, equipped with many computers used for musical composition; the beautiful chapel, where all the senior boys have to read in turn; the fine swimming pool, which they can use freely in the evenings; the sports hall, where boys were playing basketball in their lunch hour; and the thatched Red Pavilion, which burnt down in 2001 but has been restored to its original state. Most interesting of all was the Activities Board on which boys sign up for a wide range of afternoon sports and other pastimes such as Amateur Radio, Current Affairs, Model Railways and Cookery.

The boys took me into lunch, now conducted on an informal self-service system. I enjoyed my pasta bolognese on the top table with the headmaster and members of the Fifth (top) Form, who responded readily to my questions, even pulling my leg about the regrettable lack of beating in the school these days. I saw members of staff, including the headmaster, tactfully trying to ensure that boys eat a full, balanced meal. But there is no compulsion. I was struck in the dining room and all around the school by the quiet atmosphere – it was difficult to believe that over 200 boys were enjoying their lunch break in the building. Then they all disappeared for lessons at the dignified tolling of the school bell.

How can we be sure that the recent transformation of prep schools is not a mirage which fades away when scrutinized more closely? After all, as molesworth noticed, adults have always blithely assumed that 'skools are not wot they were in my day'. But the evidence of the last two decades consists of more than paters' observations, though these can sometimes be helpful now that parents have freer contact with their children's surrogate homes. One father I met compared his children's experiences at boarding school with his own at the Dragon in the 1970s. Even though he enjoyed his schooldays, he could not imagine subjecting his own offspring to the wealth of whackings, sprinkling of 'dodgy masters' and dearth of exeats he had to put up with. He saw little of his mother, who never came to watch matches or performances at the Dragon although she actually lived in Oxford. By contrast, he and his wife visit their children's school nearly every week, providing the emotional support they think essential and assessing conditions for themselves. Apart from such parental testimony, we may rely on the evidence of new laws, policy documents such as *Every Child Matters* (2004), inspection reports, the changed appearance of schools, the demeanour of their pupils and the comments of young people who are not afraid to speak their minds. All this assures us that prep schools are more open to the world, more closely linked to families, more comfortable, more kindly and more secure than they ever were in the past.

It is also clear that some aspects of prep school life have not changed. There is still, for example, a preponderance of boys over girls among boarders. This may well help to prepare them for a business boardroom, parliamentary bench or officers' mess, dominated even now by products of the right educational mill. And early separation from home may still be designed to make men of them. Another enduring feature of these schools is their social exclusiveness. *The Tatler Good Schools Guide*, when selecting John Walker of Abberley Hall as the 'best head of a prep school' for 2009, described the experience of children at the school: 'It's like living in a grand but quirkily bohemian stately pile with some wonderful views of the Worcestershire countryside.'[44] Even day pupils of a city prep school are set apart from their contemporaries. One of the nine children interviewed by Libby Brooks for her *Story of Childhood* (2006) was a pupil at a London boys' prep school usually referred to by its initials. Nicholas 'doesn't know anybody his own age who goes to a state school'. He realizes that parents have to pay fees and tries to explain why some can afford to do so: 'People might have more money if they work very hard, or they might have more money from their ancestors.'[45] What Nicholas could not be expected to understand is that annual fees in the range of £20,000 for boarding or about £15,000 for day attendance put prep schools beyond the reach of most families, however hard they work. The effects of the credit crunch which began in 2008 may make pupils part of an even smaller elite. By January 2009 about twenty-five schools were on the market and *The Good Schools Guide* reported the smaller prep schools to be 'very vulnerable indeed'.[46]

Abundant though the evidence may be, it cannot fully penetrate the secret world of the child, which lies beyond the earshot and out of the sight of parents, teachers, inspectors, interviewers and historians. Children will always tend to keep some matters to themselves. It is doubtless as hard as it ever was for them to tell anyone if they have been the victim of paedophilia. Even if they do talk, the truth may not be brought to light. In the early 2000s, for example, the headmaster of Caldicott failed to report a child's allegation of sexual abuse to the police or the social services but tried to investigate the complaint internally. As former victim, Tom Perry, points out in *The Times*: 'No school in England . . . is under any statutory obligation to report alleged abuse to the authorities.'[47] Bullying (in any type of school) is often hushed up by both perpetrators and prey – so that it was years before a mother of my acquaintance discovered that her son was being taunted as gay by boys in his class. Nor do youngsters want adults to know about the more dangerous games they play in prep school woodlands, the unsuitable books they read after lights-out, the naughty jokes which go the rounds, the unwholesome sweets they eat or the banned items they smuggle into school premises. Even if they are not committing these offences, they are unlikely to sneak on those who are. Nicholas was most unusual in telling his teacher that another child was concealing a Gameboy in a hidden compartment of his school bag, a betrayal he later admitted to Libby Brooks. Sadly for Nicholas, 'he didn't bring it in that day and they thought I was telling a lie. Which was really, really unfair.'[48] His fury echoes that of children over the centuries but it would not normally have been witnessed by adults. Many other passions, fears, joys and tricks remain uncharted, unavailable as evidence of rising or falling educational standards. Pupils of the past might recognize more than they suppose if they were to re-join the brighter classrooms, warmer dormitories and safer playgrounds of their old prep schools.

10

'The Most Potent Memory of My Life'
The Effects of the Prep School Experience

It is often said that you can take the child out of the school but you cannot take the school out of the child. This is particularly true of prep schools because they are so distinctive and because children attend them at such a young age, often spending more time at them than they do at home, for even 'day boarders' (as day pupils are often called) usually stay at school until six or seven in the evening. The maxim certainly applies to the 200 or so subjects of this book, who over the last two centuries roughed it, learnt gentlemanly manners, played the game, prepared to sacrifice themselves for their country, competed for worldly success or simply got on with it. Uncannily, what one might call the felicific equation is roughly equal: sixty of my subjects were very happy at prep school, just over sixty were very unhappy, while ninety had mixed experiences. It is obviously not the purpose of this chapter to trace the rest of their lives. Rather, I intend to give glimpses of the ways in which the prep school experience has remained with them and with their schoolfellows.

It was during the holidays that the effects of school tended to appear first. Like Robert Graves, boys returned home 'with a different vocabulary, a different moral system, even different voices'.[1] Sisters such as Selina and Charlotte in Kenneth Grahame's *Golden Age* left behind in the nursery to prepare 'new bows and arrows, whips, boats, guns and four-in-hand harness against the return of Ulysses', would find their efforts scorned as 'rot and humbug, and only fit for kids!'[2] Other sisters had similar experiences of rejection. Doris and Harry Lessing were both glad to get back to their Rhodesian farm from their respective boarding schools in Salisbury: 'The moment the holidays began, nothing had changed. We were often up with the sun and off into the bush.' But when Harry was visited by a friend from Ruzawi prep school, which was 'modelled on English lines', the boys would sneer at Doris, going off on their own and treating her 'just as schools of that kind prescribed'.[3] When Diana Athill's brother Andrew came home from boarding school, he stayed as far away from all his family as he could, seeking the company of boys in the village: 'An exile they had made him so an exile he would be.' At home he would bully his younger cousin, whose parents were in India.[4] Almost inevitably, concluded Royston Lambert, boarding life distorted relationships and rendered 'a family's holiday-time existence unnatural'. It is true that 70 per cent of his sample said that they had learned to appreciate their home more as a result of absence, but this included senior school boarders, for whom the family is not such a 'vital respite' from the outside world.[5]

The most normal outcome of a prep school education is that pupils gain places or scholarships by competitive examination at public schools. They have often reached remarkable intellectual heights for their age but some have criticized the system as relying too much on rote learning, 'so that he who has the most of this technical memory will make the most forward schoolboy'. William Hazlitt made this point in the 1820s but it still has some relevance today. Jamie Gardiner recently studied at St John's College School with the scholarship candidates, who were brought up to GCSE standard in Latin. He admits that many of them simply forgot the information once it had served its purpose of getting them into, for example, College at Eton. Jamie did not choose this educational route – and nor has he forgotten his Latin grammar which stands him in good stead at the Perse School, Cambridge.[6] Others have been less accomplished. John Peel, who came bottom of Shrewsbury School in his first term, suspected that he had actually failed the Common Entrance at Woodlands but had been 'nodded through' because his father, Uncle Bill and both grandfathers had been at Shrewsbury.

Like many of his colleagues, the headmaster of Woodlands also tried to prepare his pubescent leavers for the more personal challenges of public school life. To John and other mystified pupils, Mr Brookes explained that 'if you have a jug already filled with water and you add more water to it, it will overflow', before hastily wishing them 'good luck' at their next school.[7] Comic and tragic stories abound of the statutory special talk delivered in the headmaster's study. He might issue mysterious warnings about 'some other boys' or, occasionally, be more explicit about the 'world full of temptations' they were about to enter. Cyril Connolly remembered this admonition: 'We must report any boy at once who tried to get into our bed, never go for a walk with a boy from another house, never make friends with anyone more than a year and a half older . . . and, above all, not "play with ourselves"'.[8] Almost no one found this sort of pi-jaw in the least bit helpful.

Quite apart from the sexual dangers, the first few years at a public school could be tough going. Osbert Lancaster drew on his experience of St Ronan's prep school and Charterhouse to describe the 'special cruelty' of the English boarding school system: 'the horrors must be endured not once but twice'. After 'long and weary terms and years', a boy would become a kingpin at prep school, exercising power (including, sometimes, the power to beat) over younger boys, before being plunged into a new regime of fagging, bullying, initiation rites and tests of arcane school vocabulary imposed by their seniors.[9] Stephen Fry argues: 'Those whose early days at public school were least happy were those who had won most prizes, rank and power at their preps.'[10] Max Hasler told me, for example, that the head boy of Abberley Hall found Winchester so difficult that he soon had to leave, while Max himself made the transition easily, having learned to cope with his earlier problems. Paul Watkins, who managed to stay the course at Eton after his experience at the Dragon, concluded that 'to go there without being prepared and trained for it must have been something like it was for Alice when she tiptoed through the looking glass.'[11] Most children survived the junior forms of their public schools and, in their turn, went on to enjoy exercising authority as they became more senior. As Sydney Smith trenchantly put it in 1810, 'Every boy is alternately tyrant and slave.'[12] Thus, concludes Kathryn Tidrick, schools kept alive 'a keen appreciation of what it was like to have power and what it was like to be without it', a useful attribute when it came to running the British Empire.

Tidrick selects as typical of the colonial governors who ruled 'by the unconscious exercise of an intuitive art', Edward Wood (Lord Irwin), Viceroy of India in the 1920s.[13] But she does not trace his qualification for power back to his childhood. A sensitive boy who had been born with no left hand, Edward began his education at St David's prep school in Reigate after the death of his three older brothers. There he received frequent letters from his father, the second Viscount Halifax, urging him to 'do all sorts of grand things', 'to do everything perfectly' and to be 'the pride and happiness of our life'. Whether Edward himself was happy neither parent knew, for they visited him only once during his time at St David's. His letters did not reveal, as his autobiography does, the canings he received on 'very slender provocation', the 'petty bullying' he was subjected to in the dormitories, his intense dislike of the school and his longing for the beloved sisters, dogs and horses he had left behind on the family estate in Yorkshire.

He progressed to Eton, which he found more 'tolerable' and to Christ Church, Oxford, where he took a first class degree. Now his father was determined that Edward should be prime minister; instead, he bore with him to India the hopes and ambitions vested in him by his parents. Tall, aloof and impassive, he never climbed to the top of the greasy pole but, after inheriting his father's peerage, he did become the foreign secretary who tried to appease Hitler.[14]

Irwin/Halifax shows how an educational process starting with prep school has helped to perpetuate Britain's 'rigid caste system', by training 'the sons of the well-born and the wealthy to regard themselves from boyhood as born to be the natural officers and captains in the army of the nation'. This was the verdict of Frederic Harrison, an Edwardian radical, but his words are echoed by right-wing commentators. John Strachey Barnes, a fascist of the 1930s, described a country divided by its school system into 'two rigid castes: the "toff" and the "bloke"'.[15] A neutral modern analyst concludes that prep schools have helped both to 'train an elite' and to 'maintain social divisions'.[16] They therefore compound the growing social inequality in Britain, with its widening gulf between rich and poor.

Various explanations have been given for the ease with which prep/public school men have taken up leading places in society. In his *Nemesis of Faith* (1849), James Anthony Froude judged the public school boy to be 'better formed by far to elbow along in after-life by the practice of elbowing among schoolboys'. While admiring the 'character, vigour and independence' thus produced, he saw that it could weaken 'religious sensibility' (as it had his own).[17] Other commentators have stressed the familiarity such a boy will have with the 'mysterious internal workings' of English institutions such as the regiment, the bar, the House of Commons and the gentlemen's club. Now, as in the past, these can act as a home from home where a man can 'live his school life over again', often encountering men he met as boys in the classroom, dormitory or sports pavilion.[18]

Some historians have blamed the old boy network for Britain's post-war decline. Alistair Horne, drawing on his own experience of Ludgrove in the 1930s, suggests that schools which scorned the arts, foreign languages, science and technology did not equip their pupils to compete in the modern world:

> While Old Ludgrovians of my age-group were smugly moving, after the Second World War, into comfortable slots in their fathers' banking firms, or into merchant banks or

estate management or Lloyd's or the Temple, their competitors in France and Germany were dirtying their hands through the ranks of BMW, Mercedes and Rhône-Poulenc, or swotting their way through European business schools.[19]

But the private schools which have survived into the twenty-first century by updating their curricula cannot be so easily dismissed. Modern politicians have to acknowledge the genuine advantages provided by fee-paying establishments. Alan Johnson, a state-educated postman who rose to become education secretary in Tony Blair's Labour government, attributed their excellence to 'the time they spend with children doing sport, music and drama and building social skills ... which employers increasingly look for first'.[20] Recent research by the Organisation for Economic Co-operation and Development (OECD) found that the gap between private and state class sizes at primary level is higher in Britain than in any other developed country; there are on average thirteen more pupils in a state primary class than in a private one.[21] These large classes, as well as lack of funding and a regime of almost constant testing, have hampered primary schools in their ability to lay on the generous range of activities provided by most prep schools.

Frequently, as earlier chapters have shown, extra-curricular pursuits have incubated future success. Tennyson was already writing poetry in the early 1800s by the time he left Louth School at the age of eleven; Harold Macmillan had not only mastered hendiadys and oxymorons at Edwardian Summer Fields, he had acted the part of Prime Minister in the school play; Benjamin Britten used the sonatas, songs, suites, waltzes, rondos, fantasias and variations composed at South Lodge in the 1920s for his *Simple Symphony*; Ian Bostridge, who performed in school productions of Britten operas, does not see how he could have ended up singing without the encouragement of his music teacher at DCPS; and David Suchet made a small start on his acting career by playing an Oyster in *Alice Through the Looking Glass* at Birchington House.

Even unpleasant school experiences could sometimes provide inspiration. The work of Lord Shaftesbury on behalf of ill-treated children seems to have stemmed from his own unhappy early days at the Manor House School, Chiswick, which gave him 'an early horror of oppression and cruelty'.[22] John le Carré's alter ego, Magnus Pym, learns amid the hardships of his prep school the useful lesson of living on several planes at once: 'The art of it was to forget everything except the ground you stood on and the face you spoke from at that moment.' This was just what Magnus needed in his future profession as a 'perfect spy'.[23] In more recent years, Paul Knight's career in social work and Nick Duffell's therapeutic workshops for 'boarding school survivors' arose from their difficult times at prep school.

For a few pupils, the experience of early boarding was so incapacitating that they left school unfit for any employment. Stephen Fry went on to Uppingham, from which he was expelled, and then to a three-month stint in Pucklechurch Prison after a compulsive bout of credit card fraud. At least he had been prepared for incarceration and 'knew how to stay cheerful and think up diversions, scams and pranks'.[24] Robin Bell progressed, after his self-propelled departure from Falconbury, to Sutton Valence public school, where he refused to eat, drink or get out of bed. He continued this passive protest against what he regarded as an 'emotional prison' until his parents took him away. 'In the depths of despair' Robin was sent to a child psychiatrist, who advised a Rudolf Steiner school designed to meet the changing needs of young people. In time, Robin concludes, 'the Steiner approach eventually won the day'. In retrospect he attributes his psychological difficulties to the fact that his 'inner emotional world became detached from the day-to-day world'.[25]

It is remarkable how many prep school alumni have written about being cut off in this way from normal feelings, even if they seemed to cope well with the experience. Across the years similar images and metaphors recur. As an Edwardian schoolboy, Siegfried Sassoon felt that the only life he could call his own was inside his play-box along with his tin of mixed biscuits. In 2000 Nick Duffell wrote that 'feelings get stored in the tuck box at the back of the heart'.[26] Leonard Woolf, who was school captain at Arlington House, described his existence there as 'a condition of almost suspended animation, a kind of underwater existence' or 'a dream world'.[27] Some years later, John Harvey-Jones used a more modern analogy to describe his time at Tormore: 'It was almost as though I had been in a deep frozen state of suspended animation during my prep school years.'[28] Others put it differently, but they often recall a comparable condition. Lord Berners experienced a 'benumbing spell'. Wilfred Bion felt 'imprisoned, unable to break out of the shell' which adhered to him. As a new boy at Newton College, Arthur Quiller-Couch hardened his 'small heart' in the face of the bullying he encountered.[29] Tim Jeal grew a 'defensive hide' which enabled him to endure anything 'if treated as routine'.[30] Michael Holroyd's way of coping with separation from home was to perform a 'vanishing trick'; but he found later that there was a penalty to be paid – 'your past vanishes with you'.[31]

Several interviewees have admitted to me the permanent effects that this Houdini act can have. George Perkin links the 'distraught state' of his twenties and the 'wreckage' of his emotional life with the ploy he used when watching his mother recede in a cloud of steam as the school train left for Caldicott: 'It was at such moments that I learned, early on, not only how to suppress all feeling and emotion, but also how not to feel anything at all.'[32] David Blandford, who repressed his emotions effectively at Brambletye, finds that the only name he can now recall from his time there is that of the boy he sat next to on his first school-train journey but lost contact with in the confusion of changing at Three Bridges. He is grateful, at least, that his mother was an active member of the Young Wives' Fellowship which ran social events he could attend in the holidays. At these he could escape from the 'boarding school ethos' and meet youngsters of both sexes (including his future wife). Rupert Morris, reckoning himself still 'a buttoned-up schoolboy' at the age of thirty, found release in a course of psychotherapy. Only then, for example, was he able to weep about the death of his father.

The scars left by prep school come in all shapes and sizes. Alistair Horne finds it difficult to dissociate the onset of his asthma from the 'miseries inflicted at Ludgrove'. A former pupil of Tormore who had spent his early childhood in Karachi gained an excruciating stammer from 'the shock of trying to learn to speak and behave like an Englishman'.[33] Another young expatriate became permanently disabled by juvenile arthritis contracted in the freezing dormitories and unhomely surroundings of Craigflower in the 1930s. He feels that his illness could well have been caused by the physical and emotional stress of being separated from his India-based parents at the age of seven.[34] There are other less obvious traces. Certain adults cannot escape from recurrent dreams of prep school, in which they might kill their headmaster or get suffocated by a bully. Other ex-boarders report that they still find it difficult to say goodbye, or to do or say anything not approved by the mob code, or to eat a communal meal, or to be told that someone is waiting to see them, or to travel by train, or to have a shower (even if it is not a cold one) or, in the case of Roald Dahl, to sit for long on a hard bench or chair without feeling 'my heart beating along the old lines that the cane made on my bottom some fifty-five years ago'.[35] Or an old boy might simply have developed an undying aversion to chalk downs, sweeping driveways, rhododendrons, bald men or milk puddings – all real examples.

But of course there were also those depicted by E. M. Forster in his *Notes on the English Character* who 'remember with regret that golden time . . . when they all worked together and played together and thought together'.[36] Library shelves abound with their memoirs. In W. F. Bushell's *School Memories*, for example, he recalls an incident from his time in the 'happy family' of Orley Farm in the 1890s: 'I can still feel the thrill of victory as I ran home first in the three-legged race with another boy.' Bushell (who does not give his Christian name) went on to become a schoolmaster and 'lived in eight different boarding houses for fifty years'.[37] Even Henry Green, a New Beacon pupil during the First World War who likened the school to 'a fascist state', could call to mind joyous times when 'we laughed, we screamed and shouted and went about in packs'.[38] A contemporary, Louis MacNeice, could hardly find words vivid enough to convey the bliss of his first summer term at Sherborne: 'It was so exciting I felt like the princess in the fairy story – you open your mouth and out come golden guineas.' In both prose and poetry, MacNeice lyrically depicted such delights as the bathing pool with its chute from which boys 'would come sailing out of the sky like Jacob's angels'. In his memory:

> The trees were full of owls, the sweets were sweet
> And life an expanding ladder.[39]

Some later twentieth-century schoolboys have felt a similar nostalgia for the scene of their gregarious early years. Tom Fort recalls with pleasure the fun he had at Maidwell Hall, 'mucking about outside, climbing trees, digging underground huts, scooping aquatic life from the fringes of the lake'. He does not recognize any of the features so hated by Andrew Motion. Despite the absence of any organized pastoral care, he and his two brothers felt 'safe, valued and cherished' at the school after the death of their father in a car crash.[40] The 'cocooned conservative social stratum' described by one Brambletye old boy was one in which children often felt comfortable. Bryan Magee came to the conclusion that the closed, structured, ordered world of Christ's Hospital was just what he needed at the age of eleven after his early years in the East End and evacuation billets. 'It imbued me with a different value system: telling the truth, keeping my word, being loyal to friends.'[41] Some of the former pupils whose memories were solicited by the Old West Downs Society acknowledged a similar debt. Patrick Forwood, who played for all the first teams, served as a patrol leader and passed his Common Entrance, is typical of these grateful alumni: 'West Downs gave a firm base on which to build self confidence and was a vital first step on the journey of life for many of the boys who spent their formative years there.'[42]

Welcome or unwelcome, memories of prep school could surface at any time in a boy's future life. They might be conjured up by tangible mementos, as they were for Siegfried Sassoon when he looked at a photograph of his former Classics master, Mr Jackson, with his class. This brought back 'precariously remembered humanities', such as the 'ripping time we'd had when he took a party of us on the Norfolk Broads'.[43] The old school building itself could perform the same Proustian trick, even if it had been greatly transformed. Anthony Horowitz 'froze solid' and his heart palpitated when Orley Farm received him as a visiting author: 'I realized just how much damage that place had done to me.'[44] Yet Andrew Motion was reported as having enjoyed himself when he went back to Maidwell Hall as Poet Laureate. We do not know, however, what he really felt as he read the boys a poem describing his bemused first arrival and a secret midnight walk to the Wilderness and the Lake which proved that he was able to come and go as he pleased.[45] Perhaps the visit assuaged the poet's anger, acting almost as the penance which Michael Croft, now a Roman Catholic convert, feels that he must offer up to atone for his own rage. For David Barton, a return to the beach at Burnham-on-Sea, on which he had played 'knights and horses' as a St Dunstan's schoolboy, was beneficial; he could 'almost feel the sand between the toes' and he remembered that he had been happy there.

Other places can act as sites of remembrance. Thackeray was in Germany when he witnessed the parting of two little boys in black from their mother and felt anew the pain of his own lone departure for school. The twentieth-century writer Simon Gray described a comparable episode in his *Smoking Diaries*. When at the age of nineteen he was visiting his old housemaster at Westminster, he recognized among the staff Mr Burn, a former teacher from his Putney prep school, Glengyle. Burn had encouraged the headmaster of Glengyle to flog Simon at least once a week with 'twelve savage strokes'. And with tumult in his stomach and a roll of his heart, Simon remembered what he had previously forgotten, that during these punishments Burn had always been voyeuristically 'loitering in a corner of the room, or his face at the window'.[46] Tim Jeal's memories were nudged at the care home to which he was conducting his mother:

> Remembering my time at boarding school, I did not have to imagine what it was like to be trapped among people I had not chosen to be with. There was something very disturbing about our changed positions. She was in an institution now, just as I had been years ago, and I could take her out as I chose.[47]

George Perkin had the same experience of a 'full circle' being completed with a scene in an old people's home: 'After my weekly visit, my mother would cling to me and say "Don't leave me."' In his own old age, George's recollections of Caldicott haunt him with ever more clarity: 'If I close my eyes I can see every detail of the school and the appearance of the masters. It is the most potent memory of my life.'[48] And Peter Squire told me two weeks before he died that the terrors of his prep school years were with him all the time.

Can one generalize from these particulars? Over the years, commentators have tried to explain the qualities and failings of the English upper and upper-middle classes in the light of their peculiar habit of expelling children from the parental nest. An eighteenth-century German observer attributed to their mode of education the 'ridiculous national pride' displayed by Englishmen, who 'despise and laugh at the infinitely inferior' way of life in other countries.[49] Victor Jacquemont, a French traveller in early nineteenth-century India, met many proud young Englishmen who had left home early for school and gone on to take up imperial posts. He admired their dignified reserve, but felt that they were 'strangers to that tenderness, that sweet abandonment to which we other continentals owe so many pleasures and consolations'. They had purchased their early independence at the cost of family affections.[50]

In the years before the First World War, Rudyard Kipling, a later version of this colonial type, praised the 'famous men' who taught pupils taken early from their mothers the self-command Englishmen needed to 'serve and love the lands they rule' without seeking praise or reward.[51] Naturally, he wanted his only son, John, to grow up with the same capacity to behave 'like a Sahib' in both victory and defeat.[52] After the war, in which John Kipling and so many other brave and stoical young men lost their lives, the system which bred the stiff upper lip attracted more criticism. Forster blamed it for sending boys forth 'with well-developed bodies, fairly well-developed minds and undeveloped hearts' – so that they remained 'Old Boys and nothing else for the rest of their lives'.[53] Cyril Connolly made a similar point. The 'glories and disappointments' experienced at boarding school were so intense that pupils could not escape from them. Their emotional development was arrested and they remained 'school-minded' long after they had left the 'hot rooms of their education'.[54]

As this book has shown, prep schools carried on trying to mould children's characters in much the same way until the late twentieth century. There is ample evidence to show that some pupils suffered psychological harm from which they never fully recovered. Others conformed to the type described by Connolly and Forster by never really escaping from their juvenile cocoon; the readiness with which some old boys have talked to me suggests the important role prep school still plays in their lives. Many have emerged as the 'useful members of society' which these schools prided themselves on producing. Changes over the last thirty years mean that prep schools now place more emphasis on the individual development of each child and they no longer aim to isolate pupils from the world. Yet this type of education still keeps children busy for a substantial part of the day, monopolizing their time even if they are not actually boarders. It still separates them from contemporaries of different social classes. And it still often segregates them from the opposite sex. The prep school experience remains an intense one, whether in glories or disappointments, and it makes indelible marks on children.

Debate continues in the press, in parliament and among parents. Commenting in *The Times* on today's gentler boarding regimes, an educational psychologist suspects that seven-year-old children are still better off with parents than with 'the enlightened individuals who now run prep schools'. A *Telegraph* article praises prep schools for standing out against the national curriculum and supposes that they are as character-building for 'today's perplexed eight-year-olds' as they were for former generations.[55] Political parties are still deliberating over what to do about an educational system which creates a class culture of a kind unknown in the rest of Europe. Parents, in the meantime, weigh the academic and economic advantages conferred by prep schools against the social and emotional hazards of an education which sets their children apart from family and neighbourhood. After all, it might be as difficult for them to adjust to normal life and relationships as it was for Tom Brown to resume friendships with the good honest village boys or for Harry Potter to return to the ordinary Muggle world. Only children will know whether they can truly echo their elders' time-worn maxim about the prep school system: 'It never did me any harm.'

Endnotes

The place of publication is London, unless otherwise stated.

Notes to Introduction: 'How Would You Know?'

1   Thomas Hughes, *Tom Brown's Schooldays* (no date), 187.
2   Winston Churchill, *My Early Life* (1959 edn), 17.
3   Diana Athill, *Yesterday Morning* (2003 edn), 133–5.
4   Stephen Fry, *Moab Is My Washpot* (1998 edn), 17.
5   Angus Wilson, *The Victorians* (2002), 278.
6   Martin Bluhm, 'Preparatory Schools', unpublished thesis, 1970, 15.
7   Ibid., 276–7.
8   www.anthonyhorowitz.com
9   Q, *Memories and Opinions* (Cambridge, 1944), 41.
10 Robert McCrum, *Wodehouse: A Life* (2004), 24.
11 P. G. Wodehouse, *Jeeves in the Offing* (1963 edn), 121.
12 e.g. Lord Berners, *First Childhood* (2000 edn), 107 and W. Somerset Maugham in his autobiographical novel, *Of Human Bondage* (1975 edn), 39.
13 Alistair Horne, *A Bundle from Britain* (1993), 90, 86.
14 Fraser Harrison, *Trivial Disputes* (1989), 96.
15 Hilary Mantel quoted in H. H. Wood and A. S. Byatt, *Memory: An Anthology* (2009), 150–1.
16 Leonard Woolf, *Sowing: An Autobiography of the Years 1880 to 1904* (1960), 59, 70.
17 General Sir Ian Hamilton, *When I Was a Boy* (1939), 90–1.
18 Fry, *Moab Is My Washpot*, 126–7.
19 Edward Lucie-Smith, 'The Lesson' in Michael Donaghy (ed.), *101 Poems about Childhood* (2005), 145 and information from John Ellwood's sister, Jane.
20 Hugo Williams, 'Leaving School' and 'A Letter to My Parents' in *Writing Home* (Oxford, 1985), 29, 32.
21 See Donald Leinster-Mackay, *The Rise of the English Prep School* (London and Philadelphia, 1984); Arthur Marshall, *Whimpering in the Rhododendrons* (1982), back cover; Michael Gilbert, *Prep School: An Anthology* (1991).
22 Hugh Cunningham, *The Invention of Childhood* (2006); Harry Hendrick, *Children, Childhood and Society* (Cambridge, 1997), 3; Anthony Fletcher, *Growing Up in England: The Experience of Childhood 1600–1914*, New Haven and London, 2008), 317–8 and Vyvyen Brendon in *The Literary Review*, July 2008.
23 Philip Masters, *Preparatory Schools Today: Some Facts and Inferences* (1966); Nick Duffell, *The Making of Them: The British Attitude to Children and the Boarding School System* (2000).
24 James Kenward, *Prep School* (1969 edn), 8; interview with David Blandford, 29 December 2009 and Henry Green, *Pack My Bag* (1992 edn), 18.
25 Peter Quennell (ed.), *Mayhew's Characters* (no date), 89.
26 Edwin Hodder, *The Life and Work of the Seventh Earl of Shaftesbury* (1886), vol. 1, 2 and Ann Humpherys, *Henry Mayhew* (Boston, 1984), 2, 57.
27 David Eliot in Anthony Horowitz, *Groosham Grange* (2004), 137.

Notes to Chapter 1: 'A Little Roughing It': Georgian Boys' Schools

1   Hughes, *Tom Brown's Schooldays*, 37–8.
2   W. M. Thackeray, *Roundabout Papers* (New York, 1925 edn), 20.
3   Ann Mozley (ed.), *Letters and Correspondence of John Henry Newman* (1891), 18.
4   John Lawson and Harold Silver, *A Social History of Education in England* (1973), 198.
5   See J. A. Froude, *Nemesis of Faith* (1988 edn), 119; Thomas Mozley, *Reminiscences Chiefly of Oriel College and the Oxford Movement* (1882), vol. 1, 114 and David Newsome, *The Parting of Friends* (1966), 38.
6   Johanna Schopenhauer quoted in Patrick Bridgewater, *Arthur Schopenhauer's English Schooling* (1988), 123.
7   Charles Dickens, *Dombey and Son* (no date), 178.
8   Anthony Trollope, *An Autobiography* (1996 edn), 7–9.
9   Alan Mould, *The English Chorister* (2007), 152, 163–4.
10 'Recollections of Christ's Hospital' in Percy Fitzgerald (ed.), *The Life, Letters, and Writings of Charles Lamb* (London and Philadelphia, 1895), vol. IV, 183 and OIOC, MSS Eur F176/3, Robert Barlow to George Barlow, 22 December 1804.
11 Andrew Roberts, *Salisbury: Victorian Titan* (1999), 8.
12 Ibid., 8–12.
13 Gordon Ray (ed.), *The Letters and Private Papers of William Makepeace Thackeray* (1945), vol. 1, 7–9.
14 W. M. Thackeray, *Vanity Fair* (1908 edn), 5.
15 W. M. Thackeray, *Christmas Books* (1897 edn), 75–7.
16 D. J. Taylor, *Thackeray* (1999), 20, 33–5, 40.
17 Mozley, *Reminiscences*, vol. 1, 27.
18 *The Life of Edward Bulwer, First Lord Lytton* by his grandson, the Earl of Lytton (1913), vol. 1, 43.
19 E. S. Purcell, *The Life of Cardinal Manning, Archbishop of Westminster* (1896), vol. 1, 11–12.
20 Benjamin Disraeli, *Coningsby* (Stroud, 2007 edn), 22.
21 Henry Coke, *Tracks of a Rolling Stone* (1905), 9–10.
22 Archibald Anson, *About Others and Myself* (1920), 46–8.
23 Coke, *Rolling Stone*, 15, 27–8.
24 Meston Batchelor, *Cradle of Empire: A Preparatory School through Nine Reigns* (Chichester, 1981).
25 Dickens, *Dombey and Son*, 179, 203.
26 John Forster, *The Life of Charles Dickens* (1872–4), 370.
27 Charles Dickens, *The Life and Adventures of Nicholas Nickleby* (1892 edn), ix.
28 Dickens, *Dombey and Son*, 209, 226.
29 Dr Wendeborn, *A View of England* (1791) quoted in Bridgewater, *English Schooling*, 275.
30 Thackeray, *Christmas Books*, 67.
31 OIOC, MSS Eur F176/54, George Barlow to his father, 16 January 1806.
32 Bridgewater, *English Schooling*, 302.
33 Coke, *Rolling Stone*, 15.
34 Mozley, *Letters and Correspondence of Newman*, vol. 1, 17, 19, 26.
35 Piers Brendon, *Hurrell Froude and the Oxford Movement* (1974), 11.
36 W. H. Dunn, *James Anthony Froude* (Oxford, 1961), 26–8.
37 Ibid., 31–4.
38 Hughes, *Tom Brown's Schooldays*, 43 and Edward Mack and Walter Armytage, *Thomas Hughes: The Life of the Author of Tom Brown's Schooldays* (1952), 16–17.
39 William Wordsworth, 'Intimations of Immortality from the Recollections of Early Childhood' in T. Creehan (ed.), *The Poetry of Wordsworth* (1965), 179.
40 Lytton Strachey, *Eminent Victorians* (1928 edn), 185.
41 'Tirocinium or A Review of Schools' in *The Life and Works of William Cowper* (no date), 590.
42 David Cecil, *Melbourne* (1955), 24 and Evelyn Ashley, *The Life and Correspondence of Lord Palmerston* (1879), vol. 1, 5–6 and vol. 2, 160.
43 Sydney Smith quoted in Hesketh Pearson, *The Smith of Smiths* (1934), 24.

44 Trollope, *Autobiography*, 7–9, 10, 12 and Victoria Glendinning, *Trollope* (1992), 36.
45 Fitzgerald (ed.), *Life, Letters and Writings of Lamb*, vol. I, 1, 5.
46 Coleridge to T. Poole, 19 February 1798 in Kathleen Raine (ed.), *The Letters of Samuel Taylor Coleridge* (1952), 14–15.
47 Thornton Leigh Hunt (ed.), *The Autobiography of Leigh Hunt* (1891), 55, 61, 75.
48 Fitzgerald (ed.), *Life, Letters and Writings of Lamb*, vol. III, 161.
49 Ibid., vol. I, 7.
50 Quoted in E. K. Chambers, *Samuel Taylor Coleridge* (Oxford, 1950 edn), 11.
51 W. J. Bate, *Coleridge* (1968), 103, 51.
52 David Wright (ed.), *The Penguin Book of English Romantic Verse* (1968), 176–7.
53 Fitzgerald (ed.), *Life, Letters and Writings of Lamb*, vol. IV, 170–4; Hunt, *Autobiography*, 74; Fitzgerald (ed.), *Life, Letters and Writings of Lamb*, vol. I, 151, 158.
54 A. H. D. Acland (ed.), *Memoir and Letters of the Right Honourable Sir Thomas Dyke Acland* (1902), 6.
55 David Forrester, *Young Doctor Pusey: A Study in Development* (1989), 7.
56 Hallam Lord Tennyson, *Tennyson: A Memoir* (1897), vol. I, 6.
57 Harold Nicolson, *Tennyson* (1960 edn), 50.
58 Pearson, *Smith of Smiths*, 21–2.
59 William Hazlitt, *Table Talk: Essays on Men and Manners* (1902 edn), 95.
60 Hughes, *Tom Brown's Schooldays*, 45.
61 W. Cowper to W. Unwin, 17 September, 5 October 1780 in *Life and Works of Cowper*, 58–60.
62 OIOC, MSS Eur E357/17, J. Swete to Mrs Yule, 19 August 1826, George to Mrs Yule, 12 August, 18 November and 20 December 1826, 23 April 1827 and George to Robert Yule, 15 August 1829.
63 Charles Dickens, *A Christmas Carol* (no date), 52–5.
64 OIOC, MSS Eur E357/17, George to Mrs Yule, 8 and 15 September 1827 and Robert to Mrs Yule, 12 March 1828.
65 Thomas Hughes, *Memoir of a Brother* (1873), 19.
66 William Stephens, *The Life and Letters of Walter Farquhar Hook* (1878), 7.
67 OIOC, MSS Eur F176/16, Charles Barlow to his father, 22 January, 5 February 1811.
68 Elizabeth Gaskell, *Cranford* (Baltimore, 1976 edn), 91–2.
69 G. O. Trevelyan, *The Life and Letters of Lord Macaulay* (1895 edn), 19–20.
70 John Clive, *Thomas Babington Macaulay* (1973), 31.
71 Thomas Pinney (ed.), *The Letters of Thomas Babington Macaulay* (Cambridge, 1974–81), vol. 1, Thomas to his parents, 3, 6, 22, 26 February 1813.
72 Ibid., 6 February, 8 May, 4 November 1813.
73 Ibid., 12 and 14 August, 1813, 31 January 1815.
74 Quoted in Clive, *Macaulay*, 34.
75 Trevelyan, *Life and Letters of Macaulay*, 485.
76 Francis Darwin (ed.), *The Life and Letters of Charles Darwin* (1887), vol. 1, 136.
77 Francis Darwin (ed.), *Autobiography of Charles Darwin* (no date), 6–8.

Notes to Chapter 2: 'The Only Way to Bring Up Boys': Victorian Prep Schools

1 Eric Evans, *The Forging of the Modern State* (London and New York, 1983), 319.
2 Taunton Commission 1868, vol. 1, 200, 89.
3 Mould, *English Chorister*, 209.
4 See Leinster-Mackay, *English Prep School*, 12.
5 Evans, *Forging of Modern State*, 319.
6 George Eliot, *The Mill on the Floss* (no date), 4–5.
7 CAC, ESHR 7/39, Baliol Brett to Reginald, no date.
8 Lady Charlotte Guest, *Extracts from her Journal 1833–1852* (1950), 164, 212–3.
9 Mrs Ellis, *The Mothers of England, their Influence and Responsibility* (1843), 282, 259–61, 272, 277.
10 Mrs Bayly, *The Life and Letters of Mrs Sewell* (1889), 117.
11 Edmund Gosse, *Father and Son* (1928 edn), 292.

12   *Memoir of Tennyson*, vol. 1, 371 and Ann Thwaite, *Emily Tennyson: The Poet's Wife* (1997 edn), 395.
13   CUL, Add. 7888, II/119, Journal of Sir James Stephen, 2, 18, 19 January 1846.
14   *Life and Letters of Darwin*, vol. 1, 381–7.
15   John Tosh, *A Man's Place: Masculinity and the Middle-Class Home in Victorian England* (New Haven and London, 1999), 104–5.
16   E. G. Browne, *A Year Among the Persians* (2002 edn), 7.
17   Frederic Harrison, *Autobiographic Memoirs* (1911), 61–3.
18   Harold Perkin, *The Age of the Railway* (Newton Abbot, 1970), 116.
19   Kenneth Grahame, *The Golden Age* (no date), 281–4 and *Pagan Papers* (1893), 54, 90.
20   Herbert Merivale, *Bar, Stage and Platform* (1902), 157.
21   David Gilmour, *Curzon* (1994), 9.
22   LMA, Monro Archive, ACC/1063/876.
23   Leinster-Mackay, *English Prep School*, 50, note 38. No source is given.
24   LMA, Monro Archive, ACC/1063/878.
25   Ibid., ACC/1063/877, 898, 902, 926.
26   Ibid., 892, 895, 954, 883, 881, 883, 900, 901.
27   Ibid., 889, 876, 878, 932, 918, 959.
28   Ibid., 886, 908, 944.
29   Ibid., 260, 273, 263, 265, 277, 261.
30   Ibid., 286, 288, 355, 298.
31   Ibid., 319, 351, 352.
32   Fletcher, *Growing Up in England*, 351.
33   Thwaite, *Emily Tennyson*, 397.
34   CAC, ESHR 7/39, undated letter.
35   Q, *Memories*, 41–2.
36   Hamilton, *When I Was a Boy*, 88–9, 166, 98.
37   John Chandos, *Boys Together: English Public Schools 1800–1864* (1984), 61.
38   George Melly, *School Experiences of a Fag at a Private and a Public School* (1854), 9, 14, 19, 29.
39   Merivale, *Bar, Stage and Platform*, 159.
40   Quoted in Leinster-Mackay, *English Prep School*, 40.
41   Charles Hardinge, *Old Diplomacy: The Reminiscences of Lord Hardinge of Penshurst* (1947), 4 and Hamilton, *When I was a Boy*, 109.
42   CAC, ESHR 7/1 and 7/39, undated letters.
43   G. Bourne, *Memories of an Eton Wet-Bob of the Seventies* (1933), 14.
44   CAC, ESHR 7/1, undated letters.
45   J. Oxley Parker, *The Oxley Parker Papers* (Colchester, 1964), 240.
46   David Newsome, *Godliness and Good Learning* (1961), 166–7, 177, 192.
47   A. C. Benson, *Memories and Friends* (1923), 27.
48   Hardinge, *Old Diplomacy*, 4.
49   Hamilton, *When I Was a Boy*, 110, 112, 99–102, 115, 117–22, 126.
50   Leinster-Mackay, *English Prep School*, 44, 50, note 55.
51   Benson, *Memories and Friends*, 33, 35, 45–6, 49, 52, 42.
52   E. F. Benson, *Our Family Affairs 1876–1896* (London and New York, 1920), 77.
53   OIOC, MSS Eur E349, Campbell Papers, A. G. Campbell to his parents, 1 Feb c. 1877 and illustration in Batchelor, *Cradle of Empire*.
54   Batchelor, *Cradle of Empire*, 19.
55   Quoted in Fletcher, *Growing Up in England*, 321.
56   L. M. Faithfull, *In the House of My Pilgrimage* (1924), 29, 41.
57   Max Egremont, *Balfour* (1980), 21.
58   Lord Frederic Hamilton, *The Days Before Yesterday* (1920), 95.
59   J. W. Mackail and Guy Wyndham, *The Life and Letters of George Wyndham* (1925), 23.
60   Andrew Lycett, *Conan Doyle: The Man who Created Sherlock Holmes* (2007), 20.
61   A. Conan Doyle, *Memories and Adventures* (1930 edn), 19–22.

62   BL, Arthur Conan Doyle Papers, Arthur to his mother, 31 October 1870, undated, 30 May 1869.

63   Eliot, *Mill on the Floss*, 157–8.

64   Quoted in Batchelor, *Cradle of Empire*, 41.

65   CAC, ESHR 7/1, undated letter.

66   Newsome, *Godliness and Good Learning*, 168, 173.

67   Gosse, *Father and Son*, 210.

68   Lycett, *Conan Doyle*, 29.

69   Arthur Baldwin, *My Father: The True Story* (1955), 40.

70   Benson, *Family Affairs*, 120–1.

71   Robert Rhodes James, *Lord Randolph Churchill* (1994 edn), 19 and Winston Churchill, *Lord Randolph Churchill* (1906), 6.

72   Lord Hawke, *Recollections and Reminiscences* (1924), 22 and M. Williamson on www.cricinfo.com.

73   CAC, CHAN 2/18, Alfred to his father, 21 June 1865 and Edith Lyttelton, *Alfred Lyttelton: An Account of his Life* (London and New York, 1917), 17.

74   Arnold Lunn, *The Harrovians* (1913), 24.

75   Bourne, *Memories of Seventies*, 16–7.

76   KCC, REF 3/57/1, 3 September 1877, 3/57/2, 24 February 1878, 3/57/6, 1 June 1879.

77   Benson, *Memories and Friends*, 34.

78   Peter Green, *Kenneth Grahame* (1959), 43–4.

79   Kenneth Grahame, *The Wind in the Willows* (1993 edn), 9.

80   Admiral Sir William Goodenough, *A Rough Record* (London and New York, 1943), 14.

81   Hardinge, *Old Diplomacy*, 5.

82   Grahame, *Golden Age*, 286.

83   Hamilton, *When I was a Boy*, 126–8, 133–5, 89–91.

84   Browne, *Year Among the Persians*, 7.

85   Merivale, *Bar, Stage and Platform*, 161.

86   Eliot, *Mill on the Floss*, 70–1.

87   e.g. Batchelor, *Cradle of Empire*, 41.

Notes to Chapter 3: 'Three Stumps, One Wicket': Late Victorian and Edwardian Heyday

1   This episode forms the basis of Alex Hamilton's short story 'The Props of the Marquee' in *The Christmas Pudding that Shook the World* (1988).

2   Kathryn Tidrick, *Empire and the English Character* (1990), 220 and Donald Leinster-Mackay, 'The nineteenth-century English preparatory school: cradle and crèche of Empire?' in J. A. Mangan (ed.) *'Benefits Bestowed'? Education and British Imperialism* (Manchester, 1988), 57.

3   Peter Parker, *The Old Lie: The Great War and the Public School Ethos* (2007 edn), 56–7 and Robert Pearce, 'The Prep School and Imperialism: The Example of Orwell's St Cyprian's' in *The Journal of Educational Administration and History*, January 1991, 44.

4   Tidrick, *Empire and Character*, 217.

5   Quoted in Leinster-Mackay, *English Prep School*, Appendix 9.

6   Board of Education, *Special Report on Preparatory Schools for Boys* (1900), 8.

7   Andrew Birkin, *J. M. Barrie and the Lost Boys* (1986), 79.

8   Mike Huggins, *The Victorians and Sport* (2004), 32.

9   *Special Report*, 344–5.

10   Leinster-Mackay, *English Prep School*, 196, 193.

11   Marshall, *Whimpering in Rhododendrons*, 9–10.

12   KCL, Bryant Archive, GB99 B/2, V. M. Haskall to Mrs Bryant, September 1908.

13   KCC, REF 3/57/5, Roger Fry to his father, 27 October 1878.

14   BL, Add 48265/C3 Morley Archive, Notice to Parents from Wixenford School.

15   Robert Graves, *Goodbye To All That* (1960 edn), 24.

16   A. C. Benson, 'The Preparatory School Product' in *Special Report*, 483.

17   Leinster-Mackay, *English Prep School*, 133.

18   Quoted in Marshall, *Whimpering in Rhododendrons*, 173.
19   *Special Report*, 475, 477, 479, 345.
20   Harrison, *Memoirs*, 64.
21   CAC, WILL Box 2, 'As I Remember'.
22   Robert Skidelsky, *John Maynard Keynes: A Biography* (1986 edn), vol. 1, 69–70.
23   John Buchan, *Memory Hold-the-Door* (1945 edn), 26, 29–31.
24   *The Captain*, June 1910, July 1900; *BOP*, 1899, 1900; Jeanne MacKenzie, *The Children of the Souls* (1968), 27–8.
25   Woolf, *Sowing*, 69.
26   Graves, *Goodbye To All That*, 24–5 and Charles Graves, *The Bad Old Days* (1951), 24.
27   Christopher Douglas, *Douglas Jardine: Spartan Cricketer* (1984), 4 and SFA, *Summer Fields Magazine*, July 1914.
28   H. Oliver, 'Douglas Robert Jardine' in *Oxford Dictionary of National Biography* (Oxford, 2006).
29   R. C. Robertson-Glasgow, *46 Not Out* (1948), 25.
30   Philip Ziegler, *Mountbatten* (1985), 28–30.
31   KCC, RCB/M2 Album and M21, Diary 1899–1900 and Christopher Hassall, *Rupert Brooke* (1964), 30–2.
32   *Special Report*, 479.
33   Siegfried Sassoon, *The Old Century and Seven More Years* (1938), 196–9.
34   CAC, AMEL 6/1/30, Papa to Leopold, Xmas 1882 and 6/1/3, E. Heel to Mrs Amery, 20 February 1886.
35   Leo Amery, *My Political Life* (1953), vol. 1, 33–5 and CAC, AMEL 6/1/30, undated letters from Leo to his mother, translated by Teresa Outhwaite.
36   Colin Clifford, *The Asquiths* (2002), 12, 37–9 and H. A. Asquith, *Moments of Memory* (1937), 65–71.
37   KCL, Bryant Archive GB99 B/2, Arthur to his parents 1908–11.
38   Ibid., letters from Mrs Haskall, September 1908, 24 May 1909 and reports, 10 April, 30 July 1909, July 1911.
39   John Buchan, *Francis and Riversdale Grenfell* (London and New York, 1920), 9–10.
40   There is a copy of this diary in the Summer Fields Archive. It is owned by Graham Tapp who traced its authorship.
41   Faculty of Asian and Middle Eastern Studies, Cambridge, RDV/9, 14 November 1909, 14 May 1911 and RDA/3, November 1909, July 1911.
42   Letters of Kipling, 30 November, 29 July 1908, quoted in Elliot Gilbert (ed.), *O Beloved Kids* (1983).
43   Judith Flanders, *A Circle of Sisters* (2001), 309–10.
44   Robert Rhodes James, *Bob Boothby: A Portrait* (1991), 27.
45   Maugham, *Of Human Bondage*, 39.
46   Berners, *First Childhood*, 113, 129.
47   CSAS, Brown Family Papers, uncatalogued.
48   BL, Add 48265 C/2, Edmund to his father, 15 July 1888 and reports, 25 February, 26 July, 27 December 1888, Lent and Michaelmas 1891, 8 August 1893.
49   José Harris, *William Beveridge* (Oxford, 1997), 19 and P. N. Furbank, *E. M. Forster: A Life* (1977), vol. 1, 34–5.
50   G. K. Chesterton, *Autobiography* (1936), 74, 77.
51   Woolf, *Sowing*, 64–8.
52   Wilfred Bion, *The Long Week-end 1897–1919: Part of a Life* (Abingdon, 1982), 47, 92.
53   Alec Waugh, *The Early Years* (1962), 21–2, 27 and Evelyn Waugh, *A Little Learning* (1964), 80.
54   Berners, *First Childhood*, 133, 192, 119, 161, 121, 111, 123, 220.
55   Randolph Churchill, *Winston Churchill* (1967), vol. 1, Companion Part 1, 87–8 and CAC, CHAR 28/38.
56   Churchill, *Early Life*, 19–21.
57   Anita Leslie, *Jennie: The Life of Lady Randolph Churchill* (1969), 82.
58   Peregrine Churchill and Julian Mitchell, *Jennie, Lady Churchill* (1974), 127.

59   CAC, CHAR 28/88, Winston to Mrs Everest, June 1886.

60   Churchill and Mitchell, *Jennie*, 160.

61   Churchill, *Early Life*, 23.

62   Maurice Baring, *The Puppet-Show of Memory* (1932), 71, 77, 79.

63   KCC, REF 3/57/6–9, letters of 1879, 1880 and 1/172, Memoir; Virginia Woolf, *Roger Fry* (1991 edn), 31–5; Frances Spalding, *Roger Fry: Art and Life* (1980), 13.

64   Hugh Trevor-Roper, *A Hidden Life: The Enigma of Sir Edmund Backhouse* (1976), 243–4, 265.

65   Brian Garfield, *The Meinertzhagen Mystery: The Life and Legend of a Colossal Fraud* (Washington DC, 2007), 43–4.

66   Oswald Mosley, *My Life* (1968), 24–7.

67   Norman Kemp Smith (ed.), *Memorials of Lionel Helbert* (1926), 91.

68   Joseph Chamberlain to the housemaster at Rugby, who had saved his son, Austen, from a flogging, 8 April 1879. Quoted in Denis Judd, *Radical Joe* (1977), 86.

69   J. S. Barnes, *Half a Life* (1933), 24, 27, 30.

70   Christopher Walker, *Oliver Baldwin: A Life of Dissent* (2003), 16.

71   Rhodes James, *Boothby*, 27–8.

72   Yorkshire Archaeological Society, H. L. Bradfer-Lawrence Collection MD335/1/8/15/1, Charles to his parents and Lord Ribblesdale, *Charles Lister Letters and Recollections with a Memoir by his Father* (1917), 11.

73   Antonia White, *Frost in May* (1978 edn), 44, 156, 158.

74   Quoted in Roy Wake and Pennie Denton, *Bedales School: The First Hundred Years* (1993), 208–10.

75   James Lees-Milne, *Harold Nicolson 1886–1929* (1980), 7.

76   *Highfield School Magazine*, Lent Term and Summer Term 1913.

77   J. A. Mangan (ed.), *The Cultural Bond: Sport, Empire, Society* (1992), 17.

78   Kenneth Grahame, *Dream Days* (New York and London, 1899), 211 and Rudyard Kipling, *Just So Stories for Little Children* (1964 edn), 60.

79   Quoted in Mangan, *Cultural Bond*, 20.

Notes to Chapter 4: 'Too Young to Gird on the Sword': The First World War

1   *The Captain*, December 1914, 253–4.

2   Quoted in Chris Sparrow, *No Time to Spare? Our Boys Who Went to War* (Oxford, 2006), 102.

3   *The Captain*, September 1915, 526.

4   SFA, *Summer Fields Magazine*, April 1915, April, July 1916, March, July 1918.

5   John Betjeman, *Summoned by Bells* (1960), 44–5.

6   Henry Longhurst, *My Life and Soft Times* (1971), 29.

7   Wilkins Papers now in Regent House Library, Oxford, Phyllis to her parents, 21 September 1915, 14 June 1916.

8   KCL, Bryant Papers GB99 B/36, Philip to his parents, 28 November 1915.

9   Waugh, *Little Learning*, 85, 88–9.

10   Knebworth House Archive, V15, Antony's diary sent to his father, June 1915.

11   Green, *Pack My Bag*, 68–9.

12   Tim Jeal, *Baden-Powell: Founder of the Boy Scouts* (1989), 448–50.

13   Wilkins Papers, Phyllis to her parents, 10 March 1914.

14   KCC, FPR 2/1, Frank to his parents, September, October 1913 and father's unpublished memoir.

15   Letters quoted in Lord Lytton, *Antony: A Record of Youth* (1935), 17, 20 and Knebworth House Archive, V15, Antony to his parents, 4, 14, 18 February, 13 December 1914.

16   A. J. P. Taylor, *A Personal History* (1984 edn), 37–40.

17   Quoted in Humphrey Carpenter, *W. H. Auden* (1981), 18.

18   H. E. Davis in Richard Usborne (ed.), *A Century of Summer Fields* (1964), 126–7.

19   A. Ritchie (Burra's sister) in William Chappell (ed.), *Edward Burra: A Painter Remembered by his Friends* (1982), 19–20.

20   KCC, FPR 2/1, Frank to his parents, undated letter.

21 Peter Parker, *Christopher Isherwood: A Life Revealed* (2004), 44 and Christopher Isherwood, *Exhumations* (1966), 185.

22 BL, Add. 81306, John to his parents, undated letters.

23 Laurence Whistler, *The Laughter and the Urn* (1985), 19, 24, 28.

24 Gordon Bowker, *George Orwell* (2003), 43.

25 Francis Wheen, *Tom Driberg: His Life and Indiscretions* (1990), 24.

26 *The Captain*, April 1916, 83.

27 Betjeman, *Summoned by Bells*, 45.

28 W. H. Auden, 'Letter to Lord Byron' in Edward Mendelson (ed.) *Collected Poems* (1991 edn), 107.

29 Waugh, *Little Learning*, 88.

30 Betjeman, *Summoned by Bells*, 28.

31 Usborne, *Century of Summer Fields*, 144–7.

32 Stephen Spender, 'Day Boy' in Graham Greene (ed.), *The Old School: Essays by Divers Hands* (1934), 187–8.

33 Littleton Powys, *The Joy of It* (1937), 195 and Louis MacNeice, *The Strings are False: An Unfinished Autobiography* (1965), 65.

34 Longhurst, *My Life*, 27; David Ogilvy, *An Autobiography* (New York, 1997), 13, and G. Orwell, 'Such, Such Were the Joys' in *The Collected Essays, Journalism and Letters* (1970 edn), vol. 4, 398.

35 Carpenter, *Auden*, 17.

36 Stephen Spender, *World Within World* (1953 edn), 288.

37 *The Captain*, October 1914.

38 Wilkins Papers, Phyllis to her parents, 6 February, 21 March 1917.

39 Orwell, *Collected Essays*, vol. 4, 398, 396.

40 Ritchie in Chappell, *Edward Burra*, 20.

41 *Preparatory Schools Review*, July 1918.

42 CAC, DSND 19/1, Duncan-Sandys to his mother, 3 November 1918.

43 CAC, CHAR 28/131, John to Lady Randolph Churchill, 19 November 1919.

44 SFA, *Summer Fields Magazine*, December 1918 and Maurice Richardson, *Little Victims: Prep School Memories* (1968), 95–6.

45 Interview with Leila Brown, 4 February 2003 and Elsie Pike, *The Story of Walthamstow Hall* (Sevenoaks, 1973), 49.

46 Knebworth House Archive, Antony to his parents, 13 December 1914.

47 Michael Davie (ed.), *The Diaries of Evelyn Waugh* (1979), 8.

48 Michael Barber, *Anthony Powell: A Life* (2004), 10.

49 Powys, *Joy of It*, 195.

50 Helen Thomas, *As It Was, and World Without End* (1956), 163 and 'This is No Case of Petty Right or Wrong' in Jon Silkin (ed.), *The Penguin Book of War Poetry* (1996), 95.

51 Auden, 'Letter to Lord Byron' in Mendelson, *Collected Poems*, 107–8.

52 Christopher Headington, *Peter Pears: A Biography* (1992), 7.

53 Wheen, *Tom Driberg*, 23–4.

54 Strix, 'The Man We Killed' in Brian Inglis (ed.), *John Bull's Schooldays* (1961), 133–6.

55 Nicholas Aldridge, *Time to Spare? A History of Summer Fields* (Oxford, 1989), 1–2, 78 and Usborne, *Century of Summer Fields*, 131–2, 146.

56 Anthony Powell, *To Keep the Ball Rolling*, vol. 1: *Infants of the Spring* (1976), 64 and *Preparatory Schools Review*, December 1915.

57 Elizabeth Bowen, 'The Mulberry Tree' in Greene, *Old School*, 50.

58 Cyril Connolly, *Enemies of Promise* (1961 edn), 177, 187.

59 Duff Hart-Davis, *Peter Fleming: A Biography* (1974), 28.

60 Green, *Pack My Bag*, 77.

61 Christopher Isherwood, *Kathleen and Frank* (1971), 356–7 and *Lions and Shadows: An Education in the Twenties* (1996 edn), 9.

62 T. C. Worsley, *Flannelled Fool: A Slice of Life in the Thirties* (1967), 14, 36–7.

63 MacNeice, *Strings are False*, 76, 64 and Powys, *Joy of It*, 194, 197.

64   Miranda Carter, *Anthony Blunt: His Lives* (2001), 18.
65   Louis MacNeice, *Autumn Journal* (1939), 40.
66   Worsley, *Flannelled Fool*, 38.
67   Spender, 'Day Boy' in Greene, *Old School*, 189.
68   Leinster-Mackay, *English Prep School*, 154.
69   Spender, *World Within World*, 284–5 and Anthony Powell quoted in Barber, *Anthony Powell*, 9.
70   See Robert Pearce, 'Truth and Falsehood: George Orwell's Prep School Woes' in *The Review of English Studies, New Series*, August 1992, 367–386 for a summary of this debate.
71   Review by Cyril Connolly in *Sunday Times*, 29 September 1968.
72   Pearce, 'Truth and Falsehood', *Review of English Studies*, 380.
73   Longhurst, *My Life*, 37, 30 and John Christie, *Morning Drum* (1983), 10.
74   Jeremy Lewis, *Cyril Connolly: A Life* (1997), 48.
75   Orwell, *Collected Essays*, vol. 4, 399.
76   Pearce, 'Truth and Falsehood', *Review of English Studies*, 385.
77   Alaric Jacob, *Scenes from a Bourgeois Life* (1949), 49.
78   *The Captain*, April 1915, 85.
79   Connolly, *Enemies of Promise*, 176, 201–2.

Notes to Chapter 5: 'All the Ghastly Smells of School': The Inter-War Period

 1   Evelyn Waugh, *Decline and Fall* (1967 edn), 21 and Richard Cobb, *A Sense of Place* (1975), 17–18.
 2   Gavin Maxwell, *The House of Elrig* (Edinburgh, 2003 edn), 69.
 3   Kenward, *Prep School*, 15. This affectionate view is based on the small school attended by Kenward after the First World War, which he calls Ripple Vale. It purports to preserve a balance between the 'typically Ripplish' and the more widely typical.
 4   Horne, *Bundle from Britain*, 87.
 5   Marshall, *Whimpering in Rhododendrons*, 26–7.
 6   *Diaries of Evelyn Waugh*, 3 July 1925, 213.
 7   David Niven, *The Moon's a Balloon* (1994 edn), 16.
 8   CAC, DSND 19/1, Duncan-Sandys to his mother.
 9   Durnford School War Memorial in St George's Church and West Downs memorial now displayed at Peter Scott's nature reserve, Slimbridge.
10   Arthur Marshall, *Life's Rich Pageant* (1984), 50–1.
11   Roald Dahl, *Boy* (1992 edn), 110.
12   Margaret Drabble, *Angus Wilson* (1995), 40–3 and Angus Wilson, 'Bexhill and After' in Inglis, *John Bull's Schooldays*, 151–2.
13   Marshall, *Rich Pageant*, 33.
14   J. B. Priestley, *The Good Companions* (1962 edn), 79–80, 89, 106.
15   Waugh, *Decline and Fall*, 19.
16   Marshall, *Rich Pageant*, 33.
17   *The Falconburian*, January 1933, 19.
18   *Diaries of Evelyn Waugh*, 5 May 1925, 211.
19   Marshall, *Rich Pageant*, 33, 41.
20   Interview with Johnny Bell, 28 November 2007.
21   Waugh, *Decline and Fall*, 190.
22   Cobb, *Sense of Place*, 9.
23   Marshall, *Rich Pageant*, 42.
24   *Preparatory Schools Review*, November 1931, 259.
25   Dahl, *Boy*, 77.
26   Robert Baker, unpublished memoir, 5–6.
27   Mark Peel, *The Land of Lost Content: The Biography of Anthony Chenevix-Trench* (Durham, 1996), 17–18, 102. I should perhaps declare an interest here: my husband suffered at his hands while a boy in his house at Shrewsbury. His oft-repeated mantra went: 'I'm going to beat you, Tuppence.'

28   Ludovic Kennedy, *On My Way to the Club* (1990 edn), 40–2.

29   A. Stevens, Obituary of Anthony Storr in *Psychiatric Bulletin*, 2001, 365.

30   Taylor, *Personal History*, 52.

31   CUL, Peter Scott Papers A273, 17 July 1923 and A111, 6 September 1918, 15 September 1920.

32   www.westdowns.com – Tom Pocock in 'Memories of the Tindall Era'.

33   Humphrey Lyttelton, *I Play as I Please: The Memoirs of an Old Etonian Trumpeter* (1954), 38–9.

34   This was the appropriate name for Rev Chittenden's Hoddesdon Grange, now relocated at Seaford. Romilly disguised Mr Wheeler as Mr Dombrill.

35   Giles and Esmond Romilly, *Out of Bounds* (1935), 44, 160, 13.

36   Batchelor, *Cradle of Empire*, 87.

37   Usborne, *Century of Summer Fields*, 188–9.

38   Denton and Wake, *Bedales*, 213, 215, 224.

39   Susan Isaacs, 'Habit' in John Rickman (ed.), *On the Bringing Up of Children* (1936), 166, 205.

40   KCC, AMT/K/1, Turing Papers, Alan to his parents, 18 October 1925.

41   CAC, McKNS 8/8, David to his parents, no date.

42   *The Falconburian*, February 1933, 34.

43   Martin Pugh, *We Danced All Night: A Social History of Britain Between the Wars* (2008), 202–3.

44   Dahl, *Boy*, 51.

45   Barnes, *Half a Life*, 25.

46   Alexander Maitland, *Wilfred Thesiger: A Life in Pictures* (2004), 13, 16.

47   Interview with Peter Squire, 23 July 2008.

48   Taylor, *Personal History*, 51–2. The idea of pupil cabinets was not confined to The Downs. At Hazelhurst, for instance, Alan Turing found himself Minister for Walks and had to answer questions during a 'Private Business' debate in 1925.

49   Nicholas Henderson, *Old Friends and Modern Instances* (2000), 31–2.

50   Quoted in Nicholas Aldridge, *G. B. Master, Monster or Myth?* (Ilfracombe, 2008), 89–90.

51   Julian Amery, *Approach March: A Venture in Autobiography* (1973), 40, 42.

52   CAC, AMEJ 3/1, 27 January 1929.

53   H. F. Ellis, *The World of A. J. Wentworth, B.A.* (1964), 9, 18, 75. Ellis was a former master at Highfield School, on which his series was modelled.

54   Nicholas Blake (penname of C. Day Lewis), *A Question of Proof* (1963 edn), 184.

55   Romilly, *Out of Bounds*, 177, 37 and Kevin Ingram, *Rebel: The Short Life of Esmond Romilly* (1985), 26.

56   *The Falconburian*, February 1931, 23.

57   Interview with Johnny Bell.

58   Dahl, *Boy*, 98, 90.

59   Horne, *Bundle from Britain*, 92–3.

60   www.westdowns.com – Tom Pocock.

61   Maxwell, *House of Elrig*, 89, 100, 106, 114.

62   CAC, DSND 19/2/1, Letters of L. Helbert, July 1918 and 1 July 1919.

63   CUL, Peter Scott Papers A111, 30 September 1918, A268, 25 July 1919, A113, Report 1920.

64   Amery, *Approach March*, 38 (original letter in SFA) and CAC, AMEJ 3/1, 7 May 1928.

65   Henderson quoted in Usborne, *Century of Summer Fields*, 238.

66   Obituary in *Daily Telegraph*, 11 January 2008 and John Harvey-Jones, *Getting it Together: Memoirs of a Troubleshooter* (1991), 56, 73.

67   Randolph Churchill, *Twenty-One Years* (1964), 22.

68   CAC, CHAR 1/157, no date.

69   Churchill, *Twenty-One Years*, 23–5.

70   Waugh, *Little Learning*, 229.

71   Richard Rhodes James, *The Road from Mandalay* (Milton Keynes, 2007), 36.

72   CAC, RDCH 3/5/2, School Report, Summer 1924.

73   George Melly, *Owning Up: The Trilogy* (2000 edn), 171.

74   Tony Orchard, unpublished memoir, Chapter 4, 3–4.

75 Interview with George Perkin, 21 August 2008.

76 Percy Everett quoted in Piers Brendon, *Eminent Edwardians* (1979), 245.

77 Creed of the Woodcraft Folk.

78 Taylor, *Personal History*, 44.

79 Michael McLeod, *Thomas Hennell: Countryman, Artist and Writer* (Cambridge, 1988), 14.

80 Jocelyn Brooke, *The Military Orchid* (1981), 45, 55.

81 Maxwell, *House of Elrig*, 41, 90, 92–3.

82 CUL, Peter Scott Papers, A271, 29 September 1921, A272, 15 May 1922.

83 CAC, DSND 19/1, 25 May 1919.

84 Elspeth Huxley, *Peter Scott: Painter and Naturalist* (1993), 23, 30.

85 Sara Turing, *Alan S. Turing* (Cambridge, 1959), 19.

86 KCC, AMT/K/1, Summer Term 1923, 8 March 1925.

87 Judith Heimann, *The Most Offending Soul Alive: Tom Harrisson and his Remarkable Life* (Honolulu, 1999), 10.

88 Alan Ross, *Blindfold Games* (1986), 75.

89 Michael Darlow, *Terence Rattigan: The Man and his Work* (2000), 33–4 and Geoffrey Wansell, *Terence Rattigan* (1995), 25.

90 Marshall, *Rich Pageant*, 58.

91 Andrew Lycett, *Ian Fleming* (1995), 11.

92 Frank Giles, *Sundry Times* (1986), 4–5 and interview with Peter Squire.

93 Cobb, *Sense of Place*, 13 and Malcolm Yorke, *Keith Vaughan: His Life and Work* (1990), 28, 30.

94 Michael Yates quoted in Carpenter, *Auden*, 143.

95 CAC, MCKN 8/7, 17 June 1923, undated 1923.

96 Ibid., 4 September 1929 and 9/26, letters of condolence to Pamela McKenna, October 1931.

97 *Oldie*, February 2003 and interview with George Perkin.

98 Waugh, *Decline and Fall*, 188.

99 Taylor, *Personal History*, 40 and Amery, *Approach March*, 39.

100 Horne, *Bundle from Britain*, 86.

101 Lord Montagu of Beaulieu, *Wheels Within Wheels: An Unconventional Life* (2000), 124.

Notes to Chapter 6: 'A Higher Sense of Sacrifice': The Second World War

1 Raleigh Trevelyan, *The Golden Oriole* (1987), 491 and *The Fortress: A Diary of Anzio and After* (1972 edn), 120.

2 William Buchan, *Rags of Time: The Fragment of an Autobiography* (Southampton, 1990), 112.

3 IWM, 83/46/1, Unpublished memoir by Capt. P. Collister.

4 Ross, *Blindfold Games*, 245.

5 Interview with Johnny Bell.

6 David Faber, *Speaking for England: Leo, Julian and John Amery – The Tragedy of a Political Family* (2005), 134.

7 Headington, *Peter Pears*, 10.

8 These qualities were noted by Charles Graves in his war diary, *Off the Record* (1944), 32–3.

9 Paul Addison, 'The Few' in *Oxford Dictionary of National Biography*.

10 Quoted in T. L. Crosby, *The Impact of Civil Evacuation in the Second World War* (1986), 131.

11 John Colville, *The Fringes of Power: Downing Street Diaries 1938–1945* (1985), 278.

12 Martin Gilbert, *Finest Hour: Winston Churchill 1939–1941* (1983), 949–50.

13 Montagu, *Wheels Within Wheels*, 34–6.

14 Interview with Tom Sharpe, 15 April, 2007.

15 Article by former pupil, Simon Jenkins, *Guardian*, 23 November 2007.

16 John Burningham, *When We Were Young: A Compendium of Childhood* (2004), 240–1.

17 Batchelor, *Cradle of Empire*, 99, 94, 100–1.

18 Douglas Hurd, *Memoirs* (2003), 25–7 and unpublished correspondence from Twyford.

19 Batchelor, *Cradle of Empire*, 98.

20   IWM, 66/316 File 1, H. Bucknell to Mr and Mrs Hammer, 21 October 1940 and Jim to his parents, 13, 20, 27 October 1940.
21   Ibid., Jim to his parents, 3, 17, 24 November 1940.
22   Ibid., File 2, Mark to his parents, 22 November 1942 and File 3, Jim to his parents, 8 January, 8 March 1942.
23   Ibid., File 1, Jim to his parents, 3, 8 December 1940, 20 July 1941.
24   Ibid., File 2, Mark to his parents, 9 July 1943, 21 January, 20 June 1944.
25   Norman Longmate, *How We Lived Then: A History of Everyday Life during the Second World War* (1973 edn), 117.
26   Eva Figes, *Little Eden: A Child at War* (1978), 33.
27   Lyn Smith, *Young Voices: British Children Remember the Second World War* (2007), 167–8.
28   Angus Calder, *The People's War: Britain 1939–1945* (1992 edn), 47, 50.
29   Bryan Magee, *Growing Up in a War* (2008), 89, 144, 161, 303.
30   *Gayhurst School Magazine*, August 1940, 3–4, December 1940, 3, September 1944, 4, September 1945, 5.
31   Interview with Rodney Barker, 20 July 2008.
32   Sebastian Faulks, *The Fatal Englishman* (1997), 226–8.
33   James Day, unpublished memoir 'My Prep School'.
34   Interview with Christopher Wood, 1 November 2007 and John le Carré, *A Perfect Spy* (1986), 141.
35   Usborne, *Century of Summer Fields*, 281.
36   Interview with Lord Charles Williams, 11 August 2008.
37   Interview in *The Times*, 5 July 2008.
38   Julian Critchley, *A Bag of Boiled Sweets: An Autobiography* (1994), 11, 8, 15, 12–13, 16.
39   Michael Heseltine, *Life in the Jungle: My Autobiography* (2000), 15–16.
40   Critchley, *Boiled Sweets*, 18–19.
41   Smith, *Young Voices*, 247–8.
42   Melly, *Owning Up*, 147, 206, 208–10.
43   Aldridge, *G.B.*, 108.
44   Aldridge, *Time to Spare*, 124.
45   Cf. Crosby, *Impact of Civil Evacuation*, 132.
46   www.westdowns.com – N. J. Hodson, Caird Biggar and Wilfred Grenville Grey in 'Memories of the Tindall Era'.
47   Figes, *Little Eden*, 12–13, 91, 61–3, 138.
48   Richmal Crompton, *William and the Evacuees* (1987 edn), 15.
49   IWM, 91/5/1 R. A. Brown, A Schoolboy's Diary for 1940, passim.
50   Peter Blencowe, *Brambletye: The Early Years 1919–1969* (East Grinstead, 2004), 86, 67, 89, 112.
51   IWM, MISC 186/2789 Recollections of the evacuation of DCPS.
52   Quoted in Neil Smith, *Dulwich and Beyond: A History of Dulwich College Preparatory School* (2005), 69.
53   J. H. Leakey, *School Errant* (1951), 69.
54   Crompton, *William and Evacuees*, 183.
55   IWM, MISC 186/2789, 'Reactions to the Evacuation of DCPS during the Second World War', Gordon Dearing, Gordon Chubb and William Gruby.
56   Smith, *Dulwich and Beyond*, 89.
57   Crosby, *Impact of Civil Evacuation*, 132.
58   Gillian Avery, *The Best Type of Girl: A History of Girls' Independent Schools* (1991), 342.
59   Longmate, *How We Lived Then*, 257.
60   *Gayhurst School Magazine*, August 1941, 7.
61   IWM, MISC 186/2789, Gordon Chubb.
62   Smith, *Young Voices*, 141.
63   Duff Cooper, *Old Men Forget* (1953), 18, 290.
64   Montagu, *Wheels Within Wheels*, 36.
65   Jessica Mann, *Out of Harm's Way* (2005), 273, 289.

66   David Harrop, 'My Recollections of World War II' and interview, September 2008.
67   Mann, *Out of Harm's Way*, 51 and 66.
68   IWM, 92/16/1, 'Byron House and the Canadian Adventure', 32–43.
69   Ibid., 'Canada Remembered', 10–11, 19, 14, 13.
70   Laurence Fleming, *Last Children of the Raj* (2004), vol. 2, 40.
71   www.bbc.co.uk/ww2peopleswar – J. A. M. Ellis, 'A Boy's Sea Voyage to India in 1940'.
72   Michael Foss, *Out of India* (2002), 156, 165, 178.
73   Michael Emtage, unpublished memoir, 'A Good English Preparatory School', passim.
74   Eric Tyndale-Biscoe, *The Story of Sheikh Bagh* (Mysore, 1945), 33, 12.
75   Fleming, *Last Children of the Raj*, vol. 2, 162, 234.
76   Interview with Michael Thomas, 3 October 2003.
77   Interview with Hilary Sweet-Escott, 1 May 2004.
78   Smith, *Young Voices*, 270.
79   DCPS newsletter quoted in Smith, *Dulwich and Beyond*, 82 and Magee, *Growing Up in War*, 34.
80   Evelyn Waugh, *Put Out More Flags* (Boston, 1942), 96.

Notes to Chapter 7: 'How to be Topp': The Post-War World

 1   Arthur Harrison, *How Was That, Sir? A Memoir of the Preparatory Schools* (1975), 42, 45.
 2   Edward Blishen, *Uncommon Entrance* (1974), 28. Blishen describes this as a 'novelised auto-biography'.
 3   *Public Schools and the General Education System* (1944), 68.
 4   Leinster-Mackay, *English Prep School*, 272.
 5   David Kynaston, *Austerity Britain 1945–51* (2007), 153–4.
 6   Jeremy Lewis, *Playing for Time* (1987), 69.
 7   Harrison, *How was That*, 42.
 8   Andrew Loog Oldham, *Stoned* (2000), 8–11.
 9   Lewis, *Playing for Time*, 60.
10   Interview with Richard Phillips, 20 December 2008.
11   M. H. Spencer in Usborne, *Century of Summer Fields*, 295.
12   Interview with Ann Rosenthal, 10 July 2008.
13   Andrew Motion, *In the Blood: A Memoir of My Childhood* (2006), 218.
14   Leinster-Mackay, *English Prep School*, 280.
15   Blishen, *Uncommon Entrance*, 128.
16   Interview with Philip Steadman, 3 October 2008.
17   Michael Holroyd, *Basil Street Blues: A Family Story* (2000 edn), 161.
18   Memories of Piers Brendon.
19   Geoffrey Willans and Ronald Searle, *The Compleet Molesworth* (1985 edn), 136–7.
20   Interview with Henley Smith, 25 January 2008.
21   Interviews with 'Michael Croft', 20 October 2008 and 'Simon Taggart', 27 September 2008.
22   Richard Branson, *Losing My Virginity* (1999), 30, obituary of Richard Vickers in *Daily Telegraph*, 25 August 2002 and interview with Rupert Morris, 21 November 2008.
23   Holroyd, *Basil Street Blues*, 51–2, 156–8, 163–4.
24   www.westdowns.com – Nick Bloxam's collection, *West Downs Magazine*, 1949, 25–6.
25   Conversation with Tim Heald, 30 October 2008 and Robin Oakley, *Inside Track* (2001), 33.
26   Avery, *Best Type of Girl*, 201.
27   Smith, *Dulwich and Beyond*, 110.
28   John Simpson, *Strange Places, Questionable People* (1998), 43.
29   Willans and Searle, *Compleet Molesworth*, 112.
30   Anthony Holden, *Charles Prince of Wales* (1979), 101–8.
31   Interviews with Anthony Heath, 18 April 2007 and Paul Knight, 20 October 2008.
32   See Paul Fussell, *The Great War and Modern Memory* (New York, 1975), passim.
33   Interview with 'Simon Taggart'.

34 Usborne, *Century of Summer Fields*, 302.

35 Aldridge, *Time to Spare*, 151–6.

36 Anthony Buckeridge, *Jennings Goes to School* (1996 edn), 24, 59 and *Take Jennings, For Instance* (1959), 256.

37 Interview with Sir Martin Gilbert, 18 August 2008.

38 Interview with David FitzGerald, 21 April 2007. A similar car club rally delights the heart of the lonely new boy, 'Jumbo' Roach, when he is befriended by Jim Prideax, a former spy teaching at his prep school. See John le Carré, *Tinker Tailor Soldier Spy* (1974 edn), 127–8.

39 Interview with Ken Saunders, 30 October 2008.

40 Interview with Peter Pugh, 7 October 2008.

41 Interview with Henley Smith.

42 Interview with Philip Steadman and holiday diaries for 1951, 1952, 1953, 1954.

43 Obituaries of Norman Hale in *The Times* 22 October and *Telegraph* 21 October, 2008.

44 Anthony Rudolf, *The Arithmetic of Memory* (1999), 98, 102.

45 Interview with Richard Phillips and Buckeridge, *Jennings Goes to School*, 105.

46 Interview with Ann Rosenthal.

47 Lewis, *Playing for Time*, 67–8, 63, 61.

48 Ferdinand Mount, *Cold Cream: My Early Life and Other Mistakes* (2008), 164, 155–7, 146.

49 Interview with 'Michael Croft'.

50 Willans and Searle, *Compleet Molesworth*, Foreword, 7, 106, interviews with Anthony Heath and with David Blandford, 29 December 2008.

51 Interview with Robin Baird-Smith, 3 October 2008.

52 Interview with Martin Gilbert.

53 BBC Radio 4, *Desert Island Discs*, 8 February 2009.

54 Interview with Peter Murray-Rust, 14 April 2008.

55 John Peel and Sheila Ravenscroft, *Margrave of the Marshes: His Autobiography* (2006), 47–8.

56 Interview with 'Simon Taggart'.

57 Tim Jeal, *Swimming with my Father: A Memoir* (2004), 71, 73–4, 78.

58 Interview with Paul Knight.

59 Harry Thompson, *Peter Cook* (1997), 11, 19 and Dominic Sandbrook, *Never Had It So Good* (2005), 574–6.

60 William Cook (ed.), *Tragically I Was an Only Twin: The Complete Peter Cook* (2003), 336–7.

Notes to Chapter 8: 'Boiled Mince and Incense': The Swinging Sixties

1 Fry, *Moab Is My Washpot*, 16, 63–4, 113, 132.

2 'Annus Mirabilis' in Anthony Thwaite (ed.), *Philip Larkin: Collected Poems* (1988), 167.

3 Martin Rowson, *Stuff* (2007), 97, 128–30, 133.

4 Interviews with Vivian Bickford-Smith, 7 July 2007 and Tom Ponsonby, 19 January 2009.

5 R. J. Henderson, *A History of King's College Choir School* (Cambridge, 1981), 97.

6 Stephen Robinson and Ben Weston quoted in Smith, *Dulwich and Beyond*, 125, 132.

7 Interview with David Walker, 21 November 2008.

8 Richard Vickers, *Nearly a Century: Scaitcliffe 1896–1990* (Englefield Green, 1991), 46 and interview with Rupert Morris.

9 www.westdowns.com – *West Downs Magazine* 1957–64, 5.

10 Marshall, *Whimpering in Rhododendrons*, 129–31 and interview with Hamish Pringle, 7 June 2007.

11 www.westdowns.com – J. Passmore in 'Memories of the Cornes Era'.

12 www.anthonyhorowitz.com and Robin Bell, private memoir 'Falconbury, Spiritual Death and its part in my downfall', 2008.

13 Interview with Dan Fairest, 30 November 2008.

14 Motion, *In the Blood*, 127 and Tom Fort in *Observer*, 24 December 2006.

15 Interview with Richard Aldwinckle, 23 December 2008.

16 Paul Watkins, *Stand Before Your God: An American Schoolboy in England* (New York, 1995), 37–40.

17   Michael Barber in *Oldie*, May 2000, 32–3 and Ian Gibson, *The English Vice: Beating, Sex and Shame in Victorian England and After* (1978), 311.

18   Simon Watson, *A Storm of Cherries* (Pulborough, 2006), 12. This novel about 'The Dell' draws on the author's own prep school education.

19   Garfield, *Meinertzhagen Mystery*, 43.

20   Anthony Storr, *Sexual Deviation* (1964), 100–3, 106–7.

21   Bluhm, 'Preparatory Schools', 2.

22   Royston Lambert, *The Hothouse Society* (1968), 272.

23   C. Midgley in *The Times*, 25 September 2008 and *Chosen*, BBC Documentary on More4, 30 September 2008.

24   Watson, *Storm of Cherries*, 109.

25   Interview with 'Peter Franks', 11 November 2008.

26   Interview with 'Luke Spiers', 24 March 2009.

27   Motion, *In the Blood*, 121–2, 263.

28   SFA, Short Guide for the Parents of New Boys.

29   Interview with 'David Barton', 17 November 2008.

30   Letters of Henry Lytton Cobbold in Knebworth House Archive.

31   Letters of Vivian Bickford-Smith, courtesy of Gillian Bickford-Smith.

32   Interview with Richard Aldwinckle and letters, 14 July 1963, 9 February 1964.

33   Interview with Rupert Morris and letters, 14, 24 January, 21 February, 8 May, 5 June, 11 December 1960 and undated.

34   Vickers, *Nearly a Century*, 43–4.

35   Interviews with Rupert Morris and with Henry Lytton Cobbold, 21 January 2009 and undated letters in Knebworth House Archive.

36   Royston Lambert, Roger Bullock and Spencer Milham, *The Chance of a Lifetime? A Study of Boys' and Coeducational Boarding Schools in England and Wales* (1975), 130.

37   Richard Aldwinckle to his parents, 13 October 1963.

38   Interview with Elizabeth McKellar, 16 December 2008.

39   Lambert, *Hothouse Society*, 288.

40   Watkins, *Stand Before Your God*, 8–9.

41   Motion, *In the Blood*, 172.

42   Rupert Everett, *Red Carpets and Other Banana Skins* (2006), 22, 24.

43   Lambert *et al.*, *Chance of a Lifetime*, 143.

44   Tony Hanania, *Homesick* (1997), 44. This autobiographical novel is clearly set in West Downs School.

45   Interview with Dan Fairest.

46   Masters, *Preparatory Schools Today*, 59.

47   Interview with Tony Mitton, 13 January 2009.

48   Interview with Duncan Wiltshire, 5 December 2008.

49   Interview with Tom Ponsonby.

50   Lambert, *Hothouse Society*, 289.

51   Watkins, *Stand Before Your God*, 29.

52   Patrick Cockburn, *The Broken Boy* (2006), 238, 271.

53   Henry Lytton Cobbold, 27 May, no year, Knebworth House Archive.

54   Interviews with Rupert Morris and David Walker.

55   Interview with Hamish Pringle.

56   Lambert, *Hothouse Society*, 152.

57   *St Dunstan's Magazine*, 1958–1966.

58   Aldridge, *Time to Spare*, 178.

59   Smith, *Dulwich and Beyond*, 185.

60   Watkins, *Stand Before Your God*, 77, 23.

61   www.westdowns.com – Jerry Cornes.

62   Motion, *In the Blood*, 176–7.

63   Richard Aldwinckle to his parents, 4 July, 18 October 1964.

64   Robin Bell, 'Falconbury'.

65   Dominic Sandbrook, *White Heat: A History of Britain in the Swinging Sixties* (2007 edn), 790–1.

66   Interview with Richard Aldwinckle, Henry Lytton Cobbold in Knebworth House Archive and Rupert Morris to his parents, 23 October 1960.

67   Hanania, *Homesick*, 193.

68   Mike Oldfield, *Changeling: The Autobiography* (2008), 29–30, 36.

69   Everett, *Red Carpets*, 27–8 and Aldridge, *Time to Spare*, 178.

70   Lambert, *Hothouse Society*, 97.

71   Rowson, *Stuff*, 138–40.

72   Lambert, *Hothouse Society*, 40–4 and *Chance of a Lifetime*, 144.

73   Motion, *In the Blood*, 174.

74   Additional information from Tony Mitton, 27 January 2009.

75   Lambert, *Chance of a Lifetime*, 144–5.

76   www.anthonyhorowitz.com

77   *St Dunstan's Magazine*, 1961, 1957.

78   Bluhm, 'Preparatory Schools', 23–4.

79   KCC Archive, first edition of *Fleur de Lys* (1961).

80   Interview with Tom Ponsonby.

81   Anthony Crosland, *The Future of Socialism* (1980 edn), 206. The book was first published in 1956 and revised as a paperback in 1964.

82   e.g. Bluhm, 'Preparatory Schools', 63–6.

83   Vickers, *Nearly a Century*, 81.

84   Richard Aldwinckle to his parents, 18 October 1964.

85   Lambert, *Hothouse Society*, 51.

86   Interview with Dan Fairest and Simon Sebag Montefiore, *My Affair with Stalin* (1997), 57.

87   D. C. Owen to Mr Morris, 31 March 1964.

88   Quoted in Mould, *English Chorister*, 253.

89   Peter Clarke, *Hope and Glory: Britain 1900–1990* (1996), 286.

90   Pamela Hansford Johnson, *The Honours Board* (1970), 60.

91   Lewis, *Playing for Time*, 57.

92   Prospectus for Ashfold School.

93   Hanania, *Homesick*, 111–12.

94   Montefiore, *Affair with Stalin*, 200.

95   Fry, *Moab Is My Washpot*, 126–7, 177, 152.

Notes to Chapter 9: 'The Harry Potter Effect': Modern Prep Schools

1   e.g. Gilbert, *Prep School*, xi.

2   Interview with Edmund Marler, 19 December 2008.

3   Interview with Rupert Pick, 20 November 2008.

4   Interview with 'Mark Randall', 19 January 2009.

5   Smith, *Dulwich and Beyond*, 335–6.

6   Willans and Searle, *Compleet Molesworth*, 333–5.

7   Interview with Duncan Wiltshire.

8   Obituary of Norman Hale in *The Times*, 22 October 2008.

9   Neville Ollerenshaw, *A History of the Prebendal School* (Chichester, 1984), 47.

10   John Bowlby, *Separation, Anxiety and Loss* (1998 edn), 410.

11   Lambert, *Chance of a Lifetime*, 231.

12   Masters, *Preparatory Schools Today*, 16.

13   Interview with Max Hasler, 13 December 2008.

14   P. Victor in *Independent on Sunday*, 1 May 1994.

15   Interview with Sam Mahony, 16 January 2009 and Ofsted Report on Cothill House, 2005.

16 Cunningham, *Invention of Childhood*, 226.
17 Interview with Max Hasler.
18 Smith, *Dulwich and Beyond*, 190–1, 343–4.
19 Interview with Max Hasler.
20 Interview with Sam Mahony.
21 Hansford Johnson, *Honours Board*, 241–2.
22 Interview with Rupert and Charlotte George, 25 January 2009.
23 Ofsted Reports on Old Buckenham Hall and Lockers Park, 2004.
24 Interview with Rupert and Charlotte George.
25 Interview with 'Mark Randall'.
26 Interview with Johnny Wall, 27 January 2009.
27 Jenny Avis quoted in *Australian*, 19 February 2007.
28 Genevieve Fox in *The Times Magazine*, 10 February 2007.
29 Michael Morpurgo, *The War of Jenkins' Ear* (2001 edn), 2, 55, 143, 95.
30 Horowitz, *Groosham Grange*, Preface, 47, 58, 60, 102, 154–5.
31 www.antonyhorowitz.com and Anthony Horowitz, *Point Blanc* (2005 edn), 169, 219.
32 *O, The Oprah Magazine*, January 2001.
33 J. K. Rowling, *Harry Potter and the Philosopher's Stone* (2000 edn), 53, 60, 165, 181, 92.
34 Interview with Hector Matthews, 3 February 2009 and Smith, *Dulwich and Beyond*, 191.
35 Interview with Johnny Wall.
36 Interview with David Nicholson-Thomas, 19 February 2009 and Ofsted Reports 2004 and 2008.
37 Interview with Sam Mahony and Ofsted Report 2005.
38 Interview with Victoria Barron, January 2009 and Ofsted Report 2005.
39 Interview with Jamie Gardiner, 19 February 2009 and Ofsted Report 2008.
40 Interview with Rupert and Charlotte George and Ofsted Report 2006.
41 Interview with Nell and Archie McCann conducted by Rosalind Rayfield, their grandmother, December 2008.
42 *Highfield Association Newsletter*, November 2007 and interview with Anthony Heath.
43 Sports Day Speech by Simon Hitchings reported in *St Aubyns Magazine* 2008, 1.
44 Reported in *The Kidderminster Shuttle*, 25 October 2008.
45 Libby Brooks, *The Story of Childhood: Growing Up in Modern Britain* (2006), 127–8.
46 Alexandra Frean in *The Times*, 8 January 2009.
47 Rob Evans in *Guardian*, 30 September 2008 and Tom Perry in *The Times*, 24 April 2009.
48 Brooks, *Story of Childhood*, 158.

Notes to Chapter 10: 'The Most Potent Memory of My Life': The Effects of the Prep School Experience

1 Graves, *Goodbye To All That*, 24.
2 Grahame, *Golden Age*, 285.
3 Doris Lessing, *Under My Skin* (1994), 110, 97, 114.
4 Athill, *Yesterday Morning*, 135.
5 Lambert, *Chance of a Lifetime*, 286 and Duffell, *Making of Them*, 52.
6 Hazlitt, *Table Talk*, 94 and interview with Jamie Gardiner.
7 Peel and Ravenscroft, *John Peel*, 55, 51.
8 Connolly, *Enemies of Promise*, 192–3.
9 Richard Boston, *Osbert: A Portrait of Osbert Lancaster* (1989), 44.
10 Fry, *Moab Is My Washpot*, 208.
11 Watkins, *Stand Before Your God*, 182.
12 Pearson, *Smith of Smiths*, 21.
13 Tidrick, *Empire and Character*, 218, 275.
14 The Earl of Halifax, *Fulness of Days* (1957), 46–8 and A. Roberts, *'The Holy Fox': A Biography of Lord Halifax* (1991), 6–7.

15   Harrison, *Memoirs*, 63 and Barnes, *Half a Life*, 40.

16   Bluhm, 'Preparatory Schools', 62–3.

17   Froude, *Nemesis of Faith*, 119.

18   Duffell, *Making of Them*, 157 cf. Mozley, *Reminiscences*, 114.

19   Horne, *Bundle from Britain*, 94–5.

20   John Harris, 'Networked from Birth' in *Guardian*, 9 May 2008.

21   Jessica Shepherd in *Guardian*, 10 September 2008.

22   Hodder, *Seventh Earl of Shaftesbury*, vol. 1, 2.

23   le Carré, *Perfect Spy*, 149.

24   Fry, *Moab Is My Washpot*, 413.

25   Robin Bell, 'Falconbury'.

26   Sassoon, *Old Century*, 196 and Duffell, *Making of Them*, 143.

27   Woolf, *Sowing*, 69.

28   Harvey-Jones, *Getting it Together*, 83.

29   Berners, *First Childhood*, 233, Bion, *Long Weekend*, 104 and Q, *Memories and Opinions*, 44.

30   Jeal, *Swimming with my Father*, 73–4.

31   Holroyd, *Basil Street Blues*, 169.

32   *Oldie*, February 2003 and interview with George Perkin.

33   Horne, *Bundle from Britain*, 92 and Robert Brow, 'A Personal View of the Twentieth Century', www. brow.on.ca.

34   See Brendon, *Children of the Raj*, 209–10.

35   Dahl, *Boy*, 145.

36   E. M. Forster, 'Notes on the English Character' in *Abinger Harvest* (1967 edn), 14.

37   W. F. Bushell, *School Memories* (Liverpool, 1962), 33, 13.

38   Green, *Pack My Bag*, 26, 82.

39   MacNeice, *Strings are False*, 67–8 and *Autumn Journal*, 41.

40   *Observer*, 24 December 2006.

41   Blencowe, *Brambletye*, 110 and Magee, *Growing Up in a War*, 157.

42   www.westdowns.com – Patrick Forwood.

43   Sassoon, *Old Century*, 199, 203.

44   BBC, *Desert Island Discs*, 31 December 2006.

45   www.maidwellhall.co.uk and A. Motion, 'A Midnight Walk' in *Public Property* (2002), 3.

46   Simon Gray, *The Smoking Diaries* (2004), 66–9.

47   Jeal, *Swimming with My Father*, 120.

48   Letters from George Perkin, 14 November and 7 October 2008.

49   Wendeborn, *View of England* quoted in Bridgewater, *English Schooling*, 277–8.

50   Victor Jacquemont, *Letters from India 1829–1832* (ed. C. A. Phillips, 1936), 134.

51   Rudyard Kipling, Prelude to *Stalky & Co* (1982 edn), vii–ix.

52   Rudyard Kipling to his son, 16 November 1912 in Gilbert (ed.), *O Beloved Kids*.

53   Forster, 'Notes on English Character', 14–15.

54   Connolly, *Enemies of Promise*, 271.

55   Dr Jeremy Swinson quoted in *The Times Magazine*, 10 February 2007 and M. Henderson in www.telegraph.co.uk, 5 January 2009.

Permission to quote from poems:

Lines from 'Vitaï Lampada' by Henry Newbolt: Peter Newbolt.

Lines from 'Letter to Lord Byron' by W. H. Auden and lines from 'A Letter to My Parents' and 'Leaving School' by Hugo Williams: Faber & Faber Ltd.

Lines from 'Autumn Journal' by Louis MacNeice: David Higham Associates on behalf of Faber & Faber Ltd.

Lines from 'Summoned by Bells' by John Betjeman: John Murray Publishers Ltd.

Every effort has been made to fulfil requirements with regard to reproducing copyright material. The author and publisher will be glad to rectify any omissions at the earliest opportunity.

Bibliography

UNPUBLISHED SOURCES

British Library (BL)
Arthur Conan Doyle papers, uncatalogued
John Gielgud Papers, Add. 81306
Morley Archive, Add. 48265/C2, 3, 11

Cambridge University Library (CUL)
Peter Scott Papers, A111–3, A267–74
Journal of Sir James Stephen, Add. 7888, II/119

Centre for South Asian Studies, Cambridge (CSAS)
Brown Papers, uncatalogued

Churchill Archives Centre, Cambridge (CAC)
Julian Amery Papers, AMEJ 3/1/2
Leopold Amery Papers, AMEL 6/1/3, 6/1/30
Churchill Papers, CHAR 28/38, 28/131
Duncan-Sandys Papers, DSND 19/1
Esher Papers, ESHR 7/1, 7/39
Lyttelton Papers, CHAN 2/18
McKenna Papers, McKNS 8/7–9, 9/26–7
Randolph Churchill Papers, RHCH 3/5/2
Willink Memoir, WILL Box 2

Faculty of Asian and Middle Eastern Studies,
*   Cambridge*
Rhys Davids Papers, RDV/1–3, 9

Imperial War Museum, Department of Documents
*   (IWM)*
R. A. Brown, 91/5/1
Capt. P. Collister, 83/46/1
William Drummond, 91/37/1
Gordon Dearing, MISC 186/2789
J. D. G. Hammer, 66/316/1–3
Miss L. M. Williams, 92/16/1

King's College, Cambridge (KCC)
Rupert Brooke, RCB/M2, M21
Roger Fry, REF 1/171–2, 3/57/1–9
Frank Ramsey, FPR 2/1
Alan Turing, AMT/K/1

King's College, London (KCL)
Bryant Archive, GB99, B/2, 36

Knebworth House Archive
Antony Knebworth Letters, V15
Henry Lytton Cobbold Letters, uncatalogued

London Metropolitan Archives, City of London
*   (LMA)*
Monro Archive, ACC/1063/259–355, 869–959,
    967–1020

Oriental and India Office Collections (OIOC)
Barlow Collection, Mss Eur F176/3, 16, 54
Campbell Papers, Mss Eur E349
Yule Collection, Mss Eur E357/17

Regent House Library, Oxford
Wilkins Family letters, uncatalogued

Summer Fields Archive, Oxford (SFA)
Diary of Robert Arrowsmith (copy)
Summer Fields Magazine

Private Papers
Richard Aldwinckle, Letters
Robert Baker, Memoir
Robin Bell, 'Falconbury, Spiritual Death and its
    part in my downfall'
Martin Bluhm, 'Preparatory Schools'
James Day, 'My Prep School'
Michael Emtage, 'A Good English Preparatory School'
David Harrop, 'My Recollections of World War II'
Douglas Hurd, Letters
Rupert Morris, Letters
Tony Orchard, Memoir
Philip Steadman, Holiday Diaries

Author's Interviews (* denotes pseudonym)
Richard Aldwinckle, 23 December 2008
Robin Baird-Smith, 3 October 2008

Rodney Barker, 20 July 2008
Victoria Barron, January 2009
David Barton,* 17 November 2008
Johnny Bell, 28 November 2007
Robin Bell, 23 February 2008
Vivian Bickford-Smith, 7 July 2007
David Blandford, 29 December 2008
Piers and Rupert Brendon
Leila Brown, 4 February 2003
Michael Croft,* 20 October 2008
Dan Fairest, 30 November 2008
David Fitzgerald, 21 April 2007
Peter Franks,* 11 November 2008
Jamie Gardiner, 19 February 2009
Martin Gilbert, 18 August 2008
Charlotte and Rupert George, 25 January 2008
David Harrop, September 2008
Max Hasler, 13 December 2008
Anthony Heath, 18 April 2007
Paul Knight, 20 October 2008
Henry Lytton Cobbold, 21 January 2009
Archie and Nell McCann, December 2008 (by
    Rosalind Rayfield)
Elizabeth McKellar, 16 December 2008
Sam Mahony, 16 January 2009
Edmund Marler, 19 December 2008
Hector Matthews, 3 February 2009

Tony Mitton, 13 January 2009
Rupert Morris, 21 November 2008
Peter Murray-Rust, 14 April 2008
David Nicholson-Thomas, 19 February 2009
George Perkin, 21 August 2008
Richard Phillips, 20 December 2008
Rupert Pick, 20 November 2008
Tom Ponsonby, 19 January 2009
Hamish Pringle, 7 June 2007
Peter Pugh, 7 October 2008
Mark Randall,* 19 January 2009
Ann Rosenthal (née Shire), 10 July 2008
Ken Saunders, 30 October 2008
Tom Sharpe, 15 April 2007
Henley Smith, 25 January 2008
Luke Spiers,* 24 March 2009
Peter Squire, 23 July 2008
Philip Steadman, 3 October 2008
Hilary Sweet-Escott (née Johnston), 1 May
    2004
Simon Taggart,* 27 September 2008
Michael Thomas, 3 October 2003
David Walker, 21 November 2008
Johnny Wall, 27 January 2009
Charles Williams, 11 August 2008
Duncan Wiltshire, 5 December 2008
Christopher Wood, 1 November 2007

PUBLISHED WORKS

This is a select list of important childhood memoirs and general books on the subject. The endnotes provide a running bibliography and indicate the full range of sources on which the book is based. The date of first publication is cited in the bibliography and the place of publication is London, unless otherwise stated.

Aldridge, Nicholas, *GB, Master, Monster or Myth?*, Ilfracombe, 2008.
Aldridge, Nicholas, *Time to Spare? A History of Summer Fields*, Oxford, 1989.
Athill, Diana, *Yesterday Morning*, 2002
Batchelor, Meston, *Cradle of Empire: A Preparatory School through Nine Reigns*, Chichester, 1981.
Benson, A. C., *Memories and Friends*, 1923.
Berners, Lord, *First Childhood*, 1988.
Betjeman, John, *Summoned by Bells*, 1960.
Bion, Wilfred, *The Long Week-end 1897–1918*, 1982.
Blake, Nicholas, *A Question of Proof*, 1935.
Blencowe, Peter, *Brambletye: The Early Years 1919–1969*, 2004.
Blishen, Edward, *Uncommon Entrance*, 1974.
Bridgewater, Patrick, *Arthur Schopenhauer's English Schooling*, 1988.

Brooks, Libby, *The Story of Childhood: Growing Up in Modern Britain*, 2006.
Buckeridge, Anthony, *Jennings Goes to School*, 1950.
Burningham, John, *When We Were Young: A Compendium of Childhood*, 2004.
Churchill, Randolph, *Twenty-One Years*, 1964.
Churchill, Winston, *My Early Life*, 1930.
Cobb, Richard, *A Sense of Place*, 1975.
Coke, Henry, *Tracks of a Rolling Stone*, 1905.
Connolly, Cyril, *Enemies of Promise*, 1938.
Craig, Patricia (ed.), *The Oxford Book of Schooldays*, Oxford, 1994.
Crompton, Richmal, *William and the Evacuees*, 1940.
Cunningham, Hugh, *The Invention of Childhood*, 2006.
Dahl, Roald, *Boy*, 1984.

Darwin, Francis, *The Life and Letters of Charles Darwin*, 1887.

Dickens, Charles, *A Christmas Carol*, 1843.

Dickens, Charles, *Dombey and Son*, 1846.

Dickens, Charles, *The Life and Adventures of Nicholas Nickleby*, 1839.

Duffell, Nick, *The Making of Them: The British Attitude to Children and the Boarding School System*, 2000.

Eliot, George, *The Mill on the Floss*, 1860.

Ellis, H. F., *The World of A. J. Wentworth, B.A.*, 1964.

Figes, Eva, *Little Eden: A Child at War*, 1978.

Fletcher, Anthony, *Growing Up in England: The Experience of Childhood 1600–1914*, New Haven and London, 2008.

Fry, Stephen, *Moab Is My Washpot*, 1997.

Gilbert, Michael, *Prep School: An Anthology*, 1991.

Gosse, Edmund, *Father and Son*, 1907.

Grahame, Kenneth, *The Golden Age*, 1895.

Graves, Robert, *Goodbye To All That*, 1929.

Green, Henry, *Pack My Bag*, 1940.

Greene, Graham (ed.), *The Old School: Essays by Divers Hands*, 1934.

Hamilton, Ian, *When I Was a Boy*, 1939.

Hanania, Tony, *Homesick*, 1997.

Hansford Johnson, Pamela, *The Honours Board*, 1970.

Harrison, Fraser, *Trivial Disputes*, 1989.

Heald, Tim, *Class Distinctions*, 1984.

Holroyd, Michael, *Basil Street Blues: A Family Story*, 1999.

Horne, Alistair, *A Bundle from Britain*, 1993.

Horowitz, Anthony, *Groosham Grange*, 1995.

Hughes, Thomas, *Tom Brown's Schooldays*, 1857.

Inglis, Brian (ed.), *John Bull's Schooldays*, 1961.

Jeal, Tim, *Swimming with my Father: A Memoir*, 2004.

Kenward, James, *Prep School*, 1958.

Lamb, Charles, 'Recollections of Christ's Hospital' in Percy Fitzgerald (ed.), *The Life, Letters, and Writings of Charles Lamb* vol. IV, London and Philadelphia, 1895.

Lambert, Royston, *The Hothouse Society*, 1968.

Lawson, John and Silver, Harold, *A Social History of Education in England*, 1973.

le Carré, John, *A Perfect Spy*, 1986.

le Carré, John. *Tinker Tailor Soldier Spy*, 1974.

Leakey, J. H. *School Errant*, 1951.

Leinster-Mackay, Donald, *The Rise of the English Prep School*, London and Philadelphia, 1984.

Lewis, Jeremy, *Playing for Time*, 1987.

Lunn, Alfred, *The Harrovians*, 1913.

Lytton, Lord, *Antony: A Record of Youth*, 1934.

Macaulay, T. B. (Pinney, Thomas, ed.), *Letters*, vol. 1, 1974.

Magee, Bryan, *Growing Up in a War*, 2008.

Marshall, Arthur, *Life's Rich Pageant*, 1984.

Marshall, Arthur, *Whimpering in the Rhododendrons*, 1982.

Masters, Philip, *Preparatory Schools Today: Some Facts and Inferences*, 1966.

Maugham, W. Somerset, *Of Human Bondage*, 1915.

Maxwell, Gavin, *The House of Elrig*, 1965.

Melly, George, *Scouse Mouse*, 1984.

Montefiore, Simon Sebag, *My Affair with Stalin*, 1997.

Morpurgo, Michael, *The War of Jenkins' Ear*, 1993.

Motion, Andrew, *In the Blood*, 2006.

Mould, Alan, *The English Chorister*, 2007.

Mount, Ferdinand, *Cold Cream: My Early Life and Other Mistakes*, 2008.

Newsome, David, *Godliness and Good Learning*, 1961.

Orwell, George, 'Such, Such Were the Joys' in *Collected Essays, Journalism and Letters*, vol. 4, 1968.

Parker, Peter, *The Old Lie: The Great War and the Public School Ethos*, 1987.

Richardson, Maurice, *Little Victims, Preparatory School Memoirs*, 1968.

Rowling, J. K., *Harry Potter and the Philosopher's Stone*, 1997.

Rowson, Martin, *Stuff*, 2007.

Rudolf, Anthony, *The Arithmetic of Memory*, 1999.

Sassoon, Siegfried, *The Old Century and Seven More Years*, 1938.

Smith, Lyn, *Young Voices: British Children Remember the Second World War*, 2007.

Smith, Neil, *Dulwich and Beyond: A History of Dulwich College Preparatory School*, 2005.

Spender, Stephen, *World Within World*, 1951.

Thackeray, W. M. (Ray, Gordon, ed.), *Letters and Private Papers*, 1945.

Tidrick, Kathryn, *Empire and the English Character*, 1990.

Tosh, John, *A Man's Place: Masculinity and the Middle-Class Home in Victorian England*, New Haven and London, 1999.

Trollope, Anthony, *An Autobiography*, 1883.

Tyndale-Biscoe, Eric, *The Story of Sheikh Bagh*, Mysore, 1945.

Usborne, Richard, *A Century of Summer Fields*, 1964.

Vickers, Richard, *Nearly a Century: Scaitcliffe 1896–1990*, Englefield Green, 1991.

Watkins, Paul, *Stand Before Your God: An American Schoolboy in England*, New York, 1995.

Watson, Simon, *A Storm of Cherries*, Pulborough, 2006.

Waugh, Alec, *The Early Years*, 1962.

Waugh, Evelyn, *Decline and Fall*, 1928.

Waugh, Evelyn, *A Little Learning*, 1962.

Willans, Geoffrey and Searle, Ronald, *The Compleet Molesworth*, 1958.

Williams, Hugo, *Writing Home*, Oxford, 1985.

Wodehouse, P. G., *Jeeves in the Offing*, 1960.

Woolf, Leonard, *Sowing: An Autobiography of the Years 1880–1904*, 1960.

WEBSITES

www.anthonyhorowitz.com

www.bbc.co.uk/ww2peopleswar

www.knebworthhouse.com

www.maidwellhall.co.uk

www.ofsted.gov.uk

www.westdowns.com

Index

Salisbury, Lord (Robert Cecil) 11, 18, 44
Sandroyd School 78, 107, 111
Sassoon, Siegfried 57, 75, 208, 211
Saunders, Ken 145
Scaitcliffe School 139–40, 141, 161, 167, 173, 178
scarlet fever 64
scholarships to public schools 42, 54, 95, 100, 113, 121, 122, 139, 140, 143, 146, 147, 149, 176, 183, 194, 196, 198, 199, 204
school council/cabinet/ pupils' parliament 102, 129, 150, 199
school magazines 6, 72, 75, 81, 85, 145
　The Falconburian 101, 104
　Fleur de Lys (King's College Choir School) 178
　Highfield School Magazine 72
　St Dunstan's Magazine 173, 177, 178
　Summer Fields Magazine 75–6, 84, 91, 103
　West Downs Magazine 142
schoolmasters/teachers 3, 5, 15, 24, 43–4, 85–6, 87, 103, 112–3, 159, 165, 175, 183, 186, 195
　see also Aldridge, Nicholas; Alington, Geoffrey; Auden, W. H.; Benson, Arthur; Blishen, Edward; Bolton, Geoffrey; Boyer, Rev James; Chenevix-Trench, Anthony; Grimes, Captain; Howell-Griffiths, David; Lewis, C. Day; Martin, Rupert; Smith, Neil; Strong, L. A. G.; Waugh, Evelyn; Wentworth, A. J.
Schopenhauer, Arthur 15
Science 147, 149, 177, 181, 188, 206
Scott, Lady Kathleen 85, 94, 99, 106
Scott, Sir Peter 98–9, 105–6, 110, 146
Scouting 77–9, 99, 104, 108, 109, 122, 127, 146, 152
Seafield Park School, Southampton 128

Seafield School, Bexhill 102, 110
Seaford School, 138, 140, 142, 148, 179
Searle, Ronald 140, 142, illustrations 8
Second World War 113, 115–35 passim, 141, 143, 153, 154, 174–5, 206
　Battle of Anzio 115
　Battle of Britain 116–18
　blitz 118–20, 123, 126, 128, 130, 135
　fall of France 128
　submarines 115, 131, 132
　war effort 119–20, 125, 130
separation from family 2, 20, 23, 30, 32, 51, 53, 62, 85, 134, 151, 152, 154, 155, 181–2, 190, 194, 201, 209
sex 18, 40, 65
　and beating 69, 162–3, 211
　sexual abuse/paedophilia 69, 86, 104, 107, 123, 152, 163–5, 202
　see also homosexuality; masturbation
Sewell, Mary 31
Shaftesbury, Lord (Antony Ashley Cooper) 7, 207
Sharpe, Tom vii, 117, illustrations 7
Sheikh Bagh School, Kashmir 134–5
Sherborne Preparatory School 83, 89, 210
shooting 27, 78, 97, 119, 199
Shrewsbury School 10, 27, 98, 204, 225 n27
Simpson, John 142
Slade, Julian 126–7
smells 4, 62, 87, 89, 90, 93, 96, 112, 124, 144, 160, 174, 176
Smith, Henley 140, 146–7
Smith, Neil 185–6, 193
Smith, Sydney 22, 205
smoking/tobacco 17, 76, 93, 95, 99, 103, 105, 130, 134, 142, 147, 151, 152, 178
　cigarette cards 80
snakes 48, 87, 108, 110, 146
Sneyd-Kynnersley, Rev H. W. 66–7, 68, 69

social class 1, 10, 29, 33, 56, 116–17, 127, 135, 137–8, 151, 178–80, 201, 206–7, 212, 213
South Lodge, Lowestoft (later Old Buckenham Hall) 111, 207
Southwell School, New Zealand 132
Speech Day 97, 138
speech impediment/stammer 19, 21, 62, 209
spelling 6, 59, 60, 61, 64, 139, 160
Spender, Stephen 83, 84, 89–90
Spiers, Luke (pseudonym) 165
spies 80, 82, 83, 125, 129, 208
Spock, Dr Benjamin 2, 159, 160, 163, 184
sport/organized games 48, 52–4, 59, 66, 108, 145, 151, 153, 172–3, 182, 193, 200, 207
　see also athletics; boxing; cricket; drill; fives; football; golf; paperchasing; rugby; tennis/racquets
Sports Day 97, 103, 104, 108, 117, 132
Squeers, Wackford 3, 14
Squire, Peter 102, 110, 112, 212
Stalin, Josef 150, 172, 179, 180
stamp collecting 45–6, 55, 57, 63, 68, 72, 122
Stancliffe Hall 162, 169, 170
Stanford C. E. F. 70, 71, 102
state/council schools 97, 117, 120, 121, 127, 137, 138, 178, 185, 191, 201, 207
　see also comprehensive schools; elementary/ primary schools; grammar schools
Steadman, Philip 139, 147
Steiner, Rudolf 208
Stephen, Sir James, Fitzjames and Leslie 32
Stirling Court 93, 96, 97, 111
Storr, Anthony 98, 163–4
storytelling/writing 45, 57, 70, 99, 142, 146, 166, 167, 171–2, 177
Strachey, James 57, 72
Stouts Hill School 159, 180, 181
Stowe School 141
Stratton Park 107
Strong L. A. G. 87